JOHN GARROOD received an Honours Degree in Physics and Electrical Engineering from Corpus Christi College, Cambridge. He continued with research work on Ferromagnetic Materials and was awarded a Ph.D. After a spell of teachin t Bryanston School, Dr. Garrood retu mbridge as a Fellow of Emmanu tured in Engineering f he has taught Head of Pl amined at all olarship and key facts

GCE A-Level Passbooks

BIOLOGY, H. Rapson, B.Sc.

CHEMISTRY, J. E. Chandler, B.Sc.
and R. J. Wilkinson, Ph.D.

PHYSICS, J. R. Garrood, M.A., Ph.D.

PURE MATHEMATICS, R. A. Parsons, B.Sc.
and A. G. Dawson, B.Sc.

GCE A-Level Passbook
Physics

J. R. Garrood, M.A., Ph.D.

key facts

Published by Intercontinental Book Productions
in conjunction with Seymour Press Ltd.
Distributed by Seymour Press Ltd.,
334 Brixton Road, London, SW9 7AG

Published 1979 by Intercontinental Book Productions, Berkshire House, Queen Street, Maidenhead, Berks., SL6 1NF in conjunction with Seymour Press Ltd.

1st edition, 1st impression 3.79.0

Made and printed by C. Nicholls & Company Ltd.
ISBN 0 85047 923 1

Contents

Base SI Units

Physical Quantities	Name	Symbol
Length	metre	m
Mass	kilogram	kg
Time	second	s
Electric current	ampere	A
Thermodynamic temperature	kelvin	K
Amount of substance	mole	mol

Derived SI Units

Physical Quantities	Name	Symbol
Frequency	hertz	Hz
Force	newton	N
Pressure	pascal	Pa
Work or Energy	joule	J
Power	watt	W
Electric charge	coulomb	C
Electric p.d.	volt	V
Electric resistance	ohm	Ω
Electric capacitance	farad	F
Magnetic flux density	tesla	T
Magnetic flux	weber	Wb
Inductance	henry	H
Radioactive activity	becquerel	Bq

Introduction

This Key Facts A-level Passbook provides a pool of subject matter which covers the widely varied demands of the U.K. examining boards, and includes most of the work for the Nuffield Physics syllabus.

At present the whole question of A-level subject matter is in a state of flux. Examination Boards are changing their requirements almost yearly, and at the time of writing, there is a very wide spread of requirements, from very traditional to what may be considered revolutionary. As a result topics which have been well established for many years (e.g. Geometrical Optics and parts of Heat) have disappeared completely from the syllabuses of some Boards, and from the Nuffield course.

There is of course no absolute syllabus, and Boards are feeling their way towards a new approach which may be more appropriate for future generations of physicists and engineers. Already the changes are evident. Many Boards have rearranged the syllabus to reflect the shift from macroscopic (bulk properties) to microscopic (behavior of atoms, molecules and nuclei). There is less history of the subject and more up-to-date application, less factual recall and more understanding, less stress on detail and accurate measurement and more on ideas and application of the facts to new situations. In short, the emphasis is changing from 'what' to 'why'. Certainly questions are more wordy and less mathematical than they used to be, and Nuffield provide all the formulae too.

With the immense spread of requirements, this book has been difficult to write. The vast majority of topics on each syllabus have been incorporated, however, and where selection has been necessary it has been on the basis of omitting topics demanded by only one or two Boards. As a result, the book contains far more than the requirement of any single Board. It is therefore **essential** that you should obtain a copy of the syllabus of your particular Board, and discuss any doubts or interpretations with your teacher. Used in conjunction with a taught course, the book should provide a useful summary of the salient facts of each topic, whichever Board's examination you take.

The book has been written in a compact, lucid style, easily readable, and presents a complete picture. Ideas are developed from first principles and then built on. Parallels are drawn between different branches of the subject where this is possible, and linked ideas are treated together (e.g. optical and X-ray spectra). There is extensive cross reference since many topics overlap and are dealt with elsewhere in the book. Particular care has been taken to build up a good molecular view and to give a realistic idea of the atom. Many examples are quoted to illustrate the layout of calculations and also to add 'feel' and colour. They are intended more as 'teaching questions' however than as actual exam questions. It is **important** therefore that you should obtain recent past examination papers of your Board for practice. At the end of each chapter there is a list of Key Terms partly to act as a check list and partly to summarize definitions.

It is hoped that this book will fulfil a need for a comprehensive textbook without padding, and form the basis of a revision course.

Remember that there are three sorts of people—those who know a subject, those who don't, and those who have notes on it. Make sure you are in the first category, and above all **enjoy** the subject.

My thanks are due to my wife and family for forebearance, to my colleagues Mr. R.M. Palmer and Dr. M. Govan for helpful discussions, to Mr. P. Thonemann for numerous suggestions, and to Mrs. Christine Bumstead and Mrs. Sue Birch for many hours of typing.

John R. Garrood 1978

Chapter 1
Mechanics and Gravitation

Statics

Statics is concerned with forces in equilibrium, i.e. balanced forces. Bodies acted upon by balanced forces are either at rest or moving with constant velocity.

Parallelogram of velocities Consider a pontoon crossing a river with a man walking diagonally across it (fig. 1i).

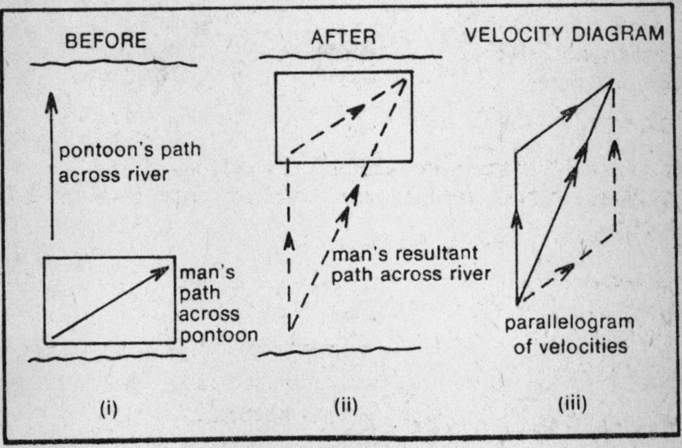

Figure 1. Parallelogram of velocities

The final position of the man relative to the ground is due both to his movement across the pontoon, and to the pontoon's movement across the river (fig. 1ii). Since the time taken to move both these distances is the same, the velocities are proportional to these distances, and a velocity diagram can be constructed to some convenient scale (fig. 1iii). The resultant velocity is seen to be the diagonal of the parallelogram formed from the two velocities being added and is usually marked with a double arrow. This rule for adding velocities also applies to all vector quantities (for example, forces, fields, momenta).

Vector addition Usually only half of the parallelogram is drawn (heavy outline in fig. 1iii) and in drawing this vector addition triangle it is important to place the two vectors end to end with the two arrows following each other.

Example A man wishes to cross a river perpendicularly. He can swim at $1\,\mathrm{m\,s^{-1}}$ in still water and the river current is $\frac{1}{2}\mathrm{m\,s^{-1}}$. In which direction does he swim?

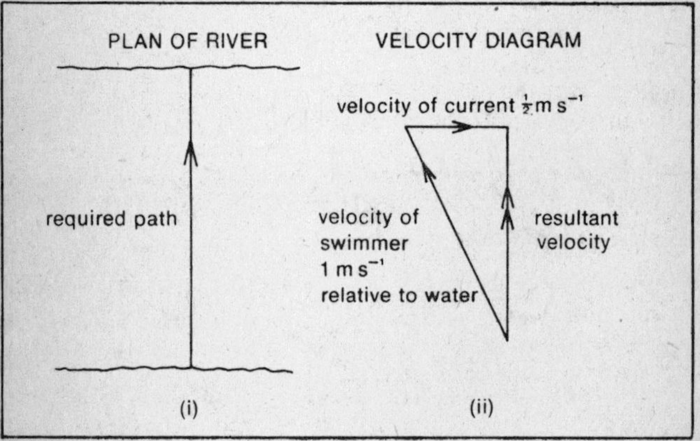

Figure 2. River crossing problem

The triangle must be that shown in fig. 2ii as the man's velocity relative to the water and the water's velocity relative to the ground are the two vectors being added. The man's velocity relative to the ground straight across the river is the resultant. It is always better to draw a separate vector diagram.

Resolution of vectors Just as two vectors can be added to make a single resultant vector, so a vector can be split up into two other vectors, with an infinite number of possibilities (fig. 3i).

It is often useful however to resolve a vector into two other mutually perpendicular vectors, and this process is known as **resolving into components.** Again, there is a large number of possibilities (fig. 3ii). There are simple relationships between a vector and its two components (fig. 3iii). The usefulness of resolving into components is that very often a force, or an acceleration (e.g. due to gravity) affects only one component and not the other, and the analysis can consider the two directions independently. Good examples are given on page 18 and page 15.

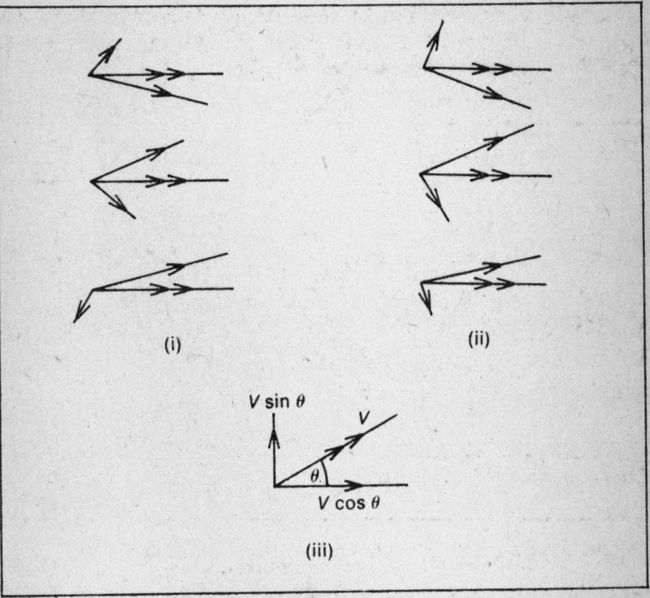

Figure 3. Resolution of vectors

Moments If a force acts on a body which is free to rotate about an axis, the force may exert a turning effect or **moment**.

The moment of a force about an axis is the product of the magnitude of the force and the **perpendicular distance** from the line of action of the force to the axis (fig. 4i).

This can easily be understood by considering a revolving door (fig. 4ii). Force *A* will not turn the door because the perpendicular distance to the pivot is zero. Force *B* will turn it with difficulty whilst force *C* is the minimum force required because the perpendicular distance is greatest (i.e. the full width of the door). Moments are measured in **newton metres** (N m).

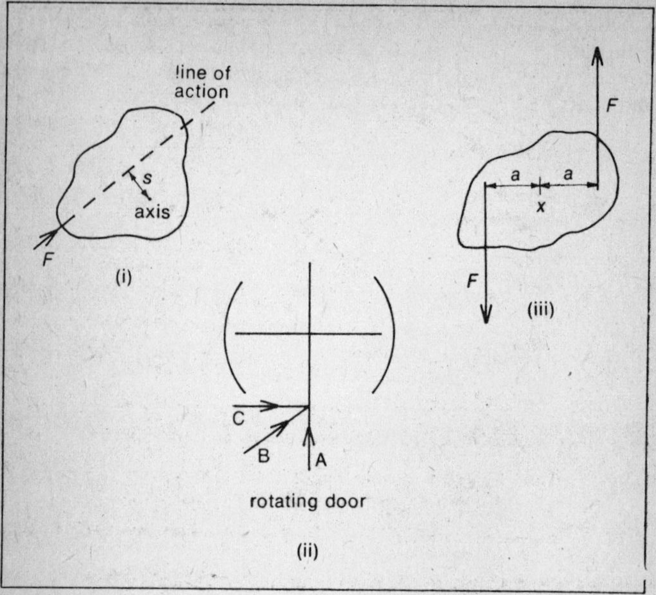

Figure 4. Moments of forces

Where two equal and opposite parallel forces act on a body (fig. 4iii), for example, electromagnetic forces on a motor armature or galvanometer coil, they are called a **couple**, and the body will rotate about an axis mid-way between the forces. In this case,

$$\text{Moment} = 2 \times Fa$$
$$= F \times 2a$$

i.e. **Moment of a couple is the product of one of the forces times the perpendicular distance between them.** If a shaft or a nut is rotated, the moment exerted is usually referred to as the **torque**.

Equilibrium If there are no net forces or moments acting on a body, it is said to be in equilibrium and it will remain either at rest or continue moving with constant velocity or angular velocity.

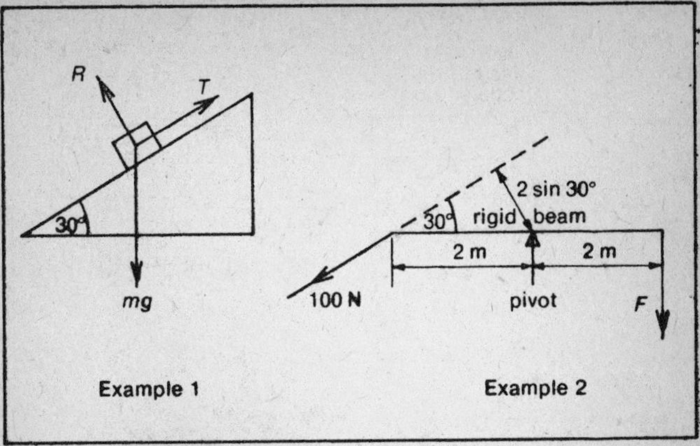

Figure 5. Equilibrium examples

These conditions can be expressed as follows:

(i) Algebraic sum of forces in any direction $\Sigma F_x = 0$

(ii) Algebraic sum of forces in the perpendicular direction $\Sigma F_y = 0$

(iii) Algebraic sum of moments about any point $\Sigma M = 0$

i.e. Turning moment clockwise = turning moment anticlockwise

Example 1 Find T and R.
The easiest way here is to resolve along the plane (since R is perpendicular to it).

Resolving along the plane, $T = mg \sin 30°$

Resolving perpendicular to the plane, $R = mg \cos 30°$

Example 2 Find F.
Taking moments about the pivot

Moment clockwise = moment anticlockwise

$$F \times 2 = 100 \times 2 \sin 30°$$

$$F = 100 \sin 30° = 50\,\text{N}$$

The centre of gravity of a body is the point through which its weight appears to act, i.e. the gravitational forces on all the particles of which the body is composed can be replaced by a single force through the centre of gravity.

Friction When two surfaces are in contact, any force tending to make them slide will be opposed by a force of friction (fig. 6i).

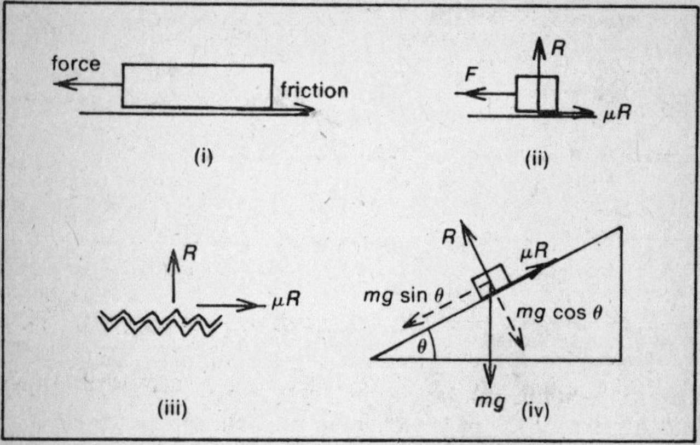

Figure 6. Frictional forces

As the lateral force is increased, so the frictional force will increase until a maximum is reached called **limiting static friction**. If the applied force is increased beyond this value, the surfaces will slide over each other and the frictional force will decrease a little, but then remain constant and independent of relative speed of the surfaces. It is then called **kinetic (or dynamic) friction**. The frictional force depends on the nature of the surfaces and on the normal reaction between them, but not on the area of contact.
Thus, when stationary (fig. 6ii)

$$F_{max} = \mu_s R \quad (\mu_s = \text{coefficient of static friction})$$

and when sliding

$$F = \mu_k R \quad (\mu_k = \text{coefficient of kinetic friction})$$

Friction is due to the roughness of the surfaces, and an idea of its origin can be obtained by considering two surfaces with meshing teeth (fig 6iii). The teeth will ride up until they slide over each other

Example (fig. 6iv). What is the steepest slope for the block just not to slip?

Resolving perpendicular to the plane: $R = mg \cos \theta$

Resolving along the plane:

$$mg \sin \theta = \mu_s R \text{ at the point of slipping}$$
$$= \mu_s mg \cos \theta$$
$$\mu_s = \tan \theta \qquad \therefore \quad \theta = \tan^{-1} \mu_s$$

Hydrostatics

Hydrostatics is concerned with fluids at rest.

Pressure

Pressure is force normal to an area per unit area.

$$P = F/A$$

The unit is **Pascal** (Pa) which is 1 newton per square metre.

Pressure at a point is the force normal to a vanishingly small area divided by that area.

$$P = \lim_{\text{area} \to 0} \left(\frac{\delta F}{\delta A}\right)$$

Pressure at a point in a fluid acts equally in all directions.

Pressure and depth The pressure at a depth h in a fluid of density ρ can be calculated by considering the weight of fluid above an area A (fig. 7i).

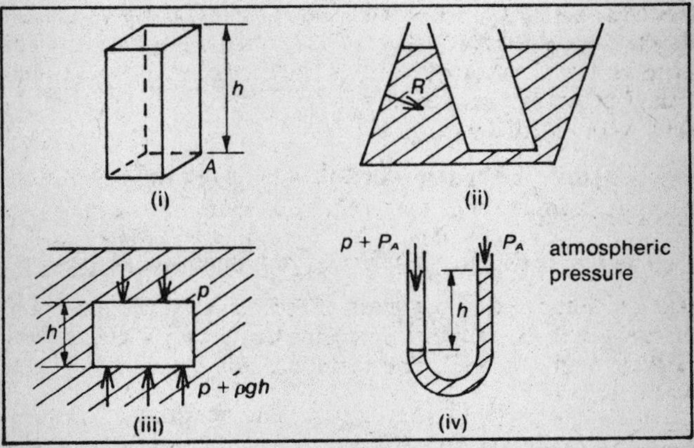

Figure 7. Hydrostatic pressures

$$\text{Volume of fluid above } A = hA$$
$$\text{Mass of fluid above } A = \rho hA$$
$$\text{Weight of fluid above } A = \rho ghA$$
$$\therefore \quad \text{Pressure over } A = \frac{\rho ghA}{A} = \rho gh$$

With tapered vessels (fig. 7ii) the walls contribute a reaction pressure which adds to the pressure due to the fluid so that the pressure is the same at all points of equal depth.

Pressure measurement A simple apparatus for measuring pressure difference is the U-tube manometer (fig. 7iv). The pressure above atmospheric (P_A in diagram) is clearly that due to the head of liquid h and is thus ρgh. This pressure is usually called the **'excess pressure'**.

The standard atmosphere used to be defined as the pressure due to a column of 76 cm of mercury.

Hence $\quad P_A = \rho gh = 13{\cdot}6 \times 10^3 \times 9{\cdot}81 \times 0{\cdot}76 = 101\,396 \text{ Pa}$

The standard atmosphere is now **defined** as 101 325 Pa.

Archimedes' principle states that when a body is fully or partially immersed in a fluid, the upthrust on it is equal to the weight of fluid displaced. This can be proved by considering the net forces acting on a submerged rectangular box (fig. 7iii).

Let the pressure acting on the upper surface be p. The pressure acting on the lower surface $= p + \rho gh$. Equating forces vertically:

$$\text{Upthrust} = \text{force on lower surface} - \text{force on upper surface}$$
$$= (p + \rho gh)A - pA = \rho ghA$$

An alternative, and completely general, proof of Archimedes' principle is to consider the equilibrium of forces acting on an arbitrary volume of fluid. The fluid has its weight acting downwards. It would therefore accelerate downwards but for the existence of an equal and opposite force acting on it which is the upthrust. Therefore since the volume of fluid is in equilibrium, upthrust = weight of fluid.

If the volume of fluid is displaced by another body of identical shape, the upthrust will still be exactly the same as it was before. Hence

Upthrust on body = weight of fluid displaced

$$= \text{volume} \times \rho g = \text{mass} \times g$$

$$= \text{weight of fluid displaced}$$

This upthrust is always present. If the upthrust is equal to the weight of a body, then it will float, e.g. a ship on water, but a submerged body resting on the bottom will still experience upthrust (provided that the water can reach the lower surface) although the upthrust will not be sufficient to support it.

Example A hot air balloon of volume 700 m^3 is filled with hot air of density 1 kg m^{-3} and floats in air of density 1.28 kg m^{-3}. If the mass of balloon and basket is 100 kg, what load can the balloon lift? (Take $g = 10$ m s^{-2})

$$\text{Upthrust} = \text{vol.} \times \rho \times g = 700 \times 1.28 \times 10 = 8960 \text{ N}$$

$$\text{Wt. of balloon, basket and hot air} = mg + \text{vol.} \times \rho \times g$$
$$= 100 \times 10 + 700 \times 1 \times 10$$
$$= 8000\,N$$

$\therefore$ Force available to lift load = 960 N, $\therefore$ load = 96 kg

Dynamics

Dynamics is concerned with unbalanced forces and resultant accelerations.

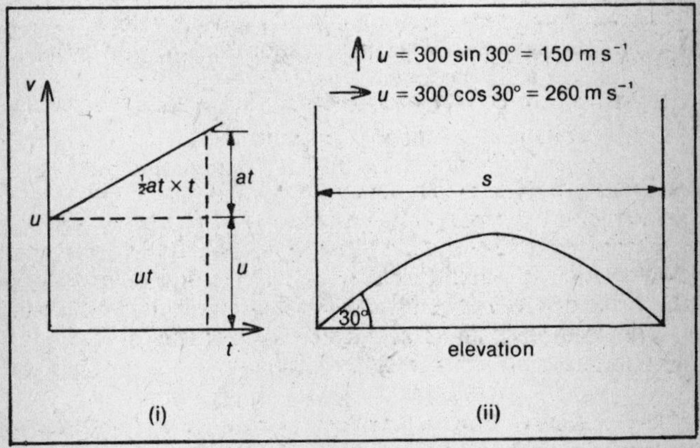

Figure 8. (i) Velocity-time graph (ii) Projectile trajectory

Equations of uniformly accelerated motion The easiest way of displaying the motion of a body is to draw a **velocity-time graph**. Since velocity × time = distance travelled, the area under the graph represents distance travelled. The graph is also a convenient way of establishing two of the three equations of uniformly accelerated motion (fig. 8i).

From the graph v can be seen to be made up of u and $a \times t$ so

$$v = u + a \times t \qquad \text{(i)}$$

The area under the graph can be seen to be made up of two areas ut and $\frac{1}{2}at \times t$ so

$$s = ut + \tfrac{1}{2}at^2 \qquad \text{(ii)}$$

The third equation can be obtained from equations (i) and (ii) by eliminating t

$$t = \frac{v - u}{a} \qquad \text{from (i)}$$

$$\therefore \quad s = u\,\frac{(v-u)}{a} + \tfrac{1}{2}a\,\frac{(v-u)^2}{a^2} \qquad \text{from (ii)}$$

$$2as = 2uv - 2u^2 + v^2 - 2uv + u^2$$

$$\therefore \quad v^2 = u^2 + 2as \qquad \text{(iii)}$$

These equations only apply if a is constant.

Projectiles Details of the trajectories of projectiles can be calculated using these equations and resolving velocity vertically and horizontally. The acceleration due to gravity only affects the vertical component.

Example Calculate the range of a projectile fired at 300 m s^{-1} at 30° to the horizontal (neglect air friction and take g = 10 m s^{-2}) (fig. 8ii).

The velocity is resolved vertically and horizontally.
Vertically $\quad u = 300 \sin 30° = 150$ m s^{-1}
Horizontally $\quad u = 300 \cos 30° = 260$ m s^{-1}

Then the time of flight to the highest point is found.
Vertically:

$$a = -10 \quad \text{(a deceleration)}$$

$$v = u + at \qquad 0 = 150 - 10t \qquad \therefore \quad t = 15 \text{ sec}$$

$$\therefore \quad \text{Total time of flight} = 2 \times 15 = 30 \text{ sec}$$

Horizontally: Distance travelled is given by $s = ut + \frac{1}{2}at^2$

$$s = 260 \times 30 + 0 \quad (\text{since } a = 0)$$
$$s = 7.8 \text{ km}$$

Mass

Mass is 'quantity of matter' and is a measure of the reluctance of a body to accelerate when acted on by a force. It is sometimes loosely referred to as a body's inertia. Unit is the **kilogram** (kg).

Momentum

Momentum is mass × velocity.

It can be transmitted from one body to another. As we shall see, momentum is always conserved in collisions whereas energy of translation usually is not. As velocity is a vector quantity, so is momentum. The unit is the **newton second**.

Newton's laws of motion

1. A body will continue in a state of rest or uniform motion in a straight line unless acted on by an unbalanced external force.
2. The rate of change of momentum of a body is proportional to the unbalanced force acting on it and takes place in the direction of the force.
3. To every action there is an equal and opposite reaction.

Comments on Newton's laws

1. This simply states that if no unbalanced force acts on a body there is no acceleration.
2. Newton actually stated this law in terms of momentum. However, if the mass and acceleration are **constant**, the law can be stated thus

$$F \propto \frac{\mathrm{d}(mv)}{\mathrm{d}t} = \frac{mv - mu}{t} = \frac{m(v - u)}{t}$$

$$\therefore F \propto ma \qquad \text{since } \frac{v - u}{t} = a$$

3. This means that if one body exerts a force on a second body then the second body exerts an equal and opposite force on the first.

Force

Force is that which causes or tends to cause acceleration and it can be calculated from both forms of Newton's second law.

The unit is the **newton** (N) which is the force which will give a mass of 1 kg an acceleration of $1\ m\ s^{-2}$. ∴ $F = ma$.

Example A fireman's hose throws 10 kg of water per second with a velocity of $30\ m\ s^{-1}$ at a door. Calculate the force acting on the door if the water does not rebound.

Force exerted by door on water

$$F = \frac{mv - mu}{t} = \frac{m}{t}(v - u) = \frac{10}{1}(0 - 30) = -300\ \text{N}$$

The minus sign means that this is a retarding force on the water, i.e. it is in the opposite direction to the water's velocity. By Newton's third law the force of the water on the door is 300 N. Another example of this is given on page 87.

Impulse The equation $F = (mv - mu)/t$ can be rewritten $Ft = mv - mu$.

The quantity Ft is known as **impulse**. Thus

Impulse = change of momentum

The unit is the **newton second** (N s) also used for momentum.

Conservation of momentum
Consider two isolated masses m_1 and m_2 colliding (fig. 9). Let m_2 be at rest for simplicity.

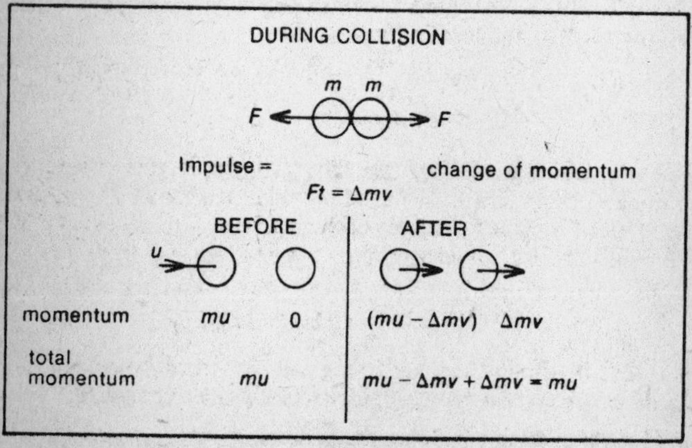

Figure 9. Conservation of momentum

By Newton's third law the forces acting on the two masses during collision are equal and opposite. Also, the time that the collision lasts is the same for both. Thus the impulse slowing the first mass down is the same as that speeding the second mass up.

Hence the first mass loses momentum whilst the second mass **gains equal momentum**. Consequently, the combined momentum of both masses remains constant. This is the **principle of conservation of momentum** which applies to any collision in which **no external forces act**. In many cases where there is an external force, the principle can still be applied since the force acting between the bodies is very much greater than the external force which can be neglected.

Collisions The principle of conservation of momentum can be applied to all collisions. There are several types of collision which can be considered:

1. Elastic collisions in which no energy is lost and the bodies separate.
2. Partially elastic collisions in which some energy is lost and the bodies separate.
3. Inelastic collisions in which the bodies stick together.

Elastic collisions will be considered later, but partially elastic collisions are no longer studied at A-level.

Applying the principle of conservation of momentum to a collision of masses m_1 and m_2, travelling at u_1 and u_2 before collision, and v_1 and v_2 after:

Momentum before collision = momentum after collision

$$m_1u_1 + m_2u_2 = m_1v_1 + m_2v_2$$

Inelastic collisions A special case will make this easier to understand. Let a mass M travelling with a velocity U collide with a mass m at rest, and let both continue with a velocity V after collision. By conservation of momentum

$$MU + 0 = (M + m)V \qquad \text{i.e. } V = \frac{M}{(M+m)}U$$

Therefore if $M \gg m$ (e.g. a moving railway carriage joining on to a small truck at rest) the velocity is almost unchanged.

But if $M \ll m$ (e.g. a moving truck joining on to a carriage at rest) the velocity becomes almost M/m of its previous value.

Example An airgun pellet of mass 10^{-3} kg is shot into a piece of plasticene on a truck which together weigh 0·499 kg. If the truck and plasticene move off at 0·5 m s^{-1} what was the velocity of the pellet?

By conservation of momentum

$$MU = (M + m)V \qquad 0{\cdot}001U = (0{\cdot}001 + 0{\cdot}499)0{\cdot}5$$

$$U = \frac{0{\cdot}25}{10^{-3}} = 250 \text{ m s}^{-1}$$

Explosions The principle of conservation of momentum can also be applied to exploding bodies, e.g. a gun and a shell. In this case, the initial momentum is zero since both gun and shell are at rest. Hence, by conservation of momentum, the combined momentum of gun and shell must still be zero after the explosion. Let the mass and final velocity of the gun be M and V, and of the shell be m and v

Then
$$0 = MV + mv$$

$$V = -\frac{m}{M}v$$

The minus sign indicates that V is a recoil velocity in the opposite direction to the shell, and it is also clear that the recoil velocity is a small fraction of the shell's velocity since $M \gg m$.

Work

Work is force times distance moved **in the direction of the force**. A force which is not moving through a distance is not doing work, e.g. a crane supporting a load does no work on the load until the load is moved upwards against the force of gravity. The unit is the **joule** (J) which is one newton moved through one metre in the direction of the force.

Energy

Energy is stored work and can take many forms – chemical, thermal, electrical, nuclear as well as mechanical energy, which can itself take several forms.

Potential energy is energy possessed by a body by virtue of its position.

Gravitational potential energy is energy possessed by a body by virtue of its position in a gravitational field. If a body is lifted h metres against a force of mg newtons (its weight) then the work done is ***mgh* joules**.

Elastic energy is work stored in stretching a spring. The calculation is more complicated since the tension in the spring varies with the extension, and in some cases this may not even be a linear relationship. Working from a tension-extension graph, this calculation of energy is easy since the area beneath the graph represents tension times extension, i.e. work done.

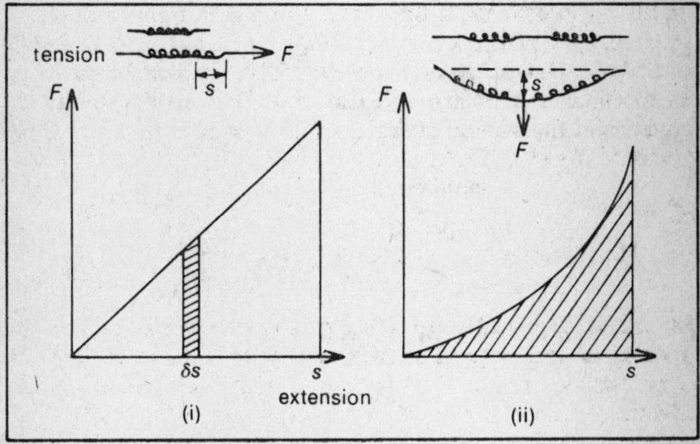

Figure 10. Calculation of strain energy

The work done δW in stretching the spring through a small distance δs (fig. 10i) is given by

$$\delta W = F\delta s$$

since the force remains approximately constant over the small distance δs. The work done is thus the shaded area on the graph. Hence the total work done is the whole area under the graph.

Thus, $$\text{Energy} = \tfrac{1}{2}Fs$$

For a non-linear spring, e.g. a spring stretched across the direction of movement (fig. 10ii), the work stored is still the area under the graph (but it is no longer $\frac{1}{2}Fs$ since the graph is curved).

Kinetic energy is the energy possessed by a body by virtue of its motion. Again, it can be found by calculating the work done by the accelerating force over the distance through which the body is accelerated.

Consider a body accelerated uniformly from rest through a distance s by a force F with acceleration a.

Work done $= F \times s$ But $F = ma$

$\therefore$ Work done $= mas$ But $v^2 = 0^2 + 2as$ i.e. $as = \frac{1}{2}v^2$

$\therefore$ Work done $= m \times \frac{1}{2}v^2 = \frac{1}{2}mv^2$

This result holds even if the acceleration is not uniform

Example A gun of mass 2 tonnes fires a shell of mass 10 kg with a velocity of 1000 m s^{-1}. Calculate the recoil velocity of the gun, and the kinetic energies of the gun and shell.

By conservation of momentum

$$0 = mv + MV$$

$$V = -\frac{m}{M}v$$

$$= -\frac{10}{2000} \times 1000 = 5 \text{ m s}^{-1}$$

Kinetic energy of gun $= \frac{1}{2}MV^2 = \frac{1}{2} \times 2000 \times 5^2 = 25$ kJ

Kinetic energy of shell $= \frac{1}{2}mv^2 = \frac{1}{2} \times 10 \times 1000^2 = 5000$ kJ

i.e. 99.5% of the energy is in the shell's motion. This is because kinetic energy depends on the square of the velocity.

Conservation of energy

Although energy may take many forms it cannot be created or destroyed. Thus the total energy of an isolated system is always constant. This is the **principle of conservation of energy.** In general, however, mechanical energy is seldom conserved, and the principle can only be used where there is no possibility of mechanical energy changing into another form.

Example of loss of mechanical energy Calculate the energy lost when the pellet of the previous example embeds itself in the plasticene.

Kinetic energy of pellet before collision $= \frac{1}{2}mv^2$

$$= \tfrac{1}{2} \times 10^{-3} \times 250^2 = 31{\cdot}2\ \text{J}$$

Kinetic energy of combination after collision

$$= \tfrac{1}{2} \times 0{\cdot}5 \times 0{\cdot}5^2 = 0{\cdot}06\ \text{J}$$

$\therefore$ loss of mechanical energy $= 31{\cdot}2 - 0{\cdot}06 = 31{\cdot}14\ \text{J}$

i.e. nearly all the mechanical energy is lost as the pellet works against the resistance of the plasticene and deforms it. This energy will reappear as heat.

Example of conservation of mechanical energy Calculate the maximum velocity of a pendulum bob if it is released from a height of 0·1 m above its lowest position. (Take g as 10 m s^{-1}).

Assuming no frictional losses, and applying the principle of conservation of energy:

Maximum potential energy relative to bottom of swing = maximum kinetic energy

$$mgh = \tfrac{1}{2}mv^2$$

$$\therefore \quad v^2 = 2gh = 2 \times 10 \times 0{\cdot}1 \qquad v = 1{\cdot}41\ \text{m s}^{-1}$$

Elastic collisions Finally, let us return to elastic collisions, and again consider a special case for clarity. Let two equal masses, m, collide, one moving at a velocity u_1 and the other at rest, and let their velocities after collision be v_1 and v_2 (along the same line).

By conservation of momentum

$$mu_1 + 0 = mv_1 + mv_2 \qquad \therefore \quad u_1 = v_1 + v_2$$

By conservation of energy (since collision is **elastic**)

$$\tfrac{1}{2}mu_1^2 + 0 = \tfrac{1}{2}mv_1^2 + \tfrac{1}{2}mv_2^2 \qquad \therefore \quad u_1^2 = v_1^2 + v_2^2$$

The solutions of these equations are:

$$\text{(i)}\ v_1 = u_1,\ v_2 = 0 \quad \text{or} \quad \text{(ii)}\ v_1 = 0,\ v_2 = u_1$$

Solution (i) is simply the case when the first mass **passes** the other without colliding (momentum and energy are obviously conserved in this case). Solution (ii) is for a collision, and the first mass comes to rest having given its entire momentum to the second – Newton's cradle, for example.

Power

Power is the rate of working, or work done per second. The unit of power is the **watt** (W) which is a rate of working of one joule per second. A powerful machine will do a given amount of work in a shorter time than a less powerful machine.

Example 1 A pump lifts 5 kg of water per second to a tank 20 metres above the pump. What power is needed?

$$\text{Work done per second} = \frac{mgh}{t} = \frac{5}{1} \times 10 \times 20 = 1000\ \text{W} = 1\ \text{kW}$$

Example 2 A car draws a trailer which exerts a drag on the car of 100 N at 20 m s^{-1}. What power is needed?

$$\text{Work done per second} = \frac{Fs}{t} = Fv = 100 \times 20 = 2\ \text{kW}$$

Example 3 50 kg of sand is deposited each second onto a conveyor belt moving at 5 m s^{-1}. Calculate (i) the force needed to keep the belt moving at 5 m s^{-1} (neglecting the friction of belt on rollers) (ii) the power required (iii) the k.e. per second given to the sand. Why are (ii) and (iii) not the same?

Force = rate of change of momentum

(i) $F = \dfrac{mv - mu}{t} = \dfrac{mv}{t}$ since $u = 0$

$= 50 \times 5 = 250$ N

(ii) Power $= F \times \dfrac{s}{t}$

$= F \times v = 250 \times 5 = 1250$ W

(iii) k.e. of sand per second $= \dfrac{\frac{1}{2}mv^2}{t} = \frac{1}{2} \times 50 \times 5^2 = 625$ W

= power absorbed by sand

The balance between (ii) and (iii) is lost in friction between the sand and the belt during the process of accelerating the sand.

Circular motion

Angular velocity

An angle in radians is defined as the arc subtended on a circle divided by the radius, i.e.

$$\theta = \frac{\text{arc}}{\text{radius}} = \frac{s}{r}$$

It should be noted that for small angles $\sin\theta = \tan\theta = \theta$. This is an acceptable approximation for examination purposes. Its validity is illustrated below.

	sin θ	**tan θ**	**θ (radians)**
1°	0·017452	0·017455	0·017453
5°	0·087155	0·087488	0·087266
10°	0·173648	0·176327	0·174533

If a particle is moving with uniform speed round a circle then two velocities may be defined:

(i) the linear velocity, $v = \dfrac{\text{distance round arc}}{\text{time taken}}$

(ii) the angular velocity, $\omega = \dfrac{\text{angle turned through}}{\text{time taken}}$

v is continually changing direction, although the speed remains constant.

ω is about a particular axis (which has direction) and hence is also a vector quantity.

$$\omega = \frac{\theta}{t}$$

but

$$\theta = \frac{s}{r}$$

$$\therefore \quad \omega = \frac{s}{rt} \quad \text{but, since } v = \frac{s}{t}$$

$$\omega = \frac{v}{r} \quad \text{or} \quad v = r\omega$$

Motion in a circle

Newton's first law states that a body continues in a state of rest or uniform motion in a straight line unless acted on by an unbalanced external force. To make a body move in a circle, therefore, requires a lateral force called the **centripetal force** (centripetal means 'centre seeking'). This force produces centripetal acceleration which changes the velocity of the body continuously as it moves round the circle (the speed remains constant but the direction is changing).

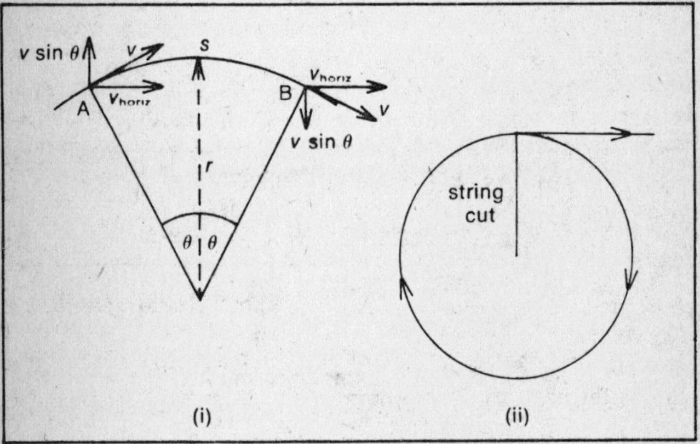

Figure 11. Centripetal acceleration

The centripetal acceleration can be calculated as follows. Consider the components perpendicular and parallel to a reference radius r (fig. 11i).

The change of vertical velocity in going from A to B is $2v \sin \theta$.
The time taken to travel from A to B is

$$\frac{\text{arc}}{\text{velocity}} = \frac{2r\theta}{v}$$

$$\therefore \quad \text{vertical acceleration} = \frac{2v^2 \sin \theta}{2r\theta} = \frac{v^2 \sin \theta}{r\theta}$$

Since $\sin \theta \rightarrow \theta$ as $\theta \rightarrow 0$

the centripetal acceleration becomes $\dfrac{v^2}{r}$

Thus the centripetal acceleration is in the direction of the radius r, i.e. towards the centre.

Since $F = ma$ the centripetal force is $\frac{mv^2}{r}$. Another useful form of this is obtained by replacing v with ωr, therefore

$$\frac{mv^2}{r} = \frac{m(\omega r)^2}{r}$$
$$= mr\omega^2$$

The concept of **centrifugal force** is not helpful since it implies that there is a force directed away from the centre. If the string keeping a whirling body in a circle is cut, the body flies off **tangentially** and not radially (fig. 11ii). (If one were **on** the body then the previous centre of rotation would **appear** to recede, but this is because of a centripetal force being absent rather than the presence of a centrifugal force.)

Examples of centripetal force

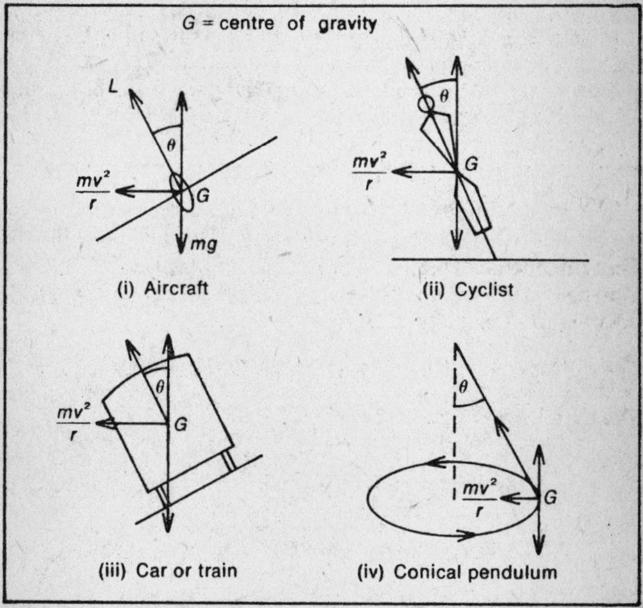

Figure 12. Centripetal forces

(i) **Banking aircraft** In this case the centripetal force is the horizontal component of the lift L (fig. 12i).

Vertically, $$L \cos \theta = mg$$

Horizontally, $$L \sin \theta = \frac{mv^2}{r}$$

Eliminating L: $$mg \tan \theta = \frac{mv^2}{r}$$

$$\therefore \quad \theta = \tan^{-1} \frac{v^2}{gr}$$

So, for instance, if the aircraft is flying at 100 m s^{-1} the angle of bank, θ, needed to turn with a radius of 1000 m is given by

$$\theta = \tan^{-1} \frac{v^2}{gr} = \tan^{-1} \frac{10^4}{10 \times 10^3} = 45°$$

It should be noted that the mass of the aircraft does not appear in the expression for the angle of bank. The same result is obtained in considering a cyclist, or car or train banked such that there is no lateral force on the track (fig. 12ii, iii). It also applies to a conical pendulum (fig. 12iv) (in which the tension of the string is equivalent to the lift of the aircraft).

(ii) **Motion in a vertical circle** For an aircraft looping the loop the gravitational force will sometimes help to provide the centripetal force. On the top of the loop, for instance, the lift will only need to provide

$$\frac{mv^2}{r} - mg$$

while at the bottom it will have to provide

$$\frac{mv^2}{r} + mg$$

If the speed is such that

$$\frac{mv^2}{r} = mg$$

then the pilot will be in a condition of weightlessness at the top of the loop.

(iii) **Variation of g with latitude** Despite the Greeks' conviction that if the earth were spinning objects would be hurled off, the centripetal force at the equator is small.

The radius of the earth is 6.37×10^6 metres, and it rotates once every 24 hours. Thus the centripetal force at the equator is given by

$$mr\omega^2 = m \times 6.37 \times 10^6 \times \left(\frac{2\pi}{24 \times 60 \times 60}\right)^2 = 0.034\, m \text{ N}$$

Thus, the force acting on the mass at the equator is $0.034\, m$ N less, so that the value of g will appear to be 0.034 m s^{-2} less, i.e. $g = (9.81 - 0.034) \text{ m s}^{-2}$.

Rotational mechanics

Moment of inertia A body free to rotate about an axis needs energy to make it rotate in much the same way as a body moving linearly does. The energy possessed by a rotating body can be calculated by considering it to consist of small particles **all rotating at the same angular velocity** (fig. 13i).

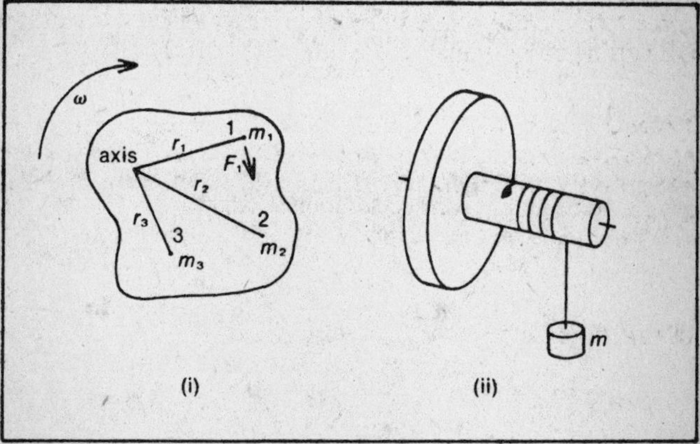

Figure 13. Moment of inertia

$$\begin{aligned}\text{The kinetic energy of particle 1} &= \tfrac{1}{2}m_1 v_1^2 \\ &= \tfrac{1}{2}m_1(r_1\omega)^2 \\ &= \tfrac{1}{2}m_1 r_1^2 \times \omega^2\end{aligned}$$

Hence, the total kinetic energy $= \frac{1}{2}(m_1r_1^2 + m_2r_2^2 + \cdots m_nr_n^2)\omega^2$

$$= \tfrac{1}{2}\omega^2\Sigma mr^2 = \tfrac{1}{2}I\omega^2$$

where I is called the **moment of inertia of the body.** Σmr^2 is shorthand for 'the sum of all the mr^2 terms' and I can be found for simple shapes by summing the mr^2 terms by integration. Values can be found in data books. The moment of inertia of a body depends primarily not on the body's mass but on its distribution, e.g. the moment of inertia of a wheel is far greater if the mass is distributed round its rim. I can also be found by experiment. The units of moment of inertia are kg m^2. One experiment for finding the value of I for a wheel and shaft is illustrated in fig. 13ii. The mass is connected by a string (which detaches itself when unwound) to a shaft. The mass falls, accelerating the wheel. The potential energy of the falling mass becomes the kinetic energy of the falling mass, plus kinetic energy of the wheel and shaft, plus frictional losses, i.e.

$$mgh = \tfrac{1}{2}mv^2 + \tfrac{1}{2}I\omega^2 + n_1f$$

where f = energy lost per turn, and n_1 = number of turns of the wheel whilst the mass is falling and accelerating the wheel. This assumes that f is independent of the speed of rotation. f is found by counting the number of turns n_2, for the wheel to come to rest after the mass has attached itself. Then $\frac{1}{2}I\omega^2 = n_2f$.

Torque and angular acceleration are related in the same way as force and linear acceleration. Consider fig. 13i again. If a force F_1 acts on the particle 1 then

$$F_1 = m_1a_1 = m_1\frac{dv_1}{dt} = m_1r_1\frac{d\omega}{dt}$$

$$\text{The moment of the force} = r_1F_1 = m_1r_1^2\frac{d\omega}{dt}$$

Hence the total moment, or torque, is given by

$$T = (m_1r_1^2 + m_2r_2^2 + \cdots m_nr_n^2)\frac{d\omega}{dt}$$

$$= \frac{d\omega}{dt}\Sigma mr^2 = I\frac{d\omega}{dt} = I\frac{d^2\theta}{dt^2}$$

This compares with the expression for the translational case

$$F = ma = m\frac{d^2s}{dt^2}$$

Work

Consider a drum with a band brake round it (fig. 14i). If the total frictional force is F (distributed evenly round the drum) then since the frictional force at all points is equidistant from the centre, the total torque is given by $T = Fr$.

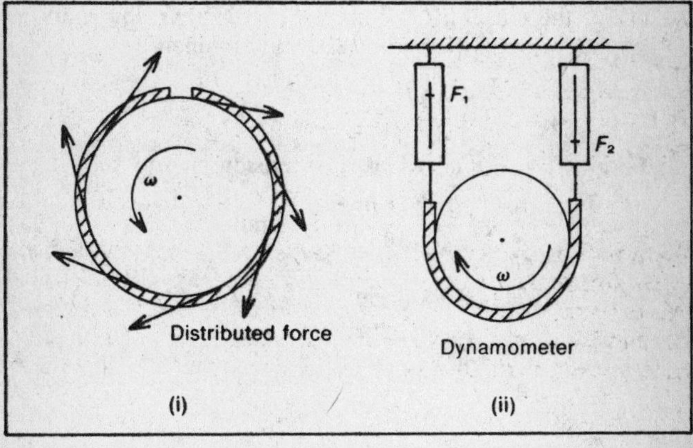

Figure 14. Band brake

The distance moved by the drum sliding against the brake band is $r\theta$, if it rotates through an angle θ.

The work done therefore is given by

$$W = F \times r\theta$$

But $\quad Fr = T \quad \therefore \quad W = T\theta$

This compares with the expression for the translational case

$$W = Fs$$

But this can be extended to power as well, since power = work done per second. Power is given by

$$P = \frac{dW}{dt} = T\frac{d\theta}{dt} \quad \text{i.e.} \quad P = T\omega$$

This compares with the expression for the translational case

$$P = Fv$$

Dynamometers for testing the power of engines work on this basis. F is the difference between the readings of the two spring balances (fig. 14ii).

$$F = F_1 - F_2 \quad \text{and} \quad T = Fr \quad \therefore \quad P = Fr\omega$$

Example A flywheel of M.I. 0.5 kg m^{-2} is accelerated by a cord with tension 20 N wound round an axle of radius 2 cm. Neglecting friction, calculate (i) the angular acceleration (ii) the k.e. of the wheel after 2 metres of cord has unwound (iii) the angular velocity of the wheel at that moment.

(i) $T = I\dfrac{d^2\theta}{dt^2} \quad \therefore \quad \dfrac{d^2\theta}{dt^2} = \dfrac{T}{I}$

Torque $T = F \times r$ where F = tension in cord

$$\therefore \quad \frac{d^2\theta}{dt^2} = \frac{Fr}{I} = \frac{20 \times 2 \times 10^{-2}}{5 \times 10^{-1}} = 0{\cdot}8 \text{ rad s}^{-2}$$

(ii) k.e. of wheel = work done

$$\tfrac{1}{2}I\omega^2 = F \times s = 20 \times 2$$
$$= 40 \text{ J}$$

(iii) $\tfrac{1}{2}I\omega^2 = 40$

$$\therefore \quad \omega^2 = \frac{40 \times 2}{5 \times 10^{-1}} = 160$$

$$\therefore \quad \omega = 12.6 \text{ rad s}^{-1}$$

(N.B. 2π rad s^{-1} = 1 r.p.s. = 60 r.p.m.)

Angular momentum

Momentum is defined as mv. **Angular momentum** (L) about an axis O is defined as the **moment of the momentum** about O.

Thus for the body in fig. 13i.

Moment of momentum of particle 1 $= m_1v_1 \times r_1 = m_1r_1^2\omega$

since $\quad v_1 = r_1\omega$

$\therefore$ Total angular momentum $L = (m_1r_1^2 + m_2r_2^2 + \cdots m_nr_n^2)\omega$

i.e. $\quad L = I\omega$

This compares with the expression for the translational case

$$P = mv$$

The units of angular momentum are joule seconds.

Conservation of angular momentum
By arguments similar to those used to establish conservation of translational momentum, it can be shown that angular momentum about a given axis is conserved in a system in which no external torque acts about the axis.

For example a ballet dancer can increase her rate of rotation if she reduces her moment of inertia by moving her arms inwards, her total angular momentum remaining constant.

Comparison of translational and angular quantities

	Translational	Angular
Newton's 2nd law	$F = m\dfrac{d^2s}{dt^2} = ma$	$T = I\dfrac{d^2\theta}{dt^2} = I\dfrac{d\omega}{dt}$
Momentum	$p = mv$	$L = I\omega$
Work	$W = Fs$	$W = T\theta$
Power	$P = Fv$	$P = T\omega$
Kinetic energy	$W = \frac{1}{2}mv^2$	$W = \frac{1}{2}I\omega^2$

Gravitation

A body on the earth's surface experiences a downward force called its weight. This force is due to the mutual attraction between the body's mass and the mass of the earth. Any two masses will attract each other, but the force is normally difficult to detect if the masses are small.

The gravitational field is a region of space in which a mass experiences a gravitational force.

Field strengths in general Several fields will be encountered in a Physics course – in particular the gravitational field, the electric field and the magnetic field.

In each case the strength of the field is measured in terms of the force it exerts on a 'unit detector'–a kilogram mass for the gravitational field, a coulomb of positive charge for the electric field, and a unit current element for the magnetic field. These are represented in theory in fig. 15. The electric and magnetic cases will be discussed later.

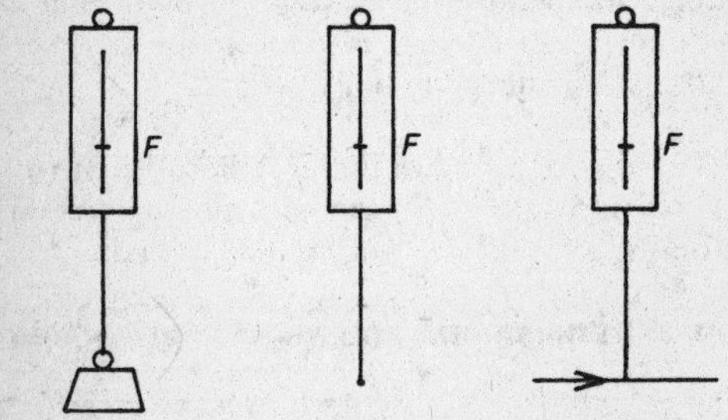

Figure 15. Field strength 'meters'

The gravitational field strength (g) is the gravitational force, F_g, in newtons acting per kilogram mass at a point in a gravitational field, i.e.

$$g = \frac{F_g}{m}$$

The units are $N\,kg^{-1}$. The value of g at the earth's surface is $9{\cdot}81\ N\,kg^{-1}$, or approximately $10\ N\,kg^{-1}$.

If a mass is released, it will fall with the **acceleration of free fall** which is, of course, numerically equal to g since $F = ma$. Its units are $m\,s^{-2}$. In this book g will be referred to as the gravitational field strength ($N\,kg^{-1}$).

Gravitational potential difference

When a mass is raised in a gravitational field, its potential energy is increased because work is done against the gravitational force. A useful additional concept is that of the potential energy per unit mass, which is then a property of the field and independent of the mass of any particular body. The gravitational potential difference (Φ) is thus defined as the potential energy per kilogram. In the earth's gravitational field (assumed to be uniform at the surface) (fig. 16i)

$$\Phi = \frac{mgh}{m} = gh$$

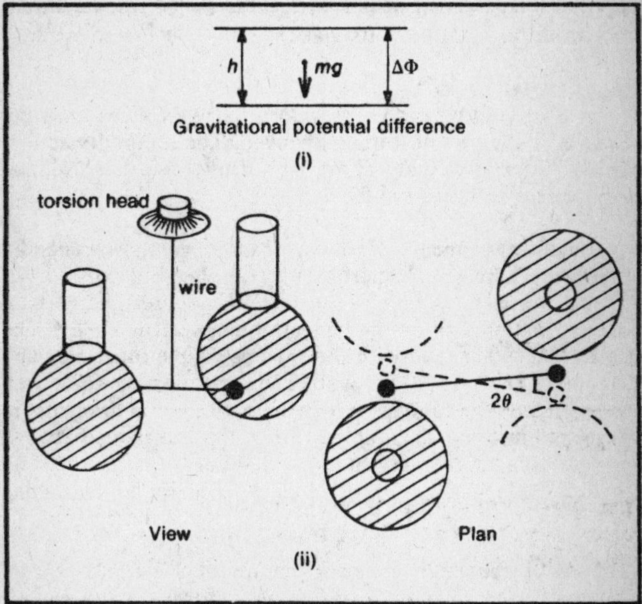

Figure 16. Gravitational p.d. and method for G

Inverse square law field

So far, only the gravitational field strength at the earth's surface has been considered, and it has been regarded as uniform. Far away from the earth, however, the field strength is very different. Newton was the first to contemplate the way in which g varies with distance. By calculations on the moon's period in going round its orbit, the radius of which is 60 times the radius of the earth, he showed that the force between the two masses must vary as $1/r^2$ where r is the distance between them. From his third law of action and reaction he deduced that the force would depend on the mass of both bodies. Thus he proposed

$$F_g \propto \frac{Mm}{r^2} \quad \text{where } M \text{ and } m \text{ are the two masses.}$$

Newton's law of gravitation thus states that

$$F_g = G\frac{Mm}{r^2}$$

where G is a constant of proportionality called the **Universal Gravitational Constant.** Its value is $6{\cdot}67 \times 10^{-11}$ N m^2 kg^{-2}.

Measurement of *G*

G can be measured in the laboratory but with some difficulty because of the minute forces involved. The method was first used by Cavendish and improved by Boys. A school version is shown schematically in fig. 16ii.

Two small lead spheres are mounted on a beam suspended by a very fine tungsten wire from a torsion head. Two flasks of mercury are brought up close to the lead spheres and gravitational attraction deflects the beam through a small angle θ. The experiment is repeated with the spheres on the other side and the total deflection (2θ) is found. The apparatus has to be well protected from vibrations (spongy mountings) and draughts (in a transparent box). The angle of deflection, distance between masses, mass of mercury and lead can all be measured, and the torsional constant of the fine wire is found by timing oscillations (knowing the moment of inertia of the beam).

Because of the inverse square nature of Newton's law of gravitation, the mass of a sphere of uniform density can be shown mathematically to act as if it were all at the centre.

Applications of Newton's law of gravitation

The mass of the earth can be found if its radius is known. Gravitational force on a mass m is given by

$$F_g = G\frac{Mm}{R^2} = mg \qquad \text{i.e. } \frac{GM}{R^2} = g$$

where M = mass of the earth, R = earth's mean radius (6380 km).

$$\therefore \quad M = \frac{gR^2}{G} = \frac{9{\cdot}8 \times 6{\cdot}38^2 \times 10^{12}}{6{\cdot}67 \times 10^{-11}} = 5{\cdot}98 \times 10^{24}\ \text{kg}$$

Satellite orbits can be calculated since the gravitational pull is providing the centripetal force when the satellite is in a stable orbit (assumed circular). Thus

$$\frac{GMm}{R^2} = \frac{mv^2}{R}$$

where R = distance of satellite from centre of earth, v = satellite velocity, M and m = mass of earth and satellite respectively.

$$\therefore \quad v^2 = \frac{GM}{R} \qquad \text{(i)}$$

Example Calculate the radius of orbit, r, necessary for a communications satellite to be in synchronous orbit (i.e. period of orbit same as that of the earth, and therefore stationary relative to the earth's surface).

Let mass of earth be M and earth's radius be R

At the satellite $$\frac{GMm}{r^2} = mr\omega^2$$

$$\therefore \quad r^3 = \frac{GM}{\omega^2}$$

But at the earth's surface for any mass m

$$\frac{GMm}{R^2} = mg \qquad \therefore \quad GM = gR^2$$

$\therefore$ Satellite orbit radius is given by

$$r^3 = \frac{gR^2}{\omega^2} = \frac{9.81 \times (6.38 \times 10^6)^2}{[2\pi/(24 \times 60 \times 60)]^2}$$

$$r = 42\,266 \text{ km}$$

Kepler's third law follows directly from equation (i) since

$$v = \text{circumferential speed} = \frac{\text{circumference}}{\text{period}} = \frac{2\pi R}{T}$$

where T = period

$$\therefore \quad \frac{4\pi^2 R^2}{T^2} = \frac{GM}{R} \qquad \text{i.e.} \quad \frac{R^3}{T^2} = \frac{GM}{4\pi^2} = \text{constant} \qquad \text{i.e.} \quad T^2 \propto R^3$$

M in this case is any central body around which smaller ones are orbiting. Kepler deduced the law empirically for planets around the sun. The constant depends on M and is therefore not the same for planets around the sun as it would be for satellites around the earth.

Kepler's laws

Kepler's laws were deduced empirically from the very accurate astronomical observations of the motions of the planets made by Tycho Brahe. They are illustrated in fig. 17.

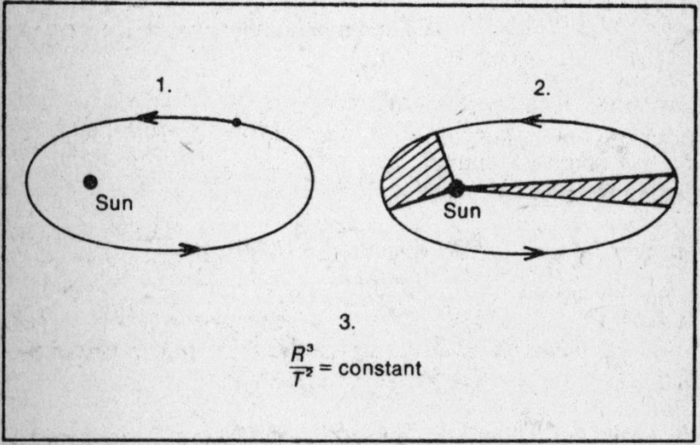

Figure 17. Kepler's law

1. The planets move in ellipses with the sun at one focus (this follows mathematically from the inverse square law).
2. The line joining the sun and the planet sweeps out equal areas in equal times (this is a consequence of conservation of angular momentum).
3. The squares of the periods of the planets round their orbits are proportional to the cubes of their major axes of the orbits (proved above for a circular orbit).

Dimensions

The method of dimensions is a powerful technique for deducing or checking the form of a physical relationship. It depends on the fact that both sides of an equation must be identical functions of the basic physical quantities – length (m), mass (kg), time (s), current (A), temperature (K), amount of substance (mol) and luminous intensity (candela). Of these, this discussion will only concern three basic quantities – mass, represented by $[M]$, length, $[L]$, and time, $[T]$, where the square brackets [] mean 'the dimension of the quantity'. Thus $v = [LT^{-1}]$ means 'the dimensions of v are those of length divided by time'. Usually the dimensions of a quantity have to be deduced from basic definitions, e.g. force = mass × acceleration = $[MLT^{-2}]$.

Checking an equation can be done by writing down the dimensions of each term. The dimensions must be the same on both sides of the equation, e.g.

$$v^2 = u^2 + 2as$$

u and v have dimensions $[LT^{-1}]$, a is $[LT^{-2}]$ and s is $[L]$.

Thus $$[LT^{-1}]^2 = [LT^{-1}]^2 + [LT^{-2}][L]$$

All are $[L^2T^{-2}]$, so that the equation is dimensionally correct. The method cannot, however, check dimensionless constants.

Deducing the form of an equation proceeds by writing down the dimensions of each possible term (up to three) and then equating the indices of each dimension.

For example, suppose we guess that centripetal force depends on mass, velocity and radius, i.e.

$$F = f(m, v, r)$$

Let the powers of m, v and r be a, b, and c respectively.

Then $$[MLT^{-2}] = [M]^a[LT^{-1}]^b[L]^c$$

Equating indices
$$[M]: 1 = a$$
$$[L]: 1 = b + c$$
$$[T]: -2 = -b$$
$$\therefore \quad a = 1, \quad b = 2, \quad c = -1$$

and the equation is $F \propto \dfrac{mv^2}{r}$

The method cannot predict any dimensionless constants (in this case 1), nor can it allow for an **incomplete** or **incorrect** list of possible physical quantities involved.

Amount of substance
The mole is defined as the amount of substance which contains

the same number of elementary entities as there are in 0.012 kg of carbon-12. This number is called the Avogadro number (N_A) and has the value 6×10^{23}.

Key terms

Speed Distance moved in unit time. Unit m s^{-1}. (1 m s^{-1} ≈ 2 m.p.h.)
Velocity Speed in a particular direction. Velocity can be positive or negative indicating opposite directions.
Acceleration Rate of change of velocity. It is a vector quantity. Unit: m s^{-2}.
Vectors Quantities that have both magnitude and direction.
Moment (turning effect). The moment of a force about an axis is the product of the force and the perpendicular distance of the axis from the line of action of the force. Unit: N m.
Torque A synonym for moment.
Equilibrium A situation in which no net forces or moments act on a body.
Friction A force between two surfaces parallel to them which opposes any applied force tending to make them slide over each other. Dynamic, or kinetic, friction is slightly less than static friction.
Pressure Normal force per unit area. Unit: Pascal (Pa). (1 Pa = 1 N m^{-2})
Archimedes' principle When a body is fully or partially immersed in a fluid, the upthrust on it is equal to the weight of fluid displaced.
Mass A measure of the quantity of matter in a body on which its inertia depends. Unit: kilogram (kg).
Weight The pull of gravity on a body. Unit: newton (N), or kilograms force (kg f).
Momentum Mass of a body multiplied by its velocity. Unit: newton second (N s) or kg m s^{-1}.
Force That which alters or tends to alter a body's state of rest or uniform motion in a straight line. Unit: newton (N).
Impulse Force multiplied by time of action of the force. Unit: newton second (N s).
Conservation of momentum If no external forces act on a closed system of colliding bodies, the total momentum of the bodies remains constant. This is true of both linear momentum and angular momentum.
Inelastic collision A collision in which two bodies do not separate, and mechanical energy is not conserved.

Elastic collision A collision in which mechanical energy is conserved, and the bodies do separate.
Work Force × distance moved in the direction of the force. Unit: joule (J).
Energy Stored work, or ability to do work. Unit: joule (J).
Potential energy Energy possessed by a body by virtue of its position.
Gravitational potential energy Energy possessed by a body by virtue of its position in a gravitational field.
Elastic energy Energy stored in a stretched spring or elastic material.
Kinetic energy Energy possessed by a body by virtue of its motion.
Conservation of energy Although energy may be transformed from one form to another, the total energy in an isolated system is always constant.
Power Rate of working, or work done per second. Unit: watt (W).
Angular velocity Angle turned through per second. Unit: radian per second (rad s^{-1}).
Centripetal force A lateral force which makes a body move in a circular path.
Centrifugal force It is better not to use this term.
Moment of inertia In circular motion, the quantity corresponding to the mass in linear motion. It is the sum of the products of the mass and the square of the perpendicular distance from the axis of all the particles in a body. Unit: kg m^2.
Angular momentum The moment of momentum about an axis. Unit: joule second (J s).
Gravitational field A region of space in which a mass experiences a gravitational force.
Newton's law of gravitation The force between two masses is proportional to their product and inversely proportional to the distance between them.
Universal gravitational constant The constant of proportionality in Newton's law of gravitation.
Mole The amount of substance which contains the same number of elementary entities as there are in 0.012 kg of carbon-12. Symbol: mol.
Avogadro number N_A. The number of elementary entities in a mole of substance (6×10^{23}) Unit: mol^{-1}.

Chapter 2
Structure and Properties of Materials

This chapter is concerned with the nature and behaviour of materials – principally solids but with a brief discussion of aspects of liquid behaviour. Gases are dealt with in chap. 3.

Atoms

The structure of atoms and the relevant experimental evidence is discussed in the chapter on Nuclear and Quantum Physics.

For this discussion, atoms are regarded as spheres with a nucleus at the centre containing the mass and positive charge but of diameter only 10^{-4} that of the atom. The rest of the atom is empty, except for several discrete shells in which there is a probability of finding electrons. Thus only about one million, millionth of the atom is solid. This is roughly equivalent to a fly in a cathedral. If your house represented a nucleus, the next nucleus in a solid would be over a hundred miles away and if matter were condensed down so that the whole of its volume consisted of nuclei, then 1 cm^3 of iron would have a mass approaching ten million tons.

Element	Atomic No.	Outer Orbital	Atomic Diameter/10^{-10} m
Li	3	L	3.0
Na	11	M	3.7
K	19	N	4.6
Ca	20	N	4.0
Cr	24	N	2.6
Ni	28	N	2.5
Cs	55	P	5.2

Table 1. Atomic diameters

Atoms are exceedingly small – diameter varying from about 1×10^{-10} to 5×10^{-10} m. The radius of an atom is, of course, that of its outer orbital. It does not vary as much as might be expected (see Table 1) since increased nuclear charge causes the inner orbitals to shrink and the extra orbitals thus cause only small increases.

Bonding

Atoms form themselves into rigid solids by interatomic bonding. This can be of four basic types – ionic, covalent, Van der Waals and metallic. Each type of bond has different characteristics.

Ionic bonds are due to the spontaneous formation of ions – atoms which have lost or gained an electron. As a result they acquire a positive or negative charge and their diameter also changes because of the loss or gain of an orbital (see Table 2). The ionic bond is thus the electrostatic attraction between positive and negative charges. The force varies as $1/x^2$ where x is the spacing between the ions. Sodium chloride is an ionic compound and the sodium ions are positive having lost their outer electrons to the chlorine ions which become negative. A positive ion can of course attract several negative ions around it as well as being repelled by other positive ions (fig. 18i).

Element	Atomic Diameter/ 10^{-10} m	Outer Orbital	Ionic Diameter/ 10^{-10} m	Outer Orbital	Ion
Li	3.0	L	1.4	K	Li^+
Na	3.7	M	2.0	L	Na^+
K	4.6	N	3.0	M	K^+
Cs	5.2	P	3.3	N	Cs^+
F	2.7	L	2.7	L	F^-
Cl	3.6	M	3.6	M	Cl^-
Br	3.9	N	3.9	N	Br^-
I	4.4	O	4.4	O	I^-

Table 2. Ionic diameters

Covalent bonds always involve the sharing of electrons. In a hydrogen molecule, for instance, each electron interacts with both nuclei so that each nucleus appears to 'possess' two electrons to complete the *K* shell. An exact description of the origin of the binding force is complex but the concentration of negative electrons between the two positive nuclei in effect binds them together (fig. 18ii). The force falls off rapidly with separation. The bond acts in a specific direction and each bond cannot affect more than one other atom.

In solids, good examples are diamond and the semiconductors germanium and silicon. All of these, being Group 4 elements, have four outer electrons, each of which form a covalent bond with one of the four neighbouring atoms.

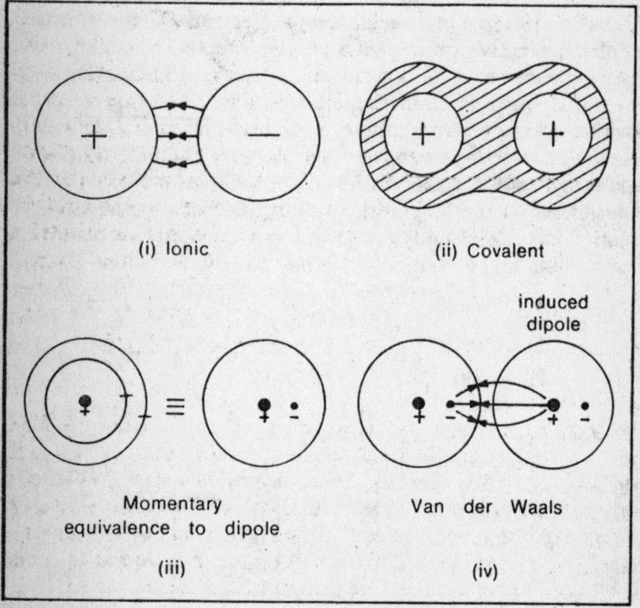

Figure 18. *Types of bond*

Van der Waals bonds are weak electrostatic forces occurring between all atoms and molecules, even though other types of bond may exist. Basically, the bonding is due to momentary asymmetrical distributions of electrons around a nucleus (fig. 18iii). As a result the atom will seem to be more positive on one side and this will cause asymmetry in a neighbouring atom by attracting electrons slightly to one side and polarizing the atom (fig. 18iv). Consequently there will be a force, weak compared with ionic and covalent forces, between the two neutral atoms called the Van der Waals force. It falls off with separation as $1/x^7$ and affects more than one atom. It is Van der Waals forces which cause the departure from ideal gas behaviour in real gases under high compression. The bonding in solid argon, neon and krypton is by Van der Waals forces which can also bond long organic molecules together, for example in waxes.

Metallic bonds occur because of the tendency for metals to lose their loosely bound outer electrons to a general 'electron gas' within the lattice. The number of free electrons in many metals, copper or silver, for instance, is about one per atom. Thus a metal consists of an array of positive ions permeated by an 'atmosphere' of free electrons (which even at room temperatures are moving extremely fast – around $300\,km\,s^{-1}$). Electrical neutrality is maintained on average over any region and there tends to be a concentration of electrons between the fixed ions. The positive ions are thus attracted to the concentration of negative charge between them and this constitutes a strong binding force. The force is again short range, extremely difficult to calculate and arbitrarily, a $1/x^6$ law is assumed. The mobile electrons account for some of the thermal and all of the electrical conduction discussed later.

Repulsion

The fact that solids and liquids are highly incompressible suggests that there are large repulsive forces between atoms if they are squashed together. These repulsive forces have been identified as being due to the penetration of the outer orbital of one atom by that of another. The nuclear charges are thus no longer completely screened from each other and tend to repel each other but an exact description of the repulsive force is complex. The repulsive force is extremely short range and very strong and has a variation of between $1/x^7$ and $1/x^{13}$.

Interatomic force curves

The net inter-atomic force can be found by combining the force of attraction and the force of repulsion.

Typically $$F_{rep} = \frac{a}{x^{13}}, \qquad F_{att} = \frac{b}{x^7}$$

$$F = F_{rep} - F_{att}; \quad F = \frac{a}{x^{13}} - \frac{b}{x^7}$$

The curves of these functions are shown in fig. 19i-iii.

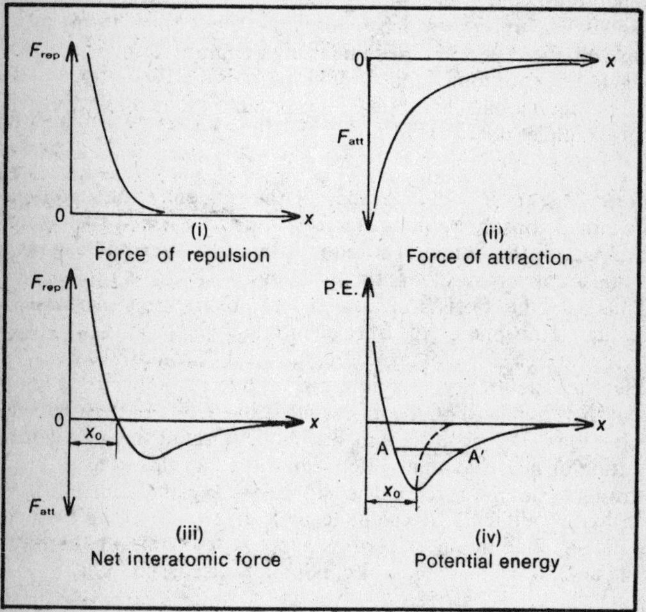

Figure 19. Intermolecular forces and energies

It can be seen that there is a value of the separation between two atoms x_0 for which the two forces exactly balance, i.e. this is the equilibrium position of the second atom relative to the first. The graph shows that for very small movements either side of the equilibrium spacing, the force/distance curve is linear (fig. 20ii point 2). This corresponds to the observed Hookes' law behaviour in tension and compression (p. 55).

Potential energy curves

Consider a force acting on a body in the direction of increasing x (fig. 20i).

Let a **repulsive force**, F, have O as its origin.

Then in moving a small distance $(-\delta x)$ against the force.

Work done $\delta W = F(-\delta x)$

So $$F = -\frac{dW}{dk} \quad \text{as} \quad \delta x \to 0$$

Thus for example, at point 3 in fig. 20iii the slope of the energy curve is maximum positive so F is maximum negative, i.e. maximum **attractive** force (point 3 in fig. 20ii).

A potential energy/separation curve can thus be calculated if the force/separation variation is known (fig. 20). The gradient at each point on the potential energy curve is equal to the force at that separation on the force curve. Three examples are given in fig. 20. At position 2 the equilibrium spacing corresponds to zero net force on the second atom and hence the gradient of the energy curve is also zero at that point. This corresponds to an energy minimum or the bottom of a potential well. The implications of the shape of this curve for a material which is heated is discussed on page 67.

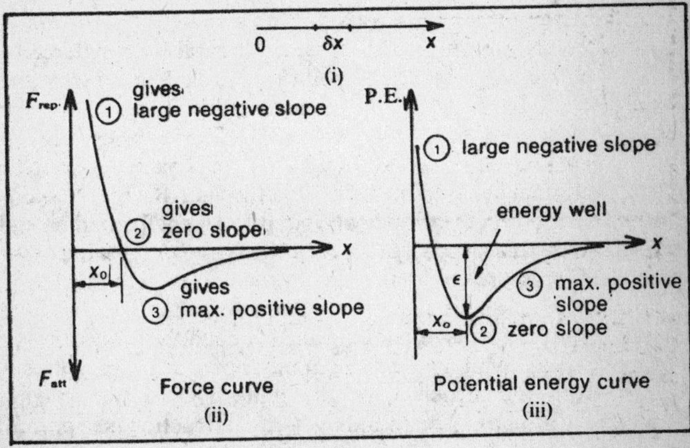

Figure 20. Derivation of potential energy curve

An estimate for the depth of the potential well, which is the bond energy ϵ, can be obtained from latent heats of vaporization or sublimation (see p. 76). If two atoms which are bonded together are separated, then the energy required to break the bond has released two atoms, i.e. each atom needed $\frac{1}{2}\epsilon$. If each atom in a solid is held by n bonds, then the energy needed to release it is $n \times \frac{1}{2}\epsilon$.

Thus for 1 mole the energy will be $N_A \times \frac{1}{2}n\epsilon$. For a typical solid $n = 12$ so the molar latent heat of sublimation is given by

$$L_{ms} = 6N_A\epsilon \qquad \therefore \quad \epsilon = \frac{L_{ms}}{6N_A}$$

For a typical liquid $n \approx 10$

so
$$L_{mv} = 5N_A\epsilon \qquad \therefore \quad \epsilon = \frac{L_{mv}}{5N_A}$$

Structure

So far the discussion has considered only atoms, or pairs of atoms. In practice of course most solids have a complex structure within a single crystal. Moreover, a solid often consists of many minute randomly orientated crystallites. Of the countless possible structures, only two possible forms of close packing found in metals will be discussed briefly.

Close packed structures are obtained by placing spheres in contact, each having six others around it and each in contact with the next (fig. 21i). The second layer will nestle in recesses formed between the first ones – but only half the recesses will be filled – the B sites of fig. 21ii. If the third layer is placed so as to be over the original spheres then the structure is ABAB . . . , and is called **hexagonal close packed** (h.c.p.). A pencil could be slid through the whole structure at any of the C sites. If, on the other hand, the C sites are covered by the third layer then the structure is ABCABC . . . , and is called **face centred cubic** (f.c.c.). There are other similar forms of packing and for each the proportion of space occupied by atoms and the number of nearest neighbours differs. Both the structure of the material and the spacing between the atoms can be found by X-ray diffraction (see p. 153).

A good analogue of a single plane of crystal structure is obtained by blowing bubbles through a very fine tube in detergent solution so that they form a 'bubble raft'. The ordered patterns, in which each bubble will have six others around it, are clear, as are changes of orientation in places corresponding to different crystallites.

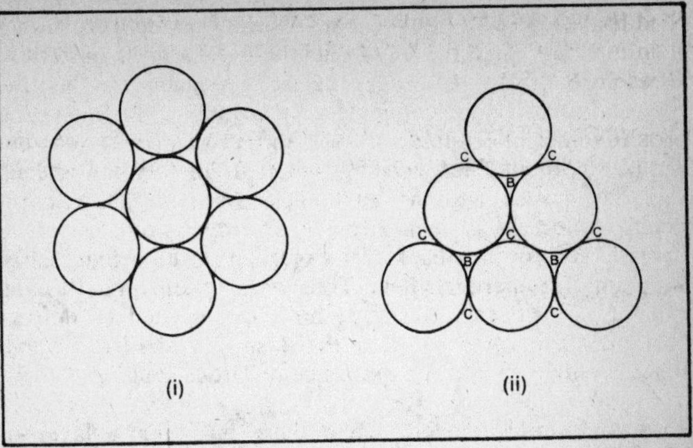

Figure 21. Close packing

Deformation of metals
If a metal is stretched beyond a small increase in length (about 1%) it will be subject to **plastic flow** with the result that it acquires a permanent deformation and will not return to its original length. This is due in the main to two mechanisms:

Slip planes are planes with atoms which can slip over each other when subjected to a shearing force (fig. 22i). There will

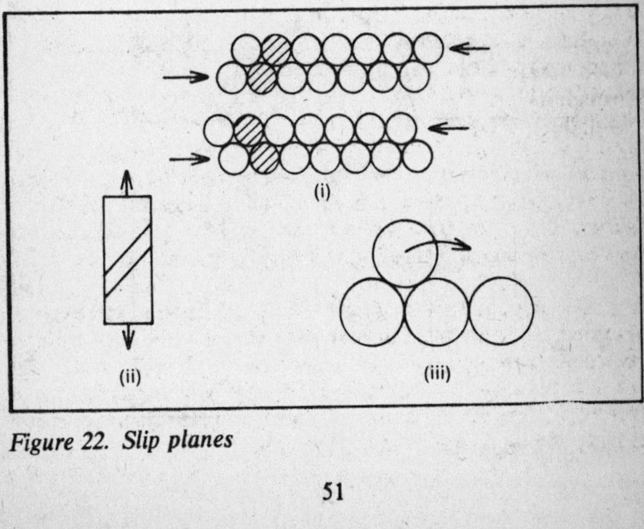

Figure 22. Slip planes

always be some crystal planes suitably orientated even with a straight tensile force (fig. 22ii). Clearly, the energy required for the atoms to 'ride over' each other is very much less than the energy to break bonds completely. It might be asked why, if a force is sufficient to start the overriding, the process does not continue without energy being supplied. In fact, after each atom has moved into the next depression, the atom it has ridden over, having been strained slightly to one side, will oscillate as it springs back to its original position (fig. 22iii) – dissipating the energy as heat. Thus work is done in deforming a metal. The measured stress, however, needed to deform most metals is one thousand times smaller than those calculated. This is due to the existence of lattice faults.

Edge dislocations occur when there is an extra layer of atoms somewhere in an otherwise regular lattice (shown in black in fig. 23i). The line along the edge of the extra plane is the **edge dislocation.** If a shear stress is applied to the lattice as shown, the atom at A will 'flick over' and rebond to the

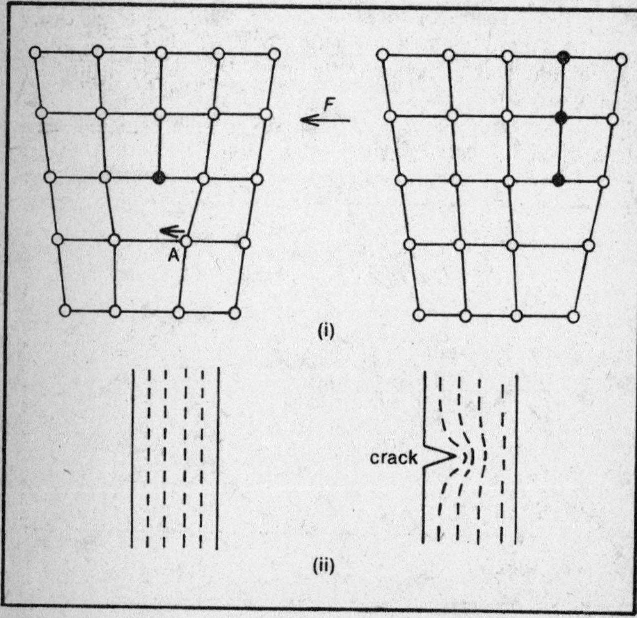

Figure 23. Edge dislocation and crack

previous extra plane, thus forming a new extra plane and causing subsequent slight readjustment of planes to give the same pattern as before. Thus the edge dislocation propogates easily through the lattice with accompanying deformation of the material, usually until it gets caught either by meeting the edge of a crystallite or another dislocation. A metal with many interlocking dislocations will be harder to deform further and is said to have **work hardened.** Edge dislocations can often be seen in bubble rafts which look superficially regular.

Brittle fracture

Most non-metals do not reach the region of plastic flow before they break. The break occurs after only one tenth to one hundredth of the breaking stress derived from elementary theory has been applied. Investigation of glass led to the discovery of minute cracks. The effect of the cracks is to concentrate stress at the tip of the crack (fig. 23ii). Bonds there will give way and the crack will propogate rapidly.

For metals, a point is reached where plastic flow causes the spontaneous formation of a 'neck' at some point (fig. 24ii). The force is then spread over fewer and fewer atoms until the bond strength is exceeded and fracture occurs, (fig. 24iii).

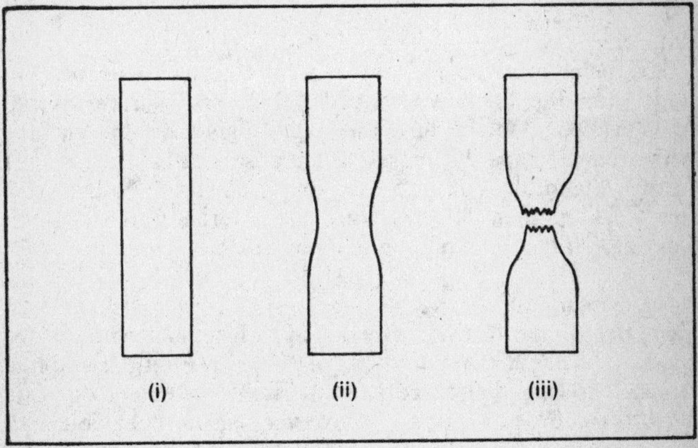

Figure 24. Necking

Rubber

A special structural arrangement is that of rubber, which

consists of very long chain molecules. These molecules are normally coiled up in random fashion, but the application of stress will cause them to straighten out with the result that some rubber can be stretched up to thirteen times its original length (fig. 25). On removing this stress, it will return to its original shape. Many polymeric solids behave in a similar way.

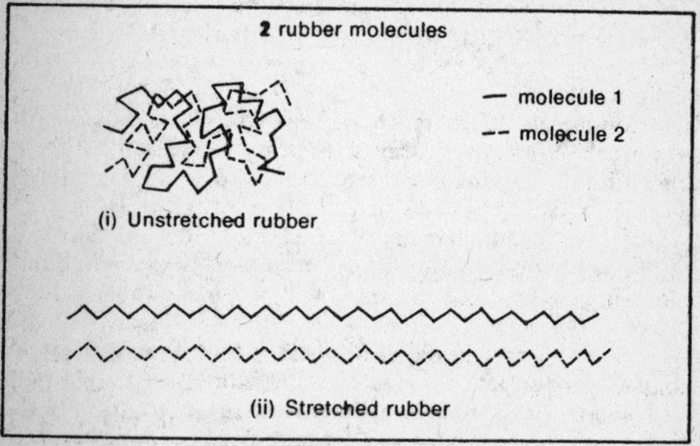

Figure 25. Stretching of rubber

Elasticity
Elastic behaviour means that a body returns to its original shape when the stress is removed and in particular, no overall work has been done because the material gives out in returning to its original shape the energy that it absorbed in stretching. If stretching continues into the region of plastic flow, irretrievable work is then done against the internal forces of the material and the deformation is irreversible.

Force-extension curves
For metals in the form of wire a typical force-extension curve is shown in fig. 26i. The first 1% or so up to P on the graph is straight showing that force is proportional to extension. P is the **limit of proportionality**. However, elastic behaviour can extend up to E, the **elastic limit**. If the load is removed, the metal will return along the curve EPO. Beyond E the metal will return along a parallel curve (dashed) but some work has been done (equal to the area enclosed by the graph) and there is a permanent extension OY when the load is removed.

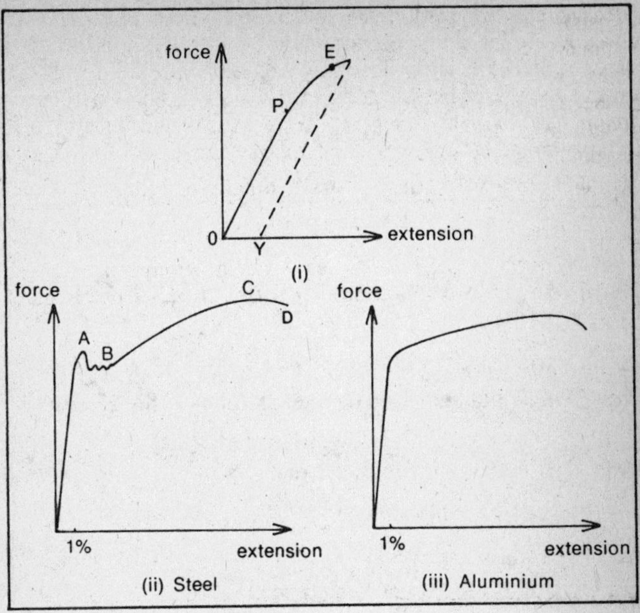

Figure 26. Force-extension curves

Typical graphs for steel and aluminium over a wide range are shown in fig. 26ii, iii. Steel shows a tendency to yield at A and can then be stretched by a slightly smaller force. Work hardening sets in at B and the maximum force is reached at C. This is the **tensile strength** of the wire. Beyond C, necking develops and the force needed to cause extension thus reduces and the wire breaks at D. For aluminium, there is no yield point but otherwise the process is similar.

Hooke's law states that below the limit of proportionality extension is proportional to tension, i.e.

$$F = kx$$

where x = extension and k is the **spring, or force constant.** The energy stored in a spring obeying Hooke's law has already been calculated on p. 23 and is given by

$$E = \tfrac{1}{2}Fx$$

$$\therefore \quad E = \tfrac{1}{2}kx^2$$

Moduli of elasticity

Values of the force constant for a particular specimen are of little general interest. The values for a particular specimen are therefore 'standardized' to apply to the material of which it is made. Force becomes force per unit area or **tensile stress** (units: Pa) and extension becomes extension per unit of original length or **linear, or tensile strain** (no units since it is a ratio).

A useful measure of the stiffness of a material is the ratio of applied stress to resultant strain – a stiff material needs much stress for little strain.

The Young modulus

The Young modulus (E) is defined as follows (fig. 27i).

$$E = \frac{\text{tensile stress}}{\text{tensile strain}} = \frac{F/A}{e/L}$$

where A = cross-sectional area
e = extension
L = unstretched length

The units of E are Pa and typical values are

Steel 2×10^{11} Pa   Nylon 2×10^{9} Pa
Brass 1×10^{11} Pa   Rubber 1×10^{6} Pa

The two other moduli are the modulus of **rigidity** and the **bulk**

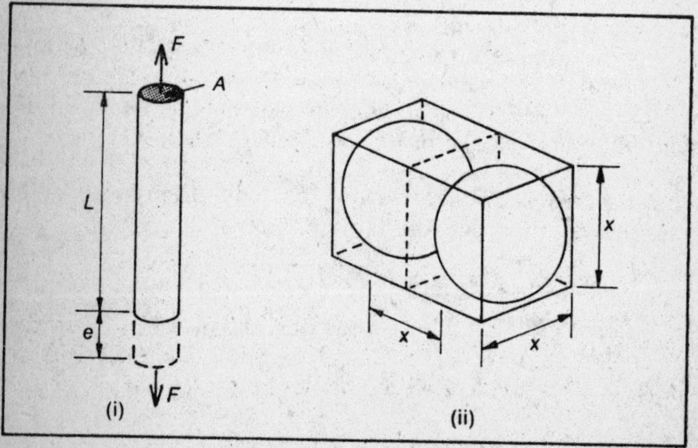

Figure 27. Elasticity

modulus. They relate to shear strain and volume strain respectively.

Example 1 A glider is launched from a hill by stretching an elastic bungee rope attached to it and then releasing the aircraft when it is fully stretched. If the rope is of cross-sectional area 5×10^{-3} m, is 25 m long and is stretched by a further 20 metres and the mass of glider and pilot is 400 kg and the Young Modulus of rubber is 1×10^6 Pa, calculate (i) initial acceleration of the glider (ii) the energy stored in the rope (iii) the aircraft's speed when the rope goes slack. (Ignore the reduction in cross-sectional area on stretching.)

$$E = \frac{F/A}{e/L}$$

$$\therefore \quad F = \frac{EA}{L} e = ke$$

where $$k = \frac{EA}{L} = \frac{10^6 \times 5 \times 10^{-3}}{25} = 200 \text{ N m}^{-1}$$

(i) $F = ke = 200 \times 20 = 4000\ N$

(ii) Elastic energy $= \frac{1}{2}ke^2 = \frac{1}{2} \times 200 \times 20^2 = 40$ kJ

(iii) Elastic energy = kinetic energy $\frac{1}{2}mv^2$

$$\therefore \quad 40 \times 10^3 = \frac{1}{2} \times 400 \times v^2$$

$$v = 14.1 \text{ m s}^{-1}$$

Example 2 Part of a building exerts a force of 1000 tonnes weight on a vertical steel stanchion 4 metres long and of total cross-sectional area 3×10^{-2} m^2. Calculate the compression of the stanchion. (Young modulus of steel $= 2 \times 10^{11}$ N m^{-2}.)

$$E = \frac{F/A}{e/L}$$

$$e = \frac{FL}{EA} = \frac{9{\cdot}8 \times 10^6 \times 4}{2 \times 10^{11} \times 3 \times 10^{-2}} = 6{\cdot}5 \text{ mm}$$

The Young modulus can be related directly to atomic quantities if a regular lattice is assumed such that one atom occupies a volume of x^3 where x is an atomic diameter (fig. 27ii).

$$\text{Young modulus } E = \frac{F/x^2}{\Delta x/x}$$

if the atoms are strained apart by Δx.
But by Hooke's law

$$F = k\Delta x$$

where k is the atomic bond spring constant.

$$\therefore \quad E = \frac{k\Delta x}{x^2} \times \frac{x}{\Delta x} = \frac{k}{x}$$

This is a useful result as it means that a value of k for an atomic bond can be calculated.

For iron $\quad E = 1{\cdot}5 \times 10^{11}$ Pa; $x \approx 3 \times 10^{-10}$ m

$$\therefore \quad k = Ex = 1{\cdot}5 \times 10^{11} \times 3 \times 10^{-10} = 45 \text{ N m}^{-1}$$

Interesting confirmation of this can be found by measuring the speed of sound in an iron rod. Theoretically (see p. 123),

$$\text{velocity of sound } v = x\sqrt{\frac{k}{m}}$$

where m = atomic mass

Now $\quad m$ = mass no. × mass of proton

So for iron, $\quad m = 56 \times 1.67 \times 10^{-27} = 9.35 \times 10^{-26}$ kg

$$v = 3 \times 10^{-10} \times \sqrt{\frac{45}{9{\cdot}35 \times 10^{-26}}} = 6{\cdot}6 \text{ km s}^{-1}$$

This agrees well with experimental values.

Measurement of the Young modulus

The simplest method is that due to Searle. Two identical wires of the same material (one a reference, the other the specimen) are suspended from a support (fig. 28). The reference wire has a fixed load to keep it straight, whilst the other is loaded with weights. Each time a weight is added the micrometer screw is adjusted until the bubble of the spirit level is central. A graph can be plotted of applied force against extension, the slope of which is the value of F/e for the wire. The Young modulus is calculated by finding the cross-sectional area from the diameter measured in several places with a micrometer, measuring the length of the wire, and substituting in the formula,

$$E = \frac{F/A}{e/L}$$

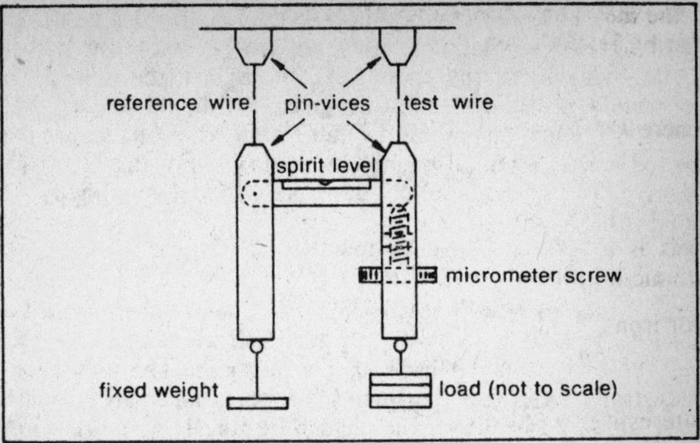

Figure 28. Searle's apparatus

Liquids

In the liquid state atoms no longer have the general order for a solid, but they still possess some local order due to the forces of attraction between them. An atom in a liquid is still in contact with other atoms, although the number is variable between four and eleven, compared with twelve in hexagonal close packing. The packing is thus looser and random and a liquid occupies roughly 10% more volume than its solid (fig.

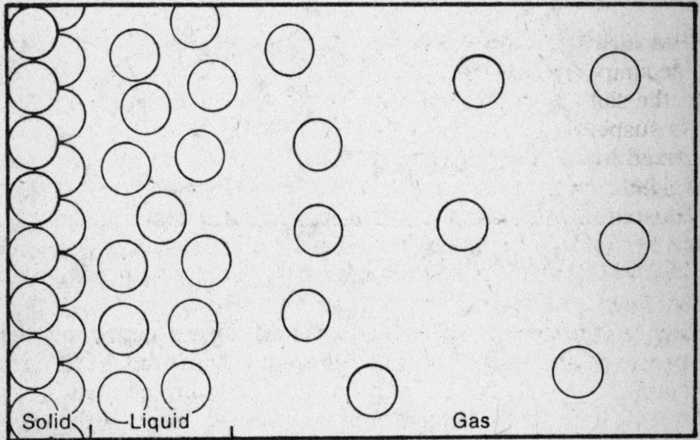

Figure 29. Solid, liquid, gas

29). (This is not true of water and ice.) A liquid also differs from a solid in that its atoms are free to move about – to jostle – because of the presence of holes, or free volume, in the random packing and this gives the liquid atoms their mobility. Since the atoms of the liquid are still very close together, the potential energy-separation curve (fig. 20iii) for them is the same, and so they, like solids, are highly incompressible.

Surface energy

The surface of any material – liquid or solid – differs from the inside in that the atoms will only have half as many bonds with neighbouring atoms. This is shown in a simplistic way in fig. 30. Attractive forces acting on the bulk atoms are balanced whilst those acting on an atom in the surface are not. Hence work would have to be done to bring an atom up to the new section of surface and the surface will therefore need energy for its formation. This energy is called the **surface energy** (γ). The units of γ are J m^{-2}.

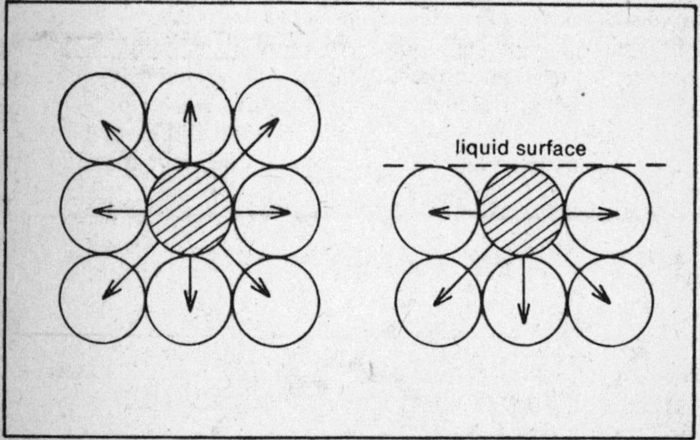

Figure 30. Surface forces

One of the results of the unbalanced forces acting on the surface atoms is to make a free drop of liquid 'draw itself' into the symmetrical shape which has the least surface area, i.e. a sphere. It seems to behave as if it were in a 'skin'. If the drop is on a solid surface, then there are forces acting between the atoms of the liquid and the atoms of the solid, as well as those only between the atoms of the liquid. If the forces of **adhesion** between solid and liquid exceed those of **cohesion** between the liquid and itself then the liquid will spread over the surface of the solid (fig. 31i). Since interatomic forces are very short range, however, even a monomolecular layer of another material can affect the adhesion and wax polish, for instance, makes water cohere into droplets again (fig. 31ii). Usually the liquid surface meets the solid surface at a definite angle. The angle measured **in the liquid** is called the **angle of contact** (fig. 31iii). For water on clean glass $\theta = 0°$; for mercury on glass $\theta = 137°$. The angle of contact can be measured by placing a strip of the solid material at an angle in the liquid. The liquid solid interface is examined and the angle adjusted until there is no distortion of the surface at the point of contact (fig. 31iv).

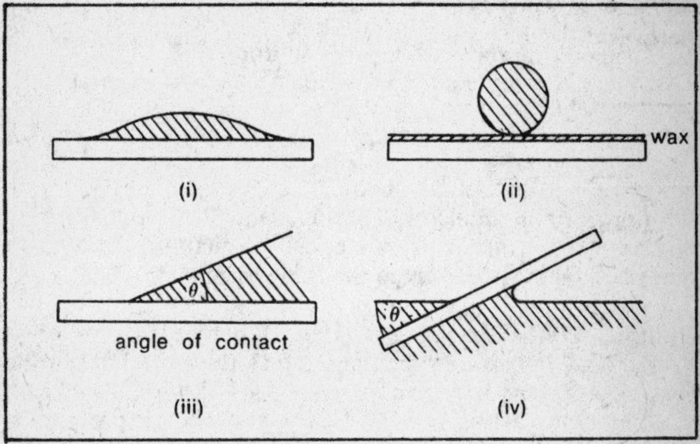

Figure 31. Surface tension

Surface tension

Consider a rectangular wire frame with one side free to move without friction and let a soap film exist across the frame (fig. 32i, ii). The area of the film can be increased by moving the sliding wire outwards. However, extra surface energy will be involved and this can only come from the work which will be done in moving the sliding wire with the force F.

Thus work done = new surface energy

$$F \times x = 2l \times x \times \gamma$$

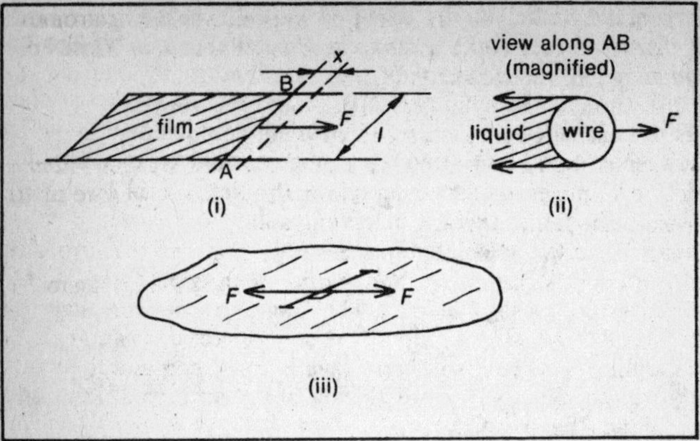

Figure 32. Surface tension

(two surfaces are formed – top and bottom).
Thus, there is a force per unit length of surface given by

$$\frac{F}{2l} = \gamma$$

This force per unit length acting in the surface, normal to the line drawn in a liquid surface is defined as the **surface tension** (fig. 32iii). It is numerically equal to the surface energy and is therefore given the same symbol γ.

Example 1 What is the least size of bubble that water at 102°C could inflate in a boiling liquid? (Neglect hydrostatic pressure). (Surface tension of water at 100°C = 58 mN m^{-1}, S.V.P. of water at 102°C = 108 770 Pa, atmospheric pressure = 101 325 Pa.)

Excess pressure in bubble = S.V.P. of water less atmospheric pressure

$$\frac{2\gamma}{r} = P_{\text{S.V.P.}} - P_A$$

$$\frac{2 \times 58 \times 10^{-3}}{r} = 108\,770 - 101\,325$$

$$\therefore \quad r = \frac{116}{7445} \times 10^{-3} = 15{\cdot}6\ \mu\text{m}$$

Cavities of suitable radius can be found in porous pot (see p. 94).

Example 2 Calculate the effect on a parallel-sided hydrometer of diameter 1 cm if the surface tension of water is 70 mN m^{-1} and the angle of contact is 0°.

Let the radius of the hydrometer be r.
Downward pull on hydrometer due to surface tension $= 2\pi r\gamma$.
This will be balanced by the extra upthrust due to more of the hydrometer submerging.
By Archimedes' principle, upthrust $= \pi r^2 h\rho g$
where h = extra depth, ρ = density of water $= 10^3$ kg m^{-3}

$$\therefore \quad \pi r^2 h\rho g = 2\pi r\gamma$$

$$h = \frac{2\gamma}{\rho g r} = \frac{2 \times 70 \times 10^{-3}}{10^3 \times 9{\cdot}8 \times 5 \times 10^{-3}} = 2{\cdot}8 \text{ mm}$$

Excess pressure in bubbles

Because of surface tension, a soap bubble will behave rather like a balloon and the pressure inside will be greater. This can readily be calculated by considering the bubble to be in two halves and equating the forces acting on each half (fig. 33i). Thus, force of excess internal pressure upwards = surface tension force for inner and outer surfaces downwards.

$$P \times \pi r^2 = 2 \times 2\pi r \times \gamma \qquad \therefore \quad P = \frac{4\gamma}{r}$$

This is the excess pressure in the bubble.

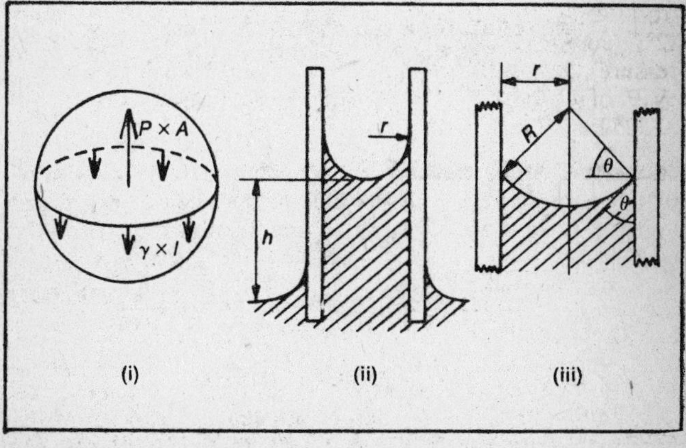

Figure 33. Forces in bubbles and capillary rise

For the excess pressure either in bubbles blown in a liquid, or inside drops of liquid, only one liquid surface is involved.

Hence
$$P \times \pi r^2 = 2\pi r \times \gamma$$
$$P = \frac{2\gamma}{r}$$

Capillary rise
If a clean capillary tube is placed in water, the adhesion between glass and water will cause the edge of the liquid to be drawn up into the tube (fig. 33ii).

A surface tension force $2\pi r\gamma$ thus holds up a column of liquid of weight $\pi r^2 h\rho g$.

So
$$2\pi r\gamma = \pi r^2 h\rho g$$
or
$$h = \frac{2\gamma}{\rho g r}$$

If the surface tension force acts at an angle of contact θ, the vertical component of the surface tension force holding up the column is $2\pi r\gamma \cos\theta$.

In this case
$$h = \frac{2\gamma \cos\theta}{\rho g r}$$

Measurement of surface tension
There are several methods, but only two will be described. In all cases the glassware must be scrupulously clean where it meets the liquid.

(i) **Capillary rise method** The capillary rise is measured, together with the radius of the tube at the relevant point, and the angle of contact. Then from the relationship described above
$$\gamma = \frac{\rho g r h}{2\cos\theta}$$

(ii) **Jaeger's method** (fig. 34i). This involves blowing bubbles in the liquid. Its ingenuity lies in not having to observe the bubble size since the minimum bubble radius is that of the tube (fig. 34i). Water is run slowly into the container, and the maximum height difference of the manometer is recorded.

Thus $$\frac{2\gamma}{r} = \rho_1 gh - \rho_2 gd$$

$$\therefore \quad \gamma = \tfrac{1}{2} rg(\rho_1 h - \rho_2 d)$$

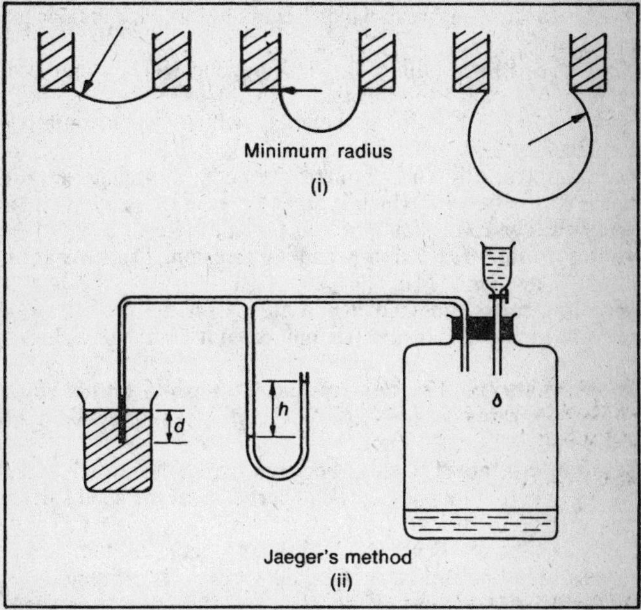

Figure 34. Jaeger's method

Key terms

Ionic bond A bond resulting from the attraction between ions of opposite charge.
Covalent bond A bond in which an electron is shared between two atoms.
Van der Waals bond A weak bond due to momentary asymmetrical distribution of electrons round a nucleus.
Metallic bond The bond which occurs in metals and is due to positive ions being attracted to a concentration of negative charge between them.
Plastic flow Permanent deformation of a solid subjected to stress.

Slip planes Planes in which atoms can slip over each other when subjected to shearing force.
Edge dislocation The line along the edge of an extra plane of atoms in a crystal lattice.
Work hardening The tendency for a metal to become harder to deform once it has been repeatedly deformed.
Brittle fracture A break which occurs before plastic flow sets in.
Limit of proportionality The limit beyond which strain is no longer proportional to stress.
Elastic limit The limit beyond which a material is permanently deformed.
Tensile strength The ultimate strength of a material; the tensile stress beyond which it breaks.
Hooke's law Extension is proportional to tension.
Spring constant Tension per unit extension. The constant in Hooke's law. Unit: $N\,m^{-1}$.
Tensile stress Tension per unit area. Unit: Pa.
Tensile strain Extension per unit length. Unit: none since it is a ratio.
Young modulus The ratio of tensile stress to tensile strain.
Surface energy The energy per unit area possessed by a liquid surface. Unit: $J\,m^{-2}$.
Angle of contact The angle between the surface of a liquid at the line where it touches the solid surface and the solid surface measured in the liquid.
Surface tension Force per unit length acting in the surface normal to a line drawn in a liquid surface. It is numerically equal to surface energy. Unit: $N\,m^{-1}$.
Capillary rise The rise in liquid level in a capillary tube due to surface tension forces.

Chapter 3
Heat and Thermodynamics

The molecular view

In considering heat it is particularly helpful to have a mental picture of the molecular scale of the system under discussion. Solids (as discussed in Chapter 2) are in the form of a lattice in which each atom or molecule is at an equilibrium position x_0 relative to the others. If energy is now given to the system it will cause the atoms to vibrate about their equilibrium position between equal points AA' on the potential energy curve in fig. 19iv. Because the energy curve is asymmetrical the centre of oscillation moves outwards causing the mean spacing x_0 to increase and hence the solid expands. As the energy of the oscillation is increased the amplitude increases to a point (at about $\frac{1}{7}x_0$) when the restraining bonds are broken and the atoms become free to move and form a liquid.

The energy possessed by the atoms or molecules of a liquid is partly vibrational and partly translational and the resultant maximum velocities of the molecules is of the same order as those in a gas at the same temperature (several hundreds of metres per second). In glass, however, (theoretically a liquid) the energy will be entirely vibrational.

If a liquid is heated some atoms gain sufficient energy to break away from the attractive forces of the rest and leave the liquid altogether to become a vapour.

In the vapour state and the gaseous state atoms or molecules are completely free. Only near the liquification point are there attractive forces of any significance. The energy of a monatomic gas is entirely translational, and the energy of the gas is the total kinetic energy of all the atoms. With polyatomic molecules, however, the energy can also take the form of both rotational kinetic energy, and oscillatory energy due to the vibration of the constituent atoms within the molecule. Clear evidence for the motion of molecules in both liquids and gases is provided by **Brownian motion**. The incessant random quivering of pollen grains in a liquid, or smoke particles in a gas, is due to temporary imbalances in the large number of molecules striking opposite sides of the particles during the random bombardment by the molecules of the liquid or gas.

In a gaseous system, molecules undergo collisions and there will be a statistical probability that after a given time the energy will be shared out equally between the various forms of motion. If some of the molecules possess greater mean kinetic energy then this energy will be shared with the other molecules by collisions until the mean kinetic energy of all the molecules is on average the same. If the atoms in one part of a solid are vibrating with more energy than the rest, then the energy will be gradually shared with the other molecules through the connecting bonds which behave like springs.
The molecules of gas in a container which is at a higher temperature, for instance, will on average gain energy by colliding with the more energetic molecules of the container wall. The process will continue until the energy has been redistributed so that all molecules – gas and container – have the same mean kinetic energy.

This picture leads to the concept of the flow of energy between regions where the mean kinetic energy of the molecules is different.

Zeroth law of thermodynamics states that if A is in thermal equilibrium with B, and B is in thermal equilibrium with C, then A will be in equilibrium with C. Whilst this does not follow with people (A and C may well not get on even though they are both friends of B) it clearly does apply to the mean kinetic energies of the molecules of A, B and C.

Heat and temperature Heat is defined as thermal energy and is measured in joules. Temperature is more difficult to define. It is the hotness of a body and will be defined here as a measure of the mean kinetic energy of the molecules. Heat can only flow from regions of higher temperature to those of lower temperature.

Measurement of temperature
From the discussion so far it would follow that there is a point at which the molecules have zero thermal energy and the temperature will then be zero. This point is called **absolute zero**.

The thermodynamic temperature scale has its zero at absolute zero, and the triple point of water is at 273·16 K (see p. 96). Temperature on this scale is a direct measure of the mean kinetic energy of the molecules. The size of the degree is the same as the Celsius degree, and there are still 100 degrees between the ice point and the steam point. The degree is called the Kelvin (K). The **ice point** is the temperature of equilibrium of ice and water at standard pressure (101 325 Pa) and the **steam point** is the temperature of equilibrium of the liquid and vapour phases of water at standard pressure. $T = t + 273$ where T = temperature in Kelvin and t = temperature in degrees Celsius.

The definition of the thermodynamic scale is too complex for further discussion here, and instead the **ideal gas** scale will be defined shortly. In the past, however, measurement of temperature was based on temperature sensitive properties of matter, and scales of temperature were based on these.

A scale of temperature needs the following:
1. a property which increases continuously with temperature.
2. two fixed points (agreed reference temperatures).
3. a numerical scale.

The two fixed points for the Celsius temperature scale are usually the ice point and the steam point. The scale between the fixed points is divided into one hundred equal parts termed degrees Celsius (°C) (formerly Centigrade).

An empirical scale can now be defined, e.g. as °C on the mercury-in-glass scale. Unfortunately two empirical scales may only agree at the two fixed points. A scale of temperature can be defined mathematically by equating the ratio of degrees to the ratio of differences of the values of the property concerned (fig. 35i)

$$\frac{\theta}{100} = \frac{X_\theta - X_0}{X_{100} - X_0} \quad \text{or} \quad \theta = \frac{X_\theta - X_0}{X_{100} - X_0} \times 100$$

where X_0, X_θ and X_{100} are the values of the property at ice point, unknown temperature and steam point respectively.

Example If the property has arisen from the ice point three quarters of the way to the steam point, then $\theta = \frac{3}{4} \times 100 = 75°C$.

Practical thermometers

A number of different properties are used.

Liquid-in-glass thermometers depend on the expansion of the liquid (though expansion of the glass affects the readings slightly). Both mercury and alcohol are commonly used. Mercury has the advantage of being easily seen and having a large working range (m.p. 39°C, b.p. 357°C). Alcohol, however, has six times the expansivity and a greater range at the lower end (m.p. −117°C).

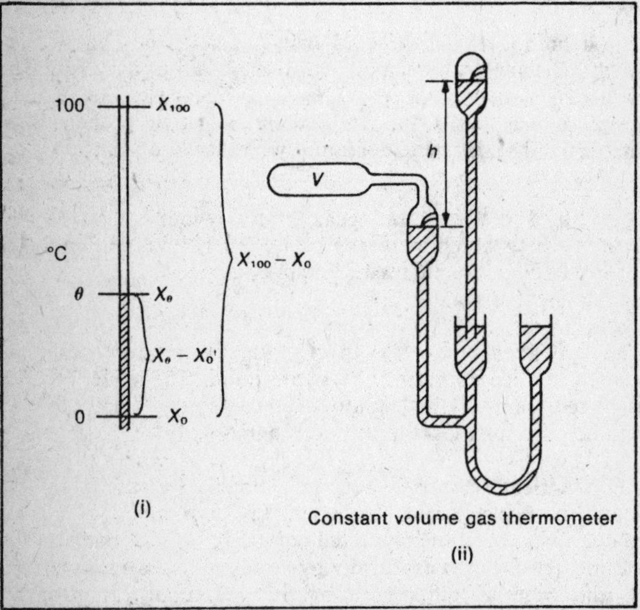

Figure 35. Constant volume gas thermometer

Constant volume gas thermometers (fig. 35ii) consist of a fixed volume of gas together with a means of measuring pressure, *p*. The bulb is heated or cooled, and the level of mercury adjusted to keep the lower level on the fixed mark. This ensures that the volume of gas remains constant. For each temperature the height (*h*) of the mercury column is recorded.

The unknown temperature can be calculated from

$$\frac{\theta}{100} = \frac{p_t - p_0}{p_{100} - p_0} = \frac{h_t - h_0}{h_{100} - h_0} \quad \text{since } p = \rho g h$$

School instruments do not usually incorporate a barometer, and the atmospheric pressure has to be measured independently and added to the readings taken. The thermometer has a large range, high sensitivity and is easily reproducible. A disadvantage is the size of the bulb. Its main use is in calibrating more conventional instruments. For accurate work, a small correction is needed for the expansion of the bulb and for the 'dead space' between the bulb and the mercury, which will not be at the temperature of the bulb.

Platinum resistance thermometers use the change of resistance of a fine platinum wire with temperature (fig. 36i). Platinum is chosen because of its resistance to corrosion. Wire is wound on a mica former. There are two pairs of leads from the probe to the Wheatstone bridge, one pair goes to the platinum resistor, R, the other pair are dummy leads to compensate for the temperature changes affecting the first pair. Thus only the resistance of the platinum wire is measured and is given by

$$\frac{R}{S} = \frac{P}{Q} \quad \text{or} \quad R = S \quad \text{if} \quad P = Q$$

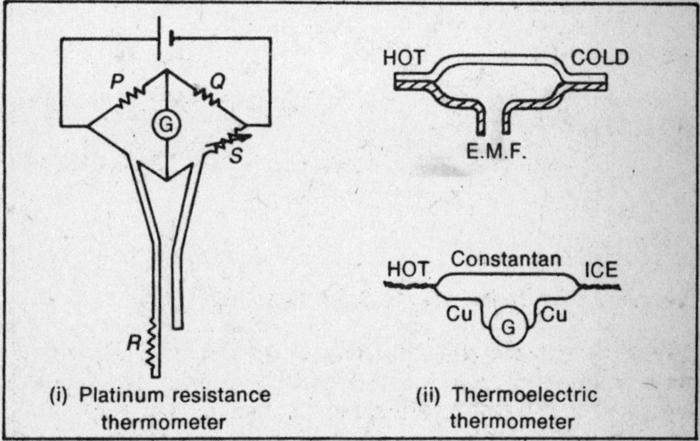

Figure 36. Electrical thermometers

Thermoelectric thermometers depend on the e.m.f. developed in a circuit consisting of two different metals where the junctions are at different temperatures. Usually one junction is maintained at 0°C in melting ice whilst the other one acts as the thermometric probe. For accurate work the e.m.f. can be measured with a potentiometer but usually a galvanometer is connected into the circuit (fig. 36ii) and the galvanometer calibrated to read temperature directly. The actual current flow will depend upon the total resistance of the circuit (including the galvanometer). A number of metal combinations are commonly used; copper/constantan up to 500°C, Chromel/Alumel (two alloys) up to 1500°C, etc.

Practical thermometers nowadays are calibrated in terms of the International Practical Temperature Scale 1968 – a practical scale based on the theoretical thermodynamic scale with eleven fixed points specified including the triple point and boiling point of water.

The ideal gas scale The pressure of a gas multiplied by its volume is a measure of its energy (see p. 84). Thus for a given

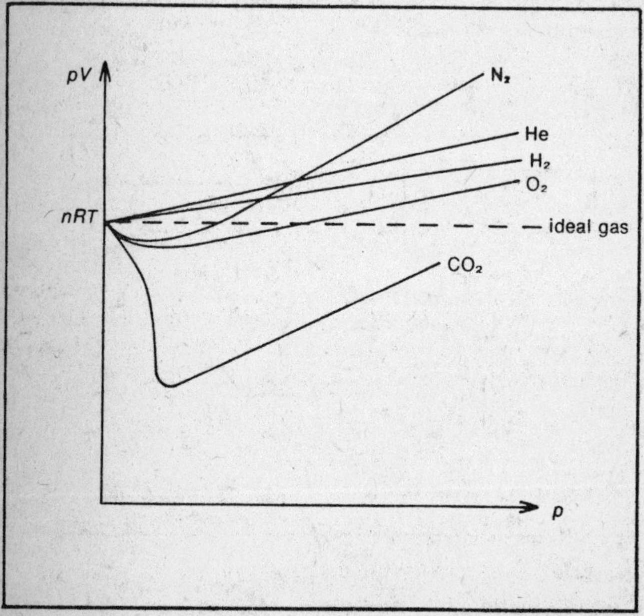

Figure 37. p-V curves

mass of gas at a particular temperature, pV should be constant, which is a statement of Boyle's law. A temperature scale could be built on values of pV being proportional to temperature. There is a problem, however, in that pV is only constant for ideal gases, and that for real gases pV varies with pressure in a complex way (due to Van der Waals forces) (fig. 37).

Ideal gas behaviour, however, can be achieved if the molecules are separated sufficiently, and this will occur if the gas is at low enough pressure. The ideal gas scale therefore takes values of pV for **zero pressure** (written $_0(pV)$).

The ideal gas scale is then defined in terms of its two fixed points – absolute zero and the triple point of water, by the equation

$$\frac{T}{273{\cdot}16} = \frac{_0(pV)_T}{_0(pV)_{273{\cdot}16}} \qquad \text{i.e.} \quad T \propto {_0(pV)_T}$$

Thermal expansion

In the molecular picture discussed, it was shown that a body when heated will expand. For small temperature changes this expansion is linear. **Linear expansivity**, α, is the increase in length per unit length per kelvin. Units are K^{-1}.

Thus $$\Delta L = L_0 \alpha t$$

where ΔL = increase in length
L_0 = original length
t = temperature rise

Therefore the new length is given by

$$\therefore \quad L = L_0 + L_0\alpha t \qquad L = L_0(1 + \alpha t)$$

Example Calculate the force in a rail of cross-sectional area 6×10^{-3} m on a railway track if it is laid at 10°C and heats up to 50°C in a heatwave. Assume it is clamped firmly to the ground. (α for steel $= 10^{-5}\ K^{-1}$, $E = 2 \times 10^{11}$ Pa)

$$\Delta L = L\alpha t$$

But $$E = \frac{F/A}{\Delta L/L}$$

$$\therefore \quad F = EA\frac{\Delta L}{L}$$

$$= EA\alpha t$$
$$= 2 \times 10^{11} \times 6 \times 10^{-3} \times 10^{-5} \times 40$$
$$= 4{\cdot}8 \times 10^{5}\ \text{N} \quad \text{(48 tonnes wt.)}$$

Heat capacities

The heat capacity (C) of a body is the heat required to raise its temperature one kelvin without change of state. The units are $\mathrm{J\,K^{-1}}$.

The specific heat capacity (c) is the heat required to raise the temperature of one kilogram of a material one kelvin without change of state. Consequently, the heat required (Q) to raise the temperature of m kilograms by θ K is given by $Q = mc\theta$. The units of c are $\mathrm{J\,kg^{-1}\,K^{-1}}$.

Determinations of specific heat capacities are usually carried out electrically.

For **solids**, a block of the material is drilled to take an electrical heater and a thermometer (fig. 38). The block is carefully lagged and the heat is switched on. The electrical energy supplied (VIt) and the resultant temperature rise (θ) are recorded. The temperature will continue to rise significantly after the heater is switched off; it is the final highest temperature reached which should be measured. Then

$$VIt = mc\theta \quad \text{i.e. } c = \frac{VIt}{m\theta}$$

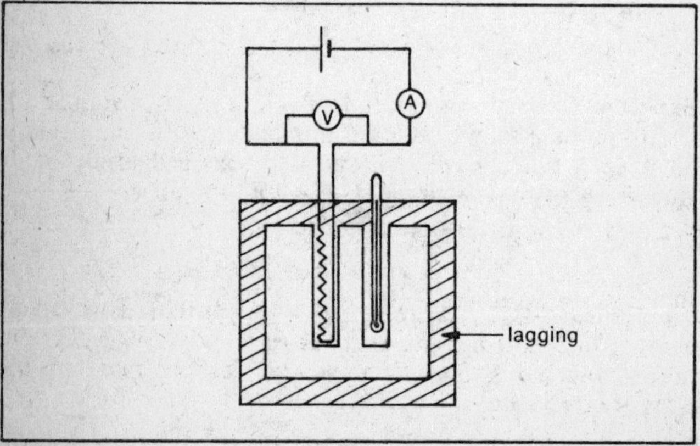

Figure 38. Determination of S.H.C.

For **liquids**, a similar method can be used but a vessel whose heat capacity is known must be used.

Continuous flow calorimeters are an alternative method for determining the S.H.C. of liquids and gases more accurately. The principle is to heat a flow of fluid continuously and measure the resultant temperature rise thus avoiding the need to know the heat capacity of the container. The calorimeter consists of a tube containing a heater and surrounded by a vacuum jacket with thermometers at the input and output (fig. 39). Once the steady state has been reached, electrical power put in is equal to the heat per second carried out by the fluid. Thus

$$VI = \frac{m}{t}c\theta \quad \text{i.e. } c = \frac{VI}{\theta} \times \frac{t}{m}$$

where m/t is the mass of fluid per second.

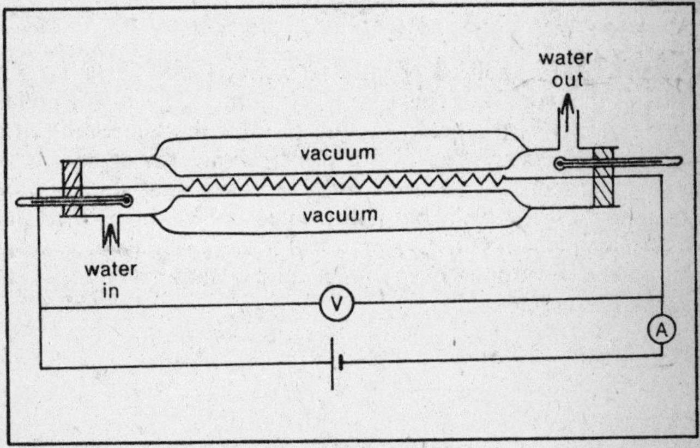

Figure 39. Continuous flow calorimeter

A refinement which can be used with constant flow calorimetry is to cancel out the heat losses by using two different rates of flow but the same temperature rise, and therefore the **same heat losses.**

For flow rate 1 $\quad V_1I_1 = \left(\frac{m}{t}\right)_1 c\theta + h$

where h is the rate of loss of heat

For flow rate 2 $$V_2I_2 = \left(\frac{m}{t}\right)_2 c\theta + h$$

Hence, by subtracting the two equations, h can be eliminated.

Specific heat capacities of a gas have many different values depending on the conditions under which expansion has occurred since both pressure and volume can vary. There are however two particular specific heat capacities which are important – that at constant pressure c_p, and that at constant volume, c_v. It is c_p which is found using a constant flow calorimeter.

The ratio of specific heat capacities of a gas (γ) is an important constant for gases, and is used in the calculations on adiabatic changes discussed on page 82.

$$\frac{c_p}{c_v} = \gamma$$

Molar heat capacities of gases (C_m) are widely used, since most of the work on gases is in terms of moles. Thus the molar heat capacity is the heat required to raise the temperature of one mole of gas one kelvin. The principal molar heat capacities are $C_{p,m}$ at constant pressure and $C_{v,m}$ at constant volume. For simplicity, these will be abbreviated to C_p and C_v. The difference between the two principal heat capacities of a gas is due to the work done in expanding at constant pressure and is discussed on page 86.

for monatomic gases $\gamma = \frac{5}{3} = 1{\cdot}66$

for diatomic gases $\gamma = \frac{7}{5} = 1{\cdot}40$

The latent heat (L) is the heat required to change the state of a given quantity of substance (solid to liquid or liquid to vapour) without any change in temperature.

The specific latent heat (l) of a substance is the heat required to change the state of one kilogram of it without any change of temperature (Units: $\mathrm{J\,kg^{-1}}$). Consequently the **heat required** to change the state of m kilograms of a substance is given by $Q = ml$.

The determination of specific latent heats is again usually carried out electrically.

The specific latent heat of fusion (l_f) of ice is found by putting a known mass of ice (m) at 0°C into a thermos flask containing water at 0°C together with an electrical heater and a thermometer (fig. 40i). The heater is connected to an electrical supply, the mixture is stirred, and the thermometer watched for the point at which the temperature starts to rise, i.e. when all the ice has melted. The electrical energy supplied (VIt) is then recorded.

Then $VIt = ml_f$ i.e. $l_f = VIt/m$

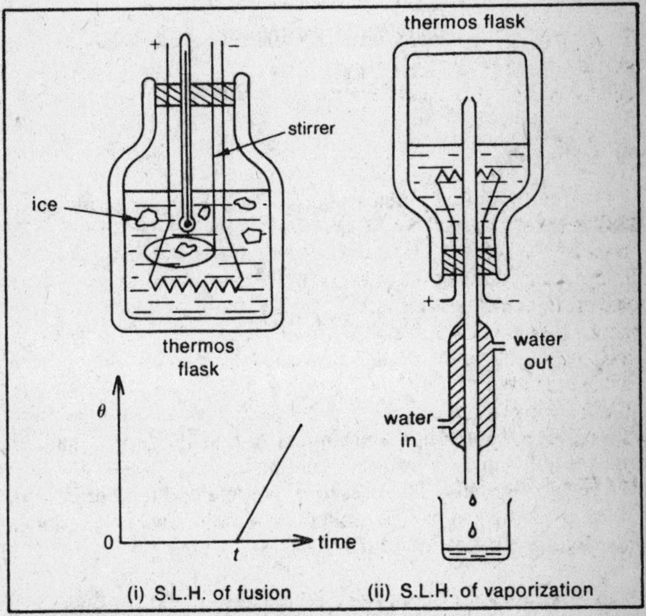

Figure 40. Determination of S.L.H.

The specific latent heat of vaporization (l_v) can be found by boiling a liquid in a thermos flask and condensing the vapour once it has left the flask. The heater is connected to an electrical supply and the apparatus left to boil for a time to reach equilibrium. The electrical energy supplied and the mass of vapour condensed in a given time are recorded.

Then $$VIt = ml_v$$

i.e. $$l_v = \frac{VIt}{m}$$

Example 1 Calculate the time (i) to boil (ii) to boil dry, 1 kilogram of water initially at 10°C in a 2 kW electric kettle of mass 0·75 kg and S.H.C. 500 J kg^{-1} K^{-1}. (S.H.C. of water = 4200 J kg^{-1} K^{-1}, S.L.H.V. of water = 2·3 MJ kg^{-1}).

For boiling:

Heat supplied = heat required to boil

$$VIt = (mc\theta)_{\text{kettle}} + (mc\theta)_{\text{water}}$$

$$2000t_1 = (0{\cdot}75 \times 500 + 1 \times 4200) \times 90$$

$$t_1 = \frac{4575 \times 90}{2000} = 206 \text{ sec } (3{\cdot}4 \text{ min})$$

For boiling dry:

Heat supplied = heat required to boil water away

$$VIt = ml_v$$

$$2000t_2 = 1 \times 2.3 \times 10^6$$

$$t_2 = 1150 \text{ sec } (19.2 \text{ min})$$

The gas laws

Gases differ from solids and liquids in that they are relatively compressible and pressure, volume and temperature can change substantially. The pressure, volume and temperature of a fixed mass of gas can be linked by simple laws and reduced to a single **equation of state.**

Boyle's law states that if temperature is kept constant then for a fixed mass of gas pressure is inversely proportional to volume.

i.e. T constant: $$p \propto \frac{1}{V}$$

or $$pV = \text{constant}$$

i.e. $$p_1V_1 = p_2V_2, \text{ etc.}$$

This can readily be established experimentally using the apparatus of fig. 41. Pressure = $\rho g(H + h)$ where H = barometric height in cm of mercury. Volume $= lA$, where A equals cross-sectional area of inside of glass tube and l = length of air sample.
Thus volume $\propto l$, and so a graph of pressure against $1/l$ should give a straight line if $p \propto 1/V$.

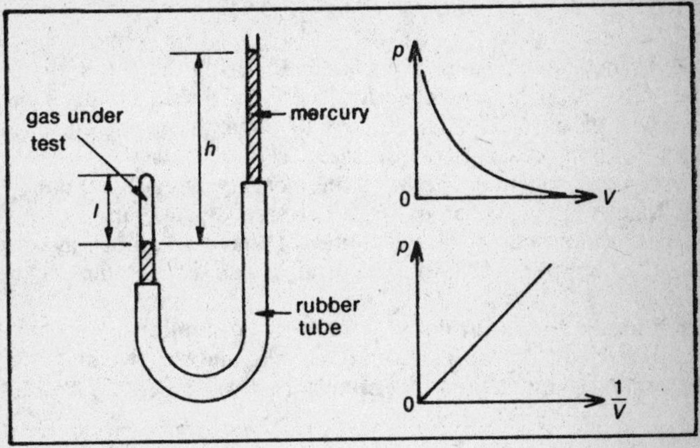

Figure 41. Boyle's law

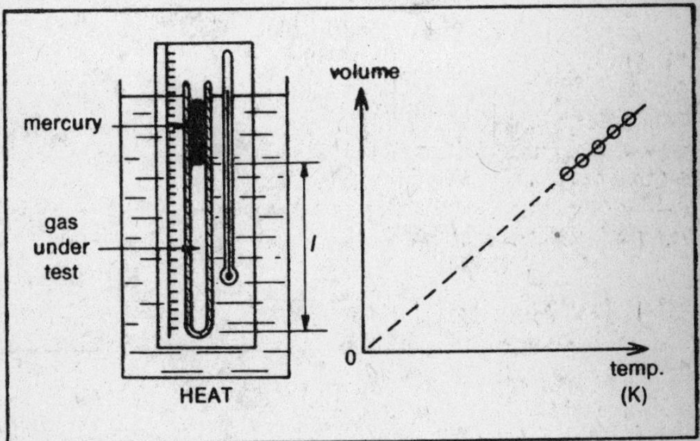

Figure 42. Charles' law

Charles' law states that if pressure is kept constant, then for a fixed mass of gas volume is proportional to absolute temperature.

i.e. p constant: $$V \propto T$$

or $$\frac{V}{T} = \text{constant}$$

i.e. $$\frac{V_1}{T_1} = \frac{V_2}{T_2}, \text{ etc.}$$

This can be established experimentally using the apparatus of fig. 42. A capillary tube with a mercury thread confines the volume of air which is allowed to expand against constant atmospheric pressure (the pressure in the capillary is equal to atmospheric plus the height of the mercury thread). Volume = lA where A equals cross-sectional area of capillary and l = length of air sample. Thus volume $\propto l$, and a graph of l against absolute temperature T gives a straight line through the origin.

The ideal gas equation is obtained by combining the previous two laws by making a change take place in two stages: 1 at constant volume and 2 at constant pressure (fig. 43).

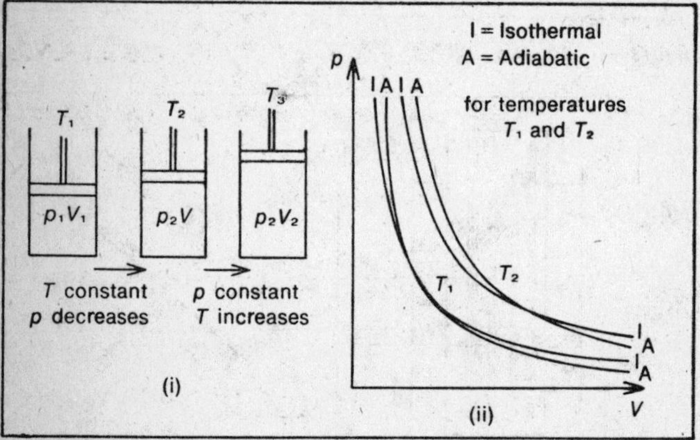

Figure 43. Isothermal and adiabatic changes

For change 1 $$p_1V_1 = p_2V$$

For change 2 $$\frac{V}{T_1} = \frac{V_2}{T_2}$$

Eliminating V: $\frac{p_1V_1}{p_2}=\frac{V_2T_1}{T_2}$ or $\frac{p_1V_1}{T_1}=\frac{p_2V_2}{T_2}$

i.e. $\frac{pV}{T}=\text{constant}$ or $pV \propto T$

Clearly the constant of proportionality will depend on the mass of gas involved. The constant for **one mole** of gas is called the **Universal Gas Constant**, R.

Thus $$pV_m = RT$$

Now one mole of any gas occupies 22·4 litres at STP.

Therefore $$R=\frac{pV_m}{T}$$

For STP $p = 101\,325$ Pa, $V_m = 22{\cdot}4\times10^{-3}\ \text{m}^3$, $T = 273{\cdot}15$ K

$$\therefore \quad R=\frac{101\,325\times22{\cdot}4\times10^{-3}}{273{\cdot}15}=8{\cdot}31\ \text{J mol}^{-1}\ \text{K}^{-1}$$

Example 1 1·5 litres of gas are evolved during a chemical experiment. The temperature of the gas is 20°C and the pressure $1{\cdot}2\times10^5$ Pa. How many moles of gas were evolved?

1 mole of gas occupies 22·4 litres at STP (0°C and 101 325 Pa). So the gas must be reduced to STP.
(It is possible to work in litres provided the same units are used on both sides of the equation.)

$$\frac{p_1V_1}{T_1}=\frac{p_2V_2}{T_2}$$

$$\therefore \quad V_2=\frac{V_1p_1T_2}{p_2T_1}=\frac{1{\cdot}5\times1{\cdot}2\times10^5\times273}{1{\cdot}013\times10^5\times293}=1{\cdot}65\ \text{litres}$$

But 1 mole occupies 22·4 litres

$$\therefore \quad \text{no. of moles}=\frac{1{\cdot}65}{22{\cdot}4}=7{\cdot}4\times10^{-2}$$

Example 2 A vessel of volume 1·5 litres contains 5 grams of bromine at 20°C. Calculate the pressure. (Atomic weight of bromine 79·9).

There are $\frac{5}{79{\cdot}9}$ moles of bromine in the vessel.

Using the ideal gas equation, $pV = nRT$

$$p = \frac{nRT}{V} = \frac{5}{79{\cdot}9} \times \frac{8{\cdot}31 \times 293}{1{\cdot}5 \times 10^{-3}} = 1.016 \times 10^5 \text{ Pa}$$

In general for a mass of **n moles** ($n = \frac{m}{M}$ where m = mass of gas and M = mass of one mole)

$$pV = nRT$$

This is the **ideal gas equation.**

In most forms of expansion, pressure, volume and temperature all change. There are however two important special cases.

Isothermal changes occur at constant temperature, and obey Boyle's law, pV = constant or $p_1V_1 = p_2V_2$. Very slow changes are usually isothermal since the temperature is restored, as heat is drawn in from the walls or passes out through them.

Adiabatic changes occur at constant heat content, i.e. heat can neither leave the gas nor enter it. Under these circumstances pV^γ = constant or $p_1V_1^\gamma = p_2V_2^\gamma$ where γ is the ratio of specific heat capacities.

Extremely rapid changes are usually adiabatic because the time is too short for heat to leave or enter the gas. Sound waves produce adiabatic changes, for example.

In adiabatic changes temperature can also change of course. Hence combining the adiabatic equation with the ideal gas equation (which is always obeyed)

$$pV^\gamma = \text{constant, and } pV = nRT$$

i.e. $$pV \times V^{\gamma-1} = \text{constant}$$

$$\therefore \quad nRT \times V^{\gamma-1} = \text{constant}$$

i.e. $$TV^{\gamma-1} = \text{constant}$$

If isothermal and adiabatic changes are plotted on a p–V graph the steeper slope of the adiabatic change can be seen (fig. 43ii).

Example During the compression stroke in the cylinder of a compressor rotating at high speed, air at 1 atmosphere is compressed to one tenth of its initial volume. Calculate the new pressure of the air. (γ for air = 1·40.)

Since the compression is very rapid the gas will gain little heat from the cylinder, and the compression will be approximately adiabatic. (It is possible to work in atmospheres provided the same unit of pressure is used on both sides of the equation.)

$$p_1 V_1^\gamma = p_2 V_2^\gamma$$

$$p_2 = p_1 \left(\frac{V_1}{V_2}\right)^\gamma = 1 \times 10^{1 \cdot 4} = 25 \cdot 1 \text{ atmospheres}$$

Real gases do not follow this behaviour precisely particularly at high pressures.

Andrews' experiments on carbon dioxide established substantial deviations from the gas laws. His apparatus was capable of applying pressures up to 100 atmospheres (fig. 44i). It consisted of two capillary tubes with a mercury thread to

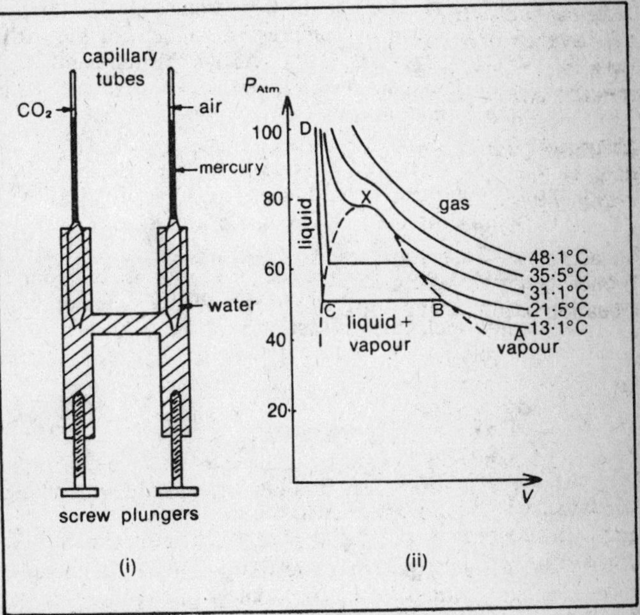

Figure 44. Andrew's curves and apparatus

seal them. One contained carbon dioxide and the other air which was assumed to obey Boyle's law thus enabling the applied **pressure** on the CO_2 to be calculated from the **volume of the air**. Pressure was applied by screwing plungers into a tank of water. His results are shown in fig. 44ii. The behaviour of a room temperature isothermal, ABCD on the diagram, shows three stages.

A–B: the gas is not following the pV hyperbola precisely due to compressibility effects (intermolecular attractions). As it is capable of being liquified at this temperature it is termed a **vapour.**
B–C: the vapour is starting to liquify and in this region both liquid and vapour are present. As the volume decreases so more of the vapour will condense thus maintaining constant pressure.
C–D: all the vapour has condensed into a liquid which is almost incompressible.

The critical temperature is the temperature above which the gas cannot be liquified by compression alone. For the carbon dioxide curves shown, it is 31·1°C. Above this temperature the isothermal never becomes horizontal – the horizontal section indicating the formation of liquid.

Above 48·1°C, the carbon dioxide follows Boyle's law fairly well, and the curves are hyperbolae. The point of inflexion (X) of the critical isothermal is called the **critical point.**

Several attempts have been made to represent this complex behaviour. The best known is Van der Waals' equation which allows for intermolecular attraction, and the volume occupied by the molecules.

Thermodynamics

Thermodynamics is the study of the interaction between heat and other forms of energy. It is concerned only with changes of energy.

Work done by a gas in expanding can be calculated by considering a cylinder with a frictionless piston (fig. 45i).

If the piston of area A is allowed to move a small distance δy

(such that the pressure does not change) then the work done by the gas is given by:

Work done = force exerted by gas × distance moved

$$\delta W = pA \times \delta y$$

But $A\delta y = \delta V$, where δV = the small change in volume

$$\therefore \quad \delta W = p\delta V$$

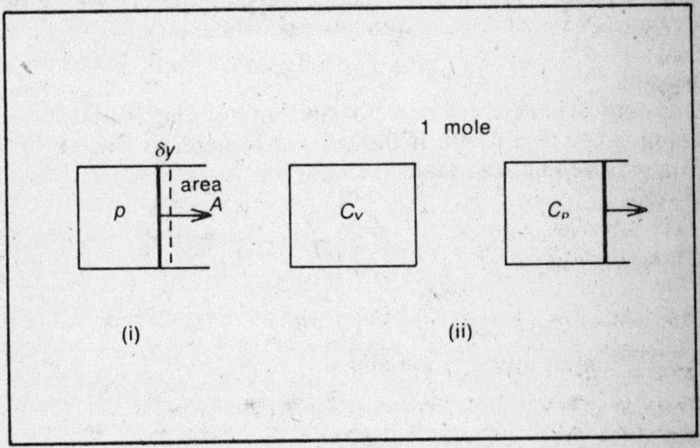

Figure 45. Work done by expanding gas

The first law of thermodynamics is a form of the law of conservation of energy, and states that in a closed system the total amount of energy of all kinds is constant. If heat is put into a closed system then

heat absorbed by the system = increase of internal energy + external work done by the system

i.e. $$\delta Q = \delta U + \delta W$$

The difference between the principal molar heat capacities can be readily calculated in terms of the work done and then expressed in terms of the temperature change.

Consider **one mole** in a sealed container (fig. 45ii). If it is heated through a small temperature rise δT then the heat required δU is given by

$$\delta U = C_v \delta T$$

The symbol δU is used because the heat is used in increasing the internal energy of the gas. Now consider the gas in a cylinder of equal volume, but fitted with a frictionless piston. The heat required is now given by

$$\delta Q = C_p \delta T$$

This time extra work has been done by the gas in expanding equal to $p\delta V$. By the first law of thermodynamics $\delta Q = \delta U + \delta W$, since δQ is both increasing the internal energy of the gas as well as doing external work. Thus

$$C_p \delta T = C_v \delta T + p\delta V$$

This expression can be further simplified by using the ideal gas equation for **one mole**. If the volume is increased by δV but the pressure kept **constant** then

$$p(V + \delta V) = R(T + \delta T)$$

i.e.

$$pV + p\delta V = RT + R\delta T$$

But

$$pV = RT$$

$$\therefore \quad p\delta V = R\delta T$$

Substituting in the equation above

$$C_p \delta T = C_v \delta T + R\delta T$$

i.e.

$$C_p - C_v = R$$

The kinetic theory of gases

The kinetic theory of gases considers a gas to consist of many small molecules in rapid random motion, and considers the force that they exert on the walls of the vessel in terms of rate of change of momentum. The following assumptions are made:

(i) the molecules behave as hard smooth spheres.
(ii) the molecules make elastic collisions with the walls of the vessel.
(iii) the molecules do not attract each other.
(iv) the molecules occupy negligible volume.
(v) the time occupied by collisions is negligible.

Using these assumptions, the behaviour of an ideal gas can be deduced. In practice, of course, real gases do not behave in this way, particularly when at high pressure. Any gas at infinitely low pressure will behave as an ideal gas, and the ideal gas scale of temperature is based on this property.

Consider a single molecule of mass m in a box of sides a, b, c (fig. 46i). Let the molecule be moving with the velocity c which has components u, v, w in directions x, y and z respectively. Consider a collision with wall A.

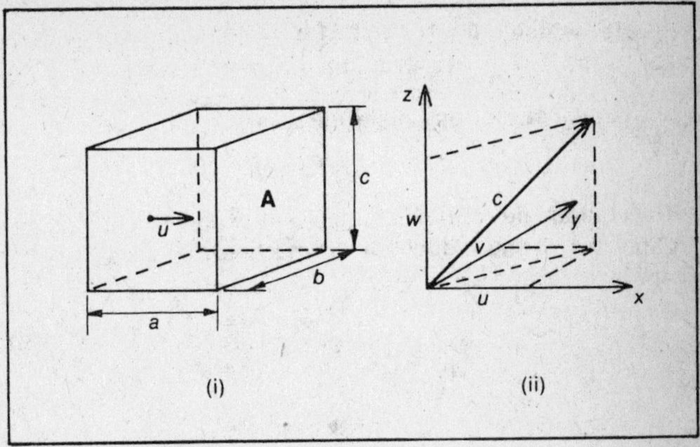

Figure 46. Kinetic theory of gases

1. Change of momentum (from $+mu$ to $-mu$) $= 2mu$

   Time taken between collisions with A (distance $2a$ at velocity u) $= \dfrac{2a}{u}$

   ∴ No. of collisions per second (reciprocal of time taken) $= \dfrac{u}{2a}$

   ∴ Rate of change of momentum (which is average force on A) $= 2mu \times \dfrac{u}{2a} = \dfrac{mu^2}{a}$

Hence if there are N molecules of velocities $u_1 \dots u_n$

Total force on A $\quad F = \dfrac{mu_1^2}{a} + \dfrac{mu_2^2}{a} + \cdots \dfrac{mu_n^2}{a}$

Total pressure on A (force per unit area) $\quad = \dfrac{F}{bc} = \dfrac{m}{abc}(u_1^2 + u_2^2 + \cdots u_n^2)$

Now $\dfrac{u_1^2 + u_1^2 + \cdots u_n^2}{N}$ is the mean of the squares of the velocities, and can be written as $\overline{u^2}$

Total pressure on A $$p_A = \frac{mN\overline{u^2}}{abc}$$

Statistically the pressure on all faces will be the same

i.e. $$p_A = p_B = p_C$$

Since mN and abc are the same for all faces

$$\overline{u^2} = \overline{v^2} = \overline{w^2}$$

Also, the velocity of any molecule c in any direction is given by

$$c^2 = u^2 + v^2 + w^2$$

by Pythagoras (fig. 45ii) where u, v and w are the components of c in the x, y and z directions respectively

$$\begin{aligned} c_1^2 + c_2^2 + \cdots c_n^2 = & \; u_1^2 + v_1^2 + w_1^2 \\ & + u_2^2 + v_2^2 + w_2^2 \\ & \cdots\cdots\cdots\cdots \\ & + u_n^2 + v_n^2 + w_n^2 \end{aligned}$$

i.e. $$\overline{c^2} = \overline{u^2} + \overline{v^2} + \overline{w^2}$$

But since $$\overline{u^2} = \overline{v^2} = \overline{w^2}$$

$$\overline{c^2} = 3\overline{u^2}$$

$$\overline{u^2} = \tfrac{1}{3}\overline{c^2}$$

Hence $$p = \frac{1}{3}\frac{Nm\overline{c^2}}{abc}$$

But Nm is the total mass of gas M and abc is the volume V

$$\therefore p = \frac{1}{3}\frac{M\overline{c^2}}{V}$$

This can be rewritten either as

$$pV = \tfrac{1}{3}Nm\overline{c^2} \quad \text{or} \quad p = \tfrac{1}{3}\rho\overline{c^2}$$

$$\rho = \text{density of the gas} = \frac{Nm}{V}$$

r.m.s. velocity ($c_{\text{r.m.s.}}$). It should be noted that $\overline{c^2}$ is **not** the same as $\bar{c}^2$ (the square of the mean speed).

For instance, let $c_1 = 4$, $c_2 = 6$ and $c_3 = 8$

Then $$\overline{c^2} = \frac{16+36+64}{3} = 38{\cdot}67$$

$$\bar{c} = \frac{4+6+8}{3} \qquad \therefore \quad \bar{c}^2 = \left(\frac{4+6+8}{3}\right)^2 = 36$$

The square root of $\overline{c^2}$ has the dimensions of velocity, and is called the root mean square velocity ($c_{r.m.s.}$).

Thus $$c_{r.m.s.} = \sqrt{\overline{c^2}} \text{ or } \overline{c^2} = c^2_{r.m.s.}$$

$c_{r.m.s.}$ can be found from the equation

$$p = \tfrac{1}{3}\rho c^2_{r.m.s.}$$

$$c_{r.m.s.} = \sqrt{\frac{3p}{\rho}}$$

p and ρ are easily measured for a gas.

For example, for air on a normal day

$$p \approx 10^5 \text{ Pa} \qquad \rho = 1{\cdot}2 \text{ kg m}^{-3}$$

$$\therefore \quad c_{r.m.s.} = \sqrt{\frac{3 \times 10^5}{1{\cdot}2}} = 500 \text{ m s}^{-1}$$

Ideal gas equation

Temperature is a measure of the mean kinetic energy of the molecules.

i.e. $$T \propto \tfrac{1}{2}m\overline{c^2}$$

$$m\overline{c^2} \propto T$$

Substituting for $m\overline{c^2}$ in $$pV = \tfrac{1}{3}Nm\overline{c^2}$$

$$pV \propto T$$

or for n moles $$pV = nRT$$

where R is the constant of proportionality for 1 mole. This is the Ideal Gas Equation which thus follows directly from the kinetic theory of gases and the definition of temperature.

Distribution of velocities

The distribution of velocities follows a Maxwellian distribution curve (fig. 47) which shows that there are a few molecules with very low velocities and a few with very high velocities, but the majority are spread around the most probable velocity. Velocities can be found with the apparatus shown in fig. 48 in which a metal is vaporized in an oven of known temperature, and a collimated beam of atoms from the oven is admitted through a narrow slit into a rapidly rotating drum. The slit cuts off a small section of the beam of atoms, and because the atoms are travelling at different velocities their times of arrival

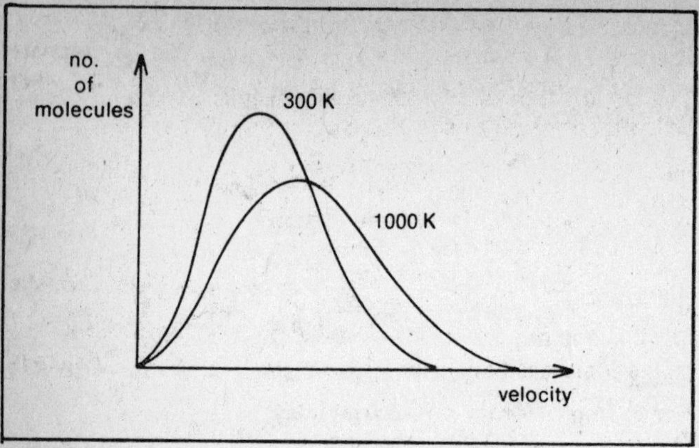

Figure 47. Distribution of molecular velocities

at the glass surface AB on the far side of the drum are different. Thus the sample of atoms is smeared out over the glass with the fastest at A and the slowest at B. The drum is rotated for some hours after which the thickness of the film which has formed is measured. A plot of film thickness against position gives the shape of the velocity distribution. As the temperature is increased the most probable velocity increases. Agreement between theory and observation is very good.

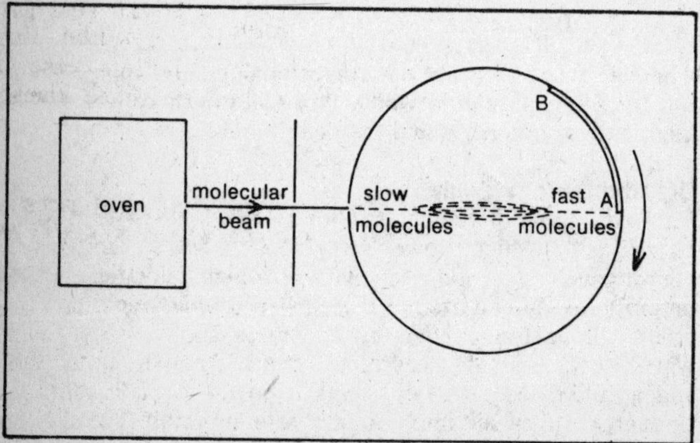

Figure 48. Rotating drum method

Calculation of mean energy of a molecule
The empirical equation $pV = RT$ for 1 mole can be compared with the theoretical equation for 1 mole, $pV = \frac{1}{3}N_A m\overline{c^2}$ where N_A is the Avogadro number

$$\tfrac{1}{3}N_A m\overline{c^2} = RT$$

hence

$$\tfrac{1}{2}m\overline{c^2} = \frac{3}{2}\frac{RT}{N_A}$$

Now $\dfrac{R}{N_A} = \dfrac{\text{Universal Gas Constant}}{\text{Avogadro Number}}$ is itself a universal constant called **Boltzmann's constant.** Its value is $1{\cdot}381 \times 10^{-23}\ \mathrm{J\,K^{-1}}$.

Hence the mean kinetic energy of a single molecule is given by

$$\tfrac{1}{2}m\overline{c^2} = 3 \times \tfrac{1}{2}kT$$

Since the molecule is free to move in three directions (x, y, z) it is said to have three **degrees of freedom**. This expression is interpreted as stating that the molecule has a mean kinetic energy of $\frac{1}{2}kT$ in each degree of freedom.

Dalton's law of partial pressures
Since there are no interatomic forces, and the molecules occupy negligible volume, the addition of extra molecules will simply increase the rate of change of momentum as molecules collide with a wall, and the new pressure becomes

$$p = \tfrac{1}{3}\rho_1\overline{c_1^2} + \tfrac{1}{3}\rho_2\overline{c_2^2} = p_1 + p_2$$

i.e. total pressure is the sum of the pressures that each gas would exert **if it occupied the whole volume by itself**. This is Dalton's law of partial pressures (it does in fact cease to hold at high pressures when the assumptions of the kinetic theory are no longer valid).

Avogadro's law
Avogadro's law states that equal volumes of different gases at the same temperature and pressure contain equal numbers of molecules.

This follows directly from the kinetic theory

$$pV = \tfrac{1}{3}n_1 m_1\overline{c_1^2} = \tfrac{1}{3}n_2 m_2\overline{c_2^2}$$

But, since the temperatures are the same

$$\tfrac{1}{2}m_1\overline{c_1^2} = \tfrac{1}{2}m_2\overline{c_2^2}$$

$$\therefore\quad n_1 = n_2$$

Liquids and vapours
A liquid produces a vapour by evaporation. There are two possible states that a vapour can take:

A saturated vapour is one which is in contact with its liquid and whose pressure, called the saturated vapour pressure (s.v.p.), remains constant for the particular temperature involved. It does not vary with volume.

An unsaturated vapour is one which is not in contact with its liquid. Its pressure varies with volume approximately according to Boyle's law. The behaviour of vapours can readily be demonstrated with the apparatus shown in principle in fig. 49i. In the apparatus the space above the mercury is initially a vacuum (fig. 49i1). If a small drop of liquid is admitted into the space and it rapidly evaporates completely then the space will contain unsaturated vapour (fig. 49i2). As more liquid is admitted some excess liquid will remain at the bottom of the space and the vapour is then saturated (fig. 49i3, 4). The

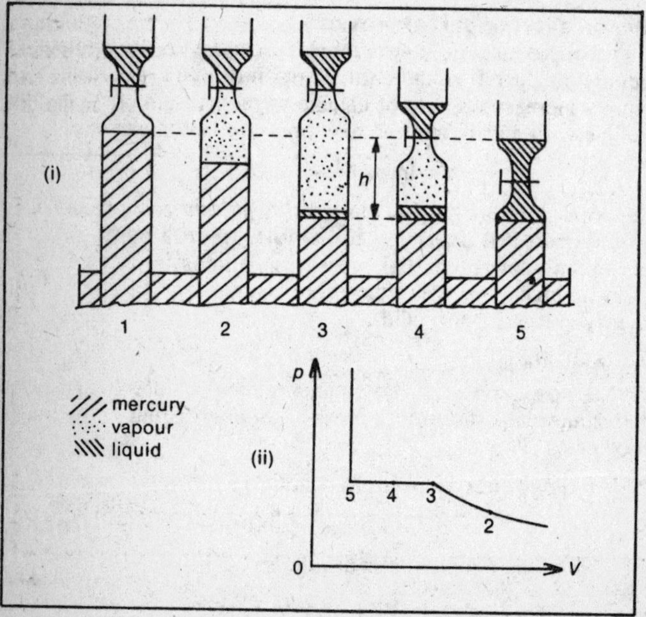

Figure 49. Saturated vapour pressure

vapour pressure is found from the depression of the mercury column (h).

$$p = \rho g h \quad \text{where} \quad \rho = \text{density of mercury}$$

If the volume of the space is changed by lowering the tube into the mercury, the s.v.p. is unchanged, and the depression of the mercury level remains the same (fig. 49i4). Ultimately as the volume is reduced further all the vapour condenses and the space is filled with liquid (fig. 49i5). These points are shown on the corresponding p-V curve for the temperature at which the experiment is conducted (fig. 49ii).

Saturated vapour pressure is thus the maximum possible pressure of a vapour at a particular temperature.

The boiling point of a liquid is defined as the temperature at which its s.v.p. is equal to the external pressure.

Variation of s.v.p. with temperature

Saturated vapour pressure can be measured by an adaptation of the apparatus of fig. 49 in which both the mercury column with the vacuum and that with the saturated vapour are placed in an enclosure such as a water bath, whose temperature can be varied. A typical result for two liquids is shown in fig. 50.

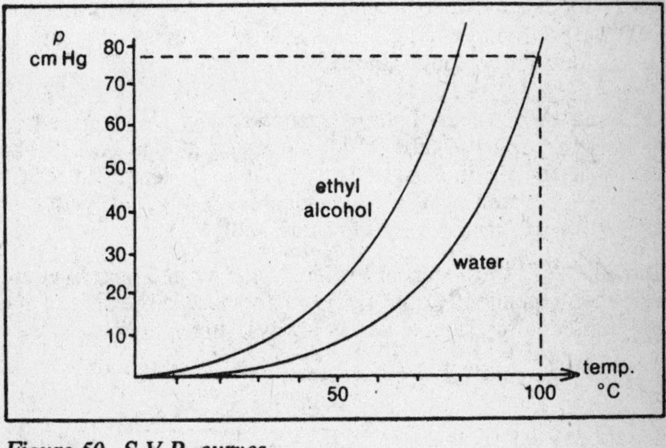

Figure 50. S.V.P. curves

A rather more accurate method is to boil the liquid under

reduced pressure, since at the boiling point the external pressure is equal to the s.v.p. The apparatus is shown in fig. 51.

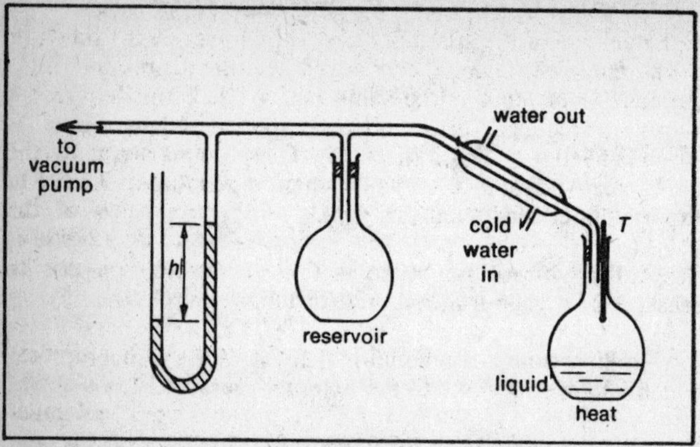

Figure 51. Determination of s.v.p.

The liquid being heated contains pieces of porous pot to prevent superheating. The reservoir is to damp out fluctuations in pressure due to uneven boiling and the pressure is measured on the manometer as H cm Hg (atmospheric pressure at the time) − h cm Hg. At each boiling point, the temperature and pressure are recorded. The condenser is to reduce the vapour passing into the vacuum pump.

Example A volume of air is trapped by a short thread of water in a capillary tube which is sealed at one end. If the length of the air is 2 cm at 0°C, what is its length at 90°C? (S.V.P. of water at 0°C is negligible, S.V.P. of water at 90°C = 7×10^4, atmospheric pressure = 10^5 Pa.)

By Dalton's Law of Partial Pressures the air and water vapour behave independently, and the total pressure is the sum of the two individual pressures, and is always atmospheric.

$$P_{\text{water vapour}} + P_{\text{air}} = P_{\text{atmospheric}} \quad \text{i.e. } P_w + P_a = P_A$$

$\therefore$ at 0°C $\quad P_a = P_A - P_w = 10^5$ Pa

at 90°C $\quad P_a = 10^5 - 7 \times 10^4 = 3 \times 10^4$ Pa

Applying the Ideal Gas Law to the expansion of the air only, and taking V to be in 'centimetres of tube'

$$\frac{P_1V_1}{T_1}=\frac{P_2V_2}{T_2}$$

$$\therefore \quad V_2=V_1\frac{P_1T_2}{P_2T_1}=\frac{2\times 10^5\times 363}{3\times 10^4\times 273}=8{\cdot}9 \text{ cm of tube}$$

The molecular view of vapours

Evaporation is a process in which molecules near to the surface of a liquid have a high enough velocity to be able to escape the attractive forces of the other molecules of the liquid and become a vapour. As the temperature of a liquid is raised more molecules acquire the necessary velocity to escape (fig. 47) and the rate of evaporation increases.

If the liquid is not heated (e.g. ether) the evaporation process may still take place at a brisk rate and the faster molecules leave the liquid. The mean energy of the rest of the molecules is therefore less, and hence the liquid cools. This effect is very evident if ether is sprayed onto one's hand. Evaporation can take place at temperatures below the boiling point, and is confined to the exposed surface of a liquid.

Latent heat of evaporation is the energy required to separate the molecules against the attractive forces between them as they pass into the gaseous state, where they are many times further apart than in the liquid. This energy is given up when the vapour subsequently condenses.

Dynamic equilibrium is the state ultimately reached when a vapour is in contact with its liquid. In this situation molecules are leaving the liquid by the mechanism discussed. Vapour molecules also collide with the liquid surface and are captured. Equilibrium is set up when the number of molecules arriving at the liquid surface per second equals the number leaving per second. The number of molecules in the vapour is then the maximum possible at that temperature, and it has become saturated.

Change of temperature affects the equilibrium by increasing the rate of evaporation. To re-establish equilibrium therefore the number of molecules in the vapour increases and hence the s.v.p. also increases. As the number of molecules with the necessary velocity to escape increases sharply with temperature (fig. 47) so does the s.v.p. (fig. 50). This is why an old aerosol can (which contains liquid Freon as a propellant) is so very dangerous if thrown onto a fire.

Change of volume affects the equilibrium by changing the density of the molecules in the vapour. If the volume is decreased, the vapour density increases proportionately, and more vapour molecules collide with the liquid and are recaptured. Thus the liquid grows at the expense of the increased density of vapour, until equilibrium is re-established.

Boiling occurs at the bottom of the liquid (or where the heat is applied) and is a process by which bubbles of vapour are able to form because the s.v.p. is equal to at least the external pressure. Because of the excess pressure inside a bubble due to surface tension, the bubbles have to nucleate on cavities or rough surfaces, otherwise the pressure inside them would be insufficient to allow them to grow and rise. This is why porous pot is placed in a flask to prevent 'bumping'. Without nucleation centres the liquid temperature can rise above the theoretical boiling point and is then superheated.

Solids also evaporate near their melting points. It is possible to have solid-vapour equilibria in the same way as liquid-vapour equilibria just described. For each substance these can be represented by a phase equilibrium diagram (fig. 52). A single phase (or state) corresponds to each area between the lines. Two phases can co-exist along each line. Three phases can

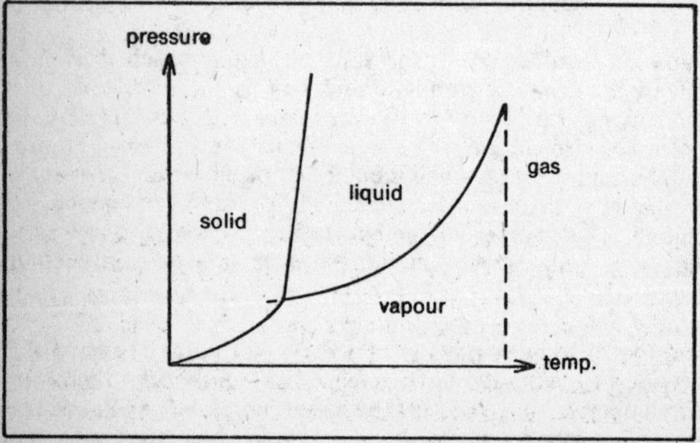

Figure 52. Phase diagram

co-exist at one unique point only – the triple point. For water this occurs at 273·16 K and is the key fixed point on the thermodynamic scale of temperature.

Thermal conductivity

The conduction of heat on the molecular model is due to two processes. In an insulator, the mechanism is one of energy being transferred by high frequency elastic waves through the lattice. In the simplest terms, a vibrating atom causes its neighbours to vibrate and so the energy spreads. In metals, however, there is also the 'electron gas' – free electrons which also possess kinetic energy. Heating one end of a metal bar will increase the kinetic energy of these electrons and they will therefore carry energy as they move. This increases the thermal conductivity of the metal by a factor of about 1000 compared with an insulator. On the macroscopic scale the process of heat conduction is mathematically identical to that of electrical conduction (in fact both are due to the free electrons) although in the case of heat conduction, there is no continual mean flow of electrons in one direction.

A temperature difference causes heat to flow. The rate of flow depends on the temperature gradient (difference in temperature per unit length), the area and the material. Thus in the steady state (when all temperatures are steady)

$$\frac{\mathrm{d}Q}{\mathrm{d}t} = -kA\frac{\mathrm{d}\theta}{\mathrm{d}s}$$

where $\frac{\mathrm{d}Q}{\mathrm{d}t}$ is rate of heat flow ($\mathrm{J\,s^{-1}}$)

$\frac{\mathrm{d}\theta}{\mathrm{d}s}$ is temp. gradient ($\mathrm{K\,m^{-1}}$)

and k is the constant of proportionality which depends on the material and is called the **thermal conductivity** of the material. The minus sign indicates that the heat flow is in the direction of decreasing temperature. The units of k are $\mathrm{J\,s^{-1}\,K^{-1}\,m^{-1}}$ or $\mathrm{W\,m^{-1}\,K^{-1}}$. For a linear flow (e.g. heat along a **lagged bar** of uniform cross-sectional area) (fig. 53) the rate of heat flow is constant down the whole bar since there is nowhere else for the heat to go, and hence the temperature gradient is constant, i.e.

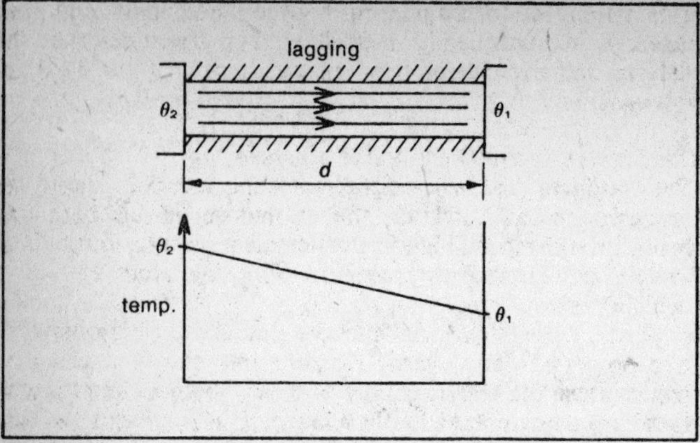

Figure 53. Uniform heat flow

$$\frac{dQ}{dt} = kA\frac{(\theta_2 - \theta_1)}{d}$$

For an **unlagged bar** neither the rate of heat flow nor the temperature gradient is constant (fig. 54). For instance, near the hot end, the rate of flow of heat down the bar is greater than at the cold end, so the rate of fall of temperature must also be greater (from $dQ/dt = -kA\ d\theta/ds$).

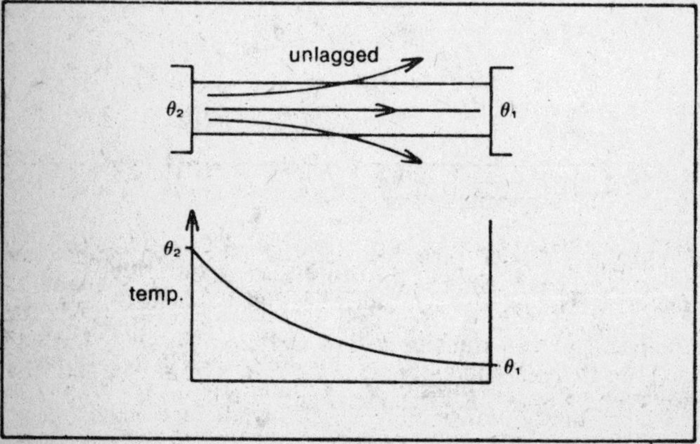

Figure 54. Non-uniform heat flow

It is important to distinguish between heat flow and heat capacity. In considering heat flow it is assumed that the material has previously been heated, and that the heat involved is only that which is passing **through** the material.

Conduction through composite layers

This situation arises when, for instance, boiler plates are covered with scale. The analysis to find the rate of heat flow through the composite layers uses the fact that the rate of heat flow through both layers is the same (fig. 55). Thus

$$\frac{dQ}{dt} = kA\frac{(\theta_2 - \theta)}{d_1} = kA\frac{(\theta - \theta_1)}{d_2}$$

The intermediate temperature θ is found in terms of θ_2 and θ_1 from the last section of the equation, and then substituted into the first section.

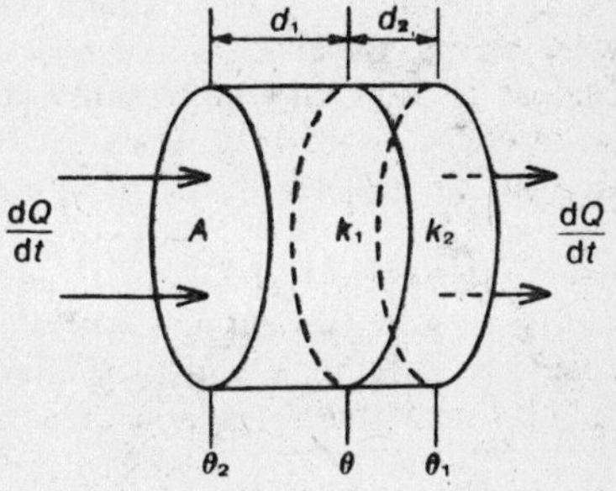

Figure 55. Composite layers

Example A boiler plate of surface area 1 sq. metre and thickness 1 cm is in contact with hot gases of temperature 300°C. Gradually a scale of thickness 2 mm builds up. Compare the heat transfer before and after the scale has built up. (The thermal conductivities of the iron plate and the scale are 50 and 1 $\mathrm{W\,m^{-1}\,K^{-1}}$ respectively.)

Before scale: $\frac{dQ}{dt} = kA\frac{(\theta_2 - \theta_1)}{d} = 50 \times 1 \times \frac{200}{10^{-2}} = 1\ \mathrm{MW}$

After scale: $$\frac{dQ}{dt} = k_1 A\frac{(\theta_2 - \theta)}{d_1} = k_2 A\frac{(\theta - \theta_1)}{d_2}$$

where k_1, d_1 and k_2, d_2 are thermal conductivities and thicknesses of plate and scale respectively, and θ is the temperature of the plate-scale interface.

$$\therefore \quad 50 \times 1 \times \frac{(300 - \theta)}{10^{-2}} = 1 \times 1 \times \frac{(\theta - 100)}{2 \times 10^{-3}}$$

$$100(300 - \theta) = 10(\theta - 100)$$

$$11\theta = 3100; \qquad \theta = 281{\cdot}8°\text{C}$$

Substituting for θ in the first half of the equation:

$$\frac{dQ}{dt} = 50 \times 1 \times \frac{(300 - 281{\cdot}8)}{10^{-2}} = 91 \text{ kW}$$

i.e. the scale reduces the heat transfer to 9% of its previous value.

Measurement of thermal conductivity

To measure thermal conductivity two separate methods are needed. The principle is to choose a test specimen and measure the heat flow for a given temperature difference.

Since $$\frac{dQ}{dt} = \frac{kA}{d}(\theta_2 - \theta_1)$$

for a good conductor (k large), d should be large and A small to get a conveniently measurable heat flow with a conveniently measurable temperature difference whilst for a bad conductor (k small), d should be small and A as large as possible.

Searle's method for a good conductor (fig. 56) uses a well lagged bar of the material, supplies one end with heat and determines the rate of heat flow reaching the far end by measuring its heating effect on a slow flow of water. Steady state conditions must, of course, have been reached. Thus

$$\frac{dQ}{dt} = \frac{M}{t}c(\theta_4 - \theta_3)$$

where $\frac{M}{t}$ = mass of water flowing per second and c = S.H.C. of water and hence

$$kA\frac{(\theta_2 - \theta_1)}{d} = \frac{Mc}{t}(\theta_4 - \theta_3) \qquad \therefore \quad k = \frac{Mc(\theta_4 - \theta_3)}{tA(\theta_2 - \theta_1)}$$

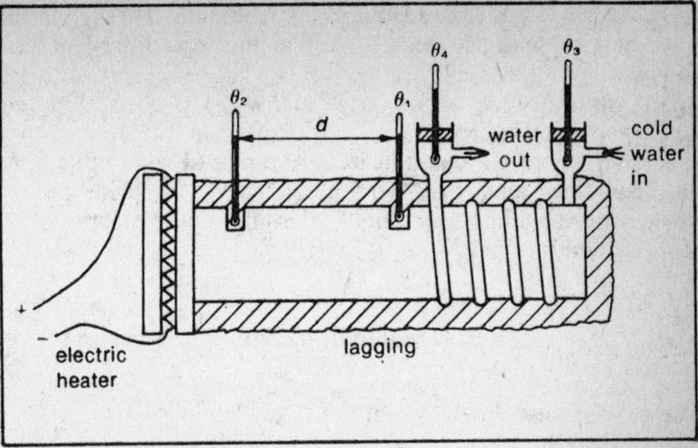

Figure 56. Searle's bar

The bar must be carefully lagged, and the water flow must be from a constant head supply. A is the cross-sectional area of the bar, calculated from its diameter.

Lees' disc method for a bad conductor uses a thin wide disc of the material sandwiched between two conducting plates fitted with thermometers (fig. 57). Again the method of finding the rate of heat flow is to measure the rate at which heat is

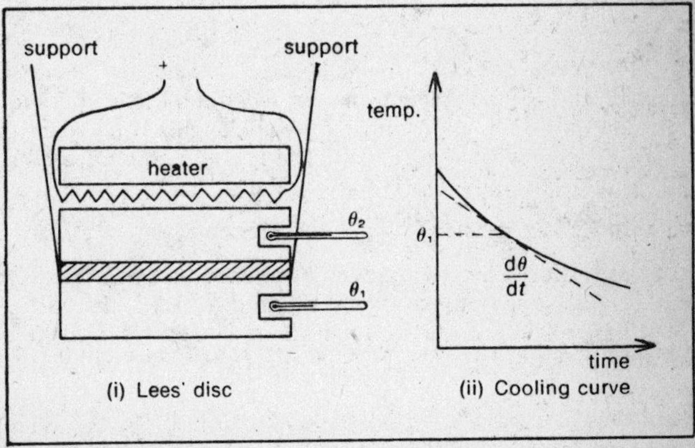

Figure 57. Lees' disc

dissipated after passing through the specimen. The apparatus is suspended with the heated plate at the top to prevent heat convecting to the cooler plate. The apparatus is left until the steady state is reached. After θ_1 and θ_2 have been recorded, the lower plate is heated to a few degrees above θ_1, and then specimen, upper plate and heater are replaced with a thick pad of insulating material. A cooling curve is then plotted (temperature against time) and the gradient of the curve $d\theta/dt$ at θ_1 is found.

Since $Q = mc\theta$

where Q = heat required to change the temperature of m kg of metal of S.H.C. c by θ K.

The rate of heat flow is given by

$$\frac{dQ}{dt} = mc\frac{d\theta}{dt}$$

Now $(d\theta/dt)_1$ is the gradient of the cooling curve at θ_1 – the temperature at which it was dissipating heat during the first part of the experiment.

$$\therefore \quad \frac{dQ}{dt} = kA\frac{(\theta_2 - \theta_1)}{dt} = mc\left(\frac{d\theta}{dt}\right)_1$$

since A, d, θ_2, θ_1, m, c and $(d\theta/dt)_1$ are all known, k can be found.

Radiation

If the radiation from an incandescent solid or liquid is analyzed in a suitable spectrometer, it is found that the radiation consists of a wide range of wavelengths, only part of which is in the visible spectrum. The rest is in the infrared or ultraviolet. The radiation is part of the electromagnetic spectrum discussed on p. 140.

Heat radiation which will heat a blackened thermometer bulb has wavelengths ranging from the red end of the visible spectrum, 740 nm, to about 1 mm, It is usually referred to as infrared radiation.

Radiation detectors for infrared are usually of two main types – in both cases the radiant energy is detected by the temperature rise it causes in the detector.

The thermopile consists of a large number of thermocouples connected in series. Radiation is allowed to fall on one set of blackened junctions whilst the other set is shielded (fig. 58i) and the resulting e.m.f. causes a current to flow through the galvanometer G.

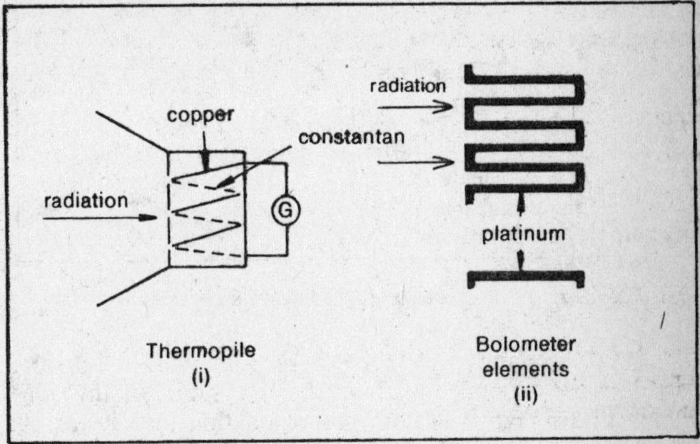

Figure 58. Thermopile and bolometer elements

The bolometer consists of a narrow, very thin blackened strip of platinum. The change in resistance is measured using a Wheatstone bridge circuit. The platinum can either take the form of a grid for general use, or of a line for use with a spectrometer (fig. 58ii, a and b).

Infrared spectrometers must avoid the use of glass since it is opaque to infrared. Lenses are replaced by concave reflectors. Prisms are made of fluorite or rock salt (fig. 59i).

There are two important theorems concerning heat radiation:

Prevost's theory of exchanges applies the idea of dynamic equilibrium to radiation. It is assumed that all bodies radiate at temperatures above absolute zero, and also that they receive radiation from their surroundings as well. A state of dynamic equilibrium is reached when the body radiates precisely the same amount of energy in a given time as it receives. It is then in thermal equilibrium with its surroundings. This is Prevost's theory of exchanges.

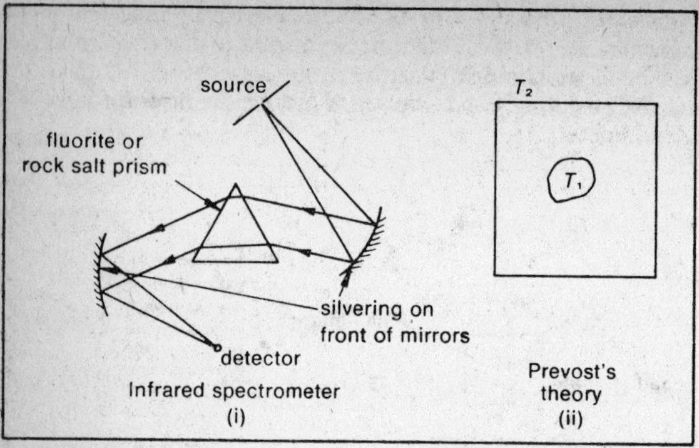

Figure 59. Infrared spectrometer and Prevost's theory

Consider a vacuum enclosure (to prevent convection) at a temperature T_2 containing a body at temperature T_1 (fig. 59ii). If $T_1 > T_2$ the body will emit more radiation than it absorbs and so its temperature will fall. If $T_2 > T_1$ it will absorb more than it emits. Consequently equilibrium is reached when T_1 equals T_2.

Good and bad absorbers The nature of a surface has a great effect on its ability to absorb radiation. Black or rough surfaces, for instance, absorb better than white or polished surfaces. If the surface is heated to the point where it is emitting more radiation than it is absorbing from its surroundings, then again it is found that black or rough surfaces emit better than white or polished surfaces. This can be demonstrated simply by placing a thermopile at equal distances from a metal cube filled with hot water, whose surfaces are painted either black or white, or are polished or rough (fig. 60i). It can be shown rigorously that **good absorbers are also good emitters**. The deepest parts of a coal fire, for instance, will be blackest when it is cold and brightest when it is hot.

Black bodies

A black body is defined as one which will absorb all the radiation falling on it. The main interest in black bodies is however the fact that they will also emit the maximum energy theoretically possible. A black body can be realized by making a heated enclosure with only a tiny hole (fig. 60ii). If the sides are curved and there is a cone opposite the hole, and the interior is matt black, then very little radiation entering the hole can emerge. When heated to incandescence, the hole will act as a black body.

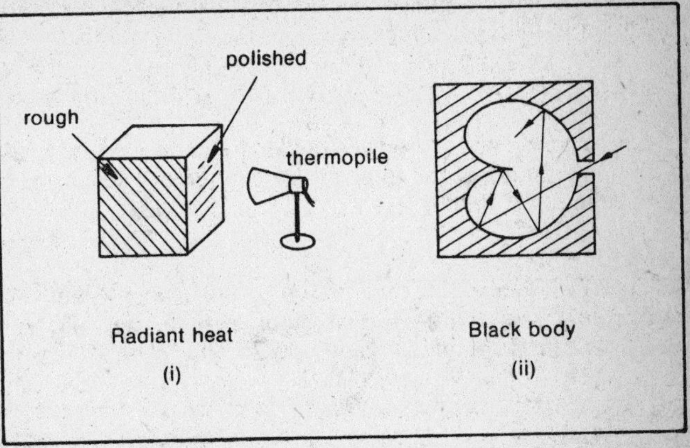

Figure 60. Radiant heat and black body

The energy distribution in black body radiation can be measured using an infrared spectrometer. Curves for such experiments are shown in fig. 61i. In plotting these curves, the

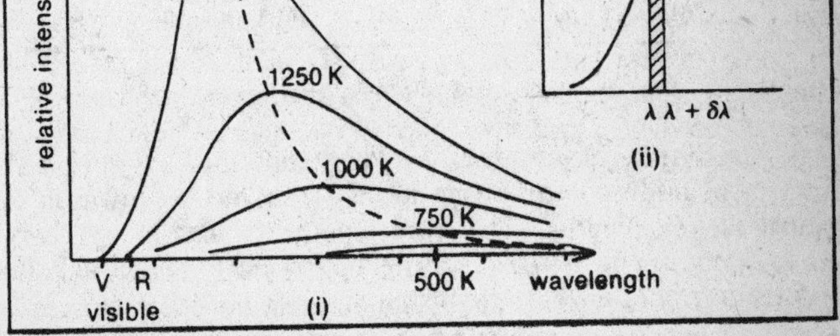

Figure 61. Black body radiation

concept of emissive power e_λ is used. e_λ is defined such that the power radiated between wavelength λ and $\lambda + \delta\lambda$ is given by $e_\lambda \delta\lambda$, which is the shaded area under the curve in fig. 60ii. Thus the total area beneath the curve gives the total power emitted, whilst the shape of the curve gives the distribution of power with wavelength. It can be seen that there is very little radiation in the visible region.

There are two laws concerning the shapes of these curves:

Stefan's law The total power radiated increases very rapidly with temperature. If the total energy emitted per square metre per second is E then

$$E = \sigma T^4$$

where T is the absolute temperature and σ is a constant. This is Stefan's law and is shown graphically in fig. 62i. σ is **Stefan's constant** and its value is $5{\cdot}7 \times 10^{-8}\ \mathrm{W\,m^{-2}\,K^{-4}}$.

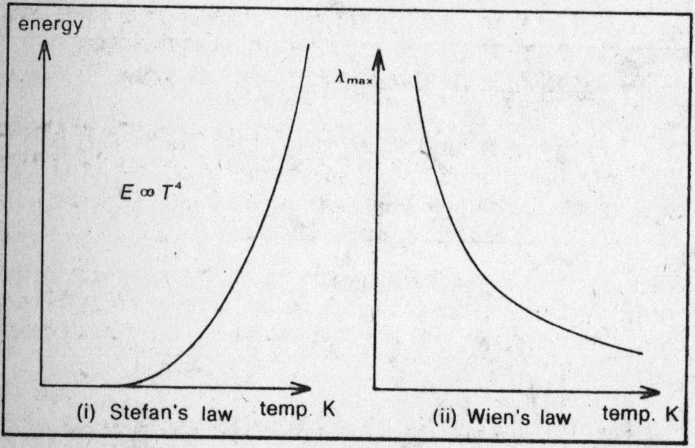

Figure 62. Stefan's law and Wien's law

Wien's displacement law As the temperature is raised the curve, in addition to getting larger, also moves towards the shorter wavelengths. The wavelength of maximum energy (λ_{max}) (fig. 61ii) is inversely proportional to the absolute temperature, i.e. $\lambda_{max} T = \text{constant}$.

This is Wien's displacement law, and the dashed line

represents this curve – a hyperbola if the scales are equal. The distribution favours the shorter wavelengths as the temperature increases. From the graph it can be seen that the visible radiation increases with temperature. This is observed as a body is heated – first there is no colour, then the colour passes through red, yellow and so on as it gets hotter.

Calculation of the energy distribution in black body radiation was attempted using Newtonian mechanics, but the formula produced did not agree with observation in the ultraviolet region (this problem in the theory was called the ultraviolet catastrophe). The problem was resolved by Planck who developed the Quantum Theory to calculate the correct distribution.

Calculation of heat radiated

To calculate the heat radiated by a black body both Stefan's law and Prevost's theory of exchanges must be used. The net power radiated is the difference between the power emitted by the body and that absorbed from its surroundings. The total rate of energy emission per unit area is thus given by

$$E = \sigma(T_1^4 - T_2^4)$$

where T_1 and T_2 are absolute temperatures of the body and its surroundings. Thus for a body of area A the total power emitted is given by

$$P = \sigma A(T_1^4 - T_2^4) \text{ watts}$$

Often, of course, the temperature of the body is very much greater than that of its surroundings. In this case $T_1^4 \gg T_2^4$, and T_2^4 can be neglected. For radiators which are not black bodies, the power emitted is less.

Example 1 Calculate the temperature of a 150 watt lamp filament of surface area 10^{-4} m^2 assuming black body behaviour.

Assuming $T_{fil}^4 \gg T_{room}^4$

Energy emitted per second $= \sigma A T_{fil}^4$ for area A

$$150 = 5{\cdot}7 \times 10^{-8} \times 10^{-4} \times T^4$$

$$\therefore \quad T^4 = \frac{1{\cdot}5 \times 10^{14}}{5{\cdot}7}$$

$$T^2 = 5{\cdot}13 \times 10^6$$

$$\therefore \quad T = 2{\cdot}265 \times 10^3\ \text{K}\ (= 1992°\text{C})$$

Example 2 A blackened metal sphere in space receives 1·5 kW per square metre continuously from the sun. What will its temperature be?

Let area of sphere be A.

Heat received from sun per second $= \dfrac{A}{2} \times 1{\cdot}5 \times 10^3$
(only half its area receives rays)

Heat radiated by entire sphere per second $= \sigma A T^4$

$$= 5{\cdot}7 \times 10^{-8} \times A \times T^4$$

But these two quantities of heat must be equal.

$$\therefore \quad \frac{A}{2} \times 1{\cdot}5 \times 10^3 = 5{\cdot}7 \times 10^{-8} \times A \times T^4$$

$$\therefore \quad T^4 = 131{\cdot}6 \times 10^8$$

$$T^2 = 11{\cdot}47 \times 10^4$$

$$T = 339\ \text{K}\ (= 66°\text{C})$$

Key terms

Brownian motion Random motion of particles in liquids or gases due to bombardment by the molecules of the liquid or gas.

Zeroth law of thermodynamics If A is in thermal equilibrium with B, and B is in thermal equilibrium with C, then A will be in equilibrium with C.

Absolute zero The lowest temperature theoretically possible, at which the thermal energy of random motion of atoms and molecules is zero.

Ideal gas scale of temperature A scale of temperature based on values of pV at zero pressure.

Constant volume gas thermometer A thermometer which measures temperature by measuring the pressure of a fixed volume of gas.

Platinum resistance thermometer A thermometer which uses the change in resistance of a fine platinum wire with temperature.

Thermoelectric thermometer A thermometer which measures temperature by measuring the e.m.f. in a circuit consisting of two different metals.
Linear expansivity Increase in length per unit length per kelvin.
Heat capacity Heat required to raise the temperature of a body by one kelvin without change of state.
Specific heat capacity Heat required to raise the temperature of one kilogram of a material by one kelvin without change of state.
Continuous flow calorimetry Methods for determining specific heat capacity of fluids by heating a flow of fluid continuously and measuring the resultant temperature rise.
Molar heat capacity Heat required to raise the temperature of one mole of substance by one kelvin.
Latent heat Heat required to change the state of a given quantity of substance without any change in temperature.
Specific latent heat Heat required to change the state of one kilogram of substance without any change in temperature.
Boyle's law If temperature is kept constant then for a fixed mass of gas pressure is inversely proportional to volume.
Charles' law If pressure is kept constant, then for a fixed mass of any gas, volume is proportional to absolute temperature.
Ideal gas equation $pV = nRT$.
Universal gas constant The constant R in the ideal gas equation for one mole of gas.
Isothermal change A change occurring at constant temperature.
Adiabatic change A change occurring such that the heat content remains constant.
Real gases Gases which do not behave as ideal gases.
Critical temperature The temperature above which a gas cannot be liquified.
First law of thermodynamics Heat put into a system equals increase of internal energy plus external work done by the system.
Dalton's law of partial pressures The total pressure exerted by a mixture of gases is the sum of the pressures that each gas would exert if it occupied the whole volume by itself.
Avogadro's law Equal volumes of different gases at the same temperature and pressure contain equal numbers of molecules.
Saturated vapour A vapour which is in equilibrium with its liquid. It cannot hold more substance in the gaseous state

unless the temperature is raised.

Unsaturated vapour A vapour that does not contain the maximum amount possible of the substance in the gaseous phase, i.e. not in equilibrium with its liquid.

Boiling point The temperature at which the s.v.p. of a liquid is equal to the external pressure.

Evaporation A continuous process at a liquid surface in which liquid molecules become vapour molecules at a temperature below the boiling point.

Dynamic equilibrium The state in which as many molecules leave the liquid in a given time as condense into the liquid.

Boiling Process in which a liquid turns to vapour throughout its volume at the boiling point.

Thermal conductivity The constant in the equation linking rate of heat flow with area and temperature gradient.

Infrared radiation Radiation, which has a heating effect, of wavelengths longer than the visible spectrum (1 mm to 740 nm).

Thermopile An infrared detector consisting of a large number of thermocouples.

Bolometer Infrared detector consisting of a blackened strip of platinum whose resistance changes are measured.

Prevost's theory of exchanges A body emits precisely the same radiant energy as it absorbs when it is in thermal equilibrium with its surroundings.

Black body A body which will absorb all the radiation falling on it.

Stefan's law Total power radiated per square metre is proportional to the fourth power of the absolute temperature.

Stefan's constant The constant of proportionality in Stefan's law.

Wien's displacement law The wavelength of maximum energy emission in a black body spectrum is inversely proportional to the absolute temperature.

Chapter 4
Oscillations and Waves

Oscillations

A body may execute oscillatory motion of many kinds but one type of periodic motion is of supreme importance in physics.

Simple harmonic motion

The periodic motion of a body subjected to a restoring force proportional to displacement from the centre of oscillation is called Simple Harmonic Motion (SHM). The period of the oscillation is independent of amplitude and the displacement varies sinusoidally with time. **The period of an oscillatory motion** is the time taken for one complete oscillation.

The amplitude is the maximum displacement either side of the centre of oscillation (equilibrium position).

The conditions for SHM are that the resultant force acting on the body must be (i) proportional to the displacement (ii) directed towards the centre (fig. 63i), i.e.

$$F = -kx$$

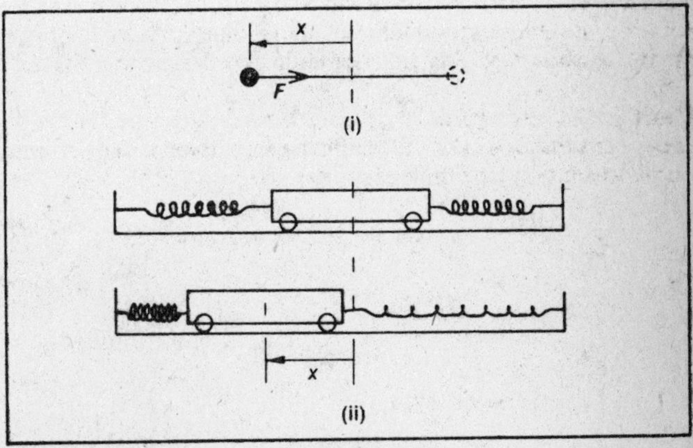

Figure 63. Simple harmonic oscillation

The minus sign means that the direction of the force is opposite to the direction of increasing x, i.e. towards the centre.

Mechanical oscillator

It will be easier to discuss a specific mechanical oscillator – a small trolley tethered by stretched springs in a box (fig. 63ii).

Let the spring constant of the combination of springs be k, the mass of the trolley be m, and the displacement x. Then the force acting on the trolley is given by

$$F = -kx$$

The minus sign indicates that the force is a restoring force towards the centre.

Now $$F = ma \qquad \therefore \quad a = \frac{F}{m}$$

$$\therefore \quad a = -\frac{k}{m}x$$

or $$\frac{d^2x}{dt^2} = -\omega^2 x, \quad \text{where } \omega^2 \text{ is written for } \frac{k}{m}$$

(The introduction of ω^2 rather than ω becomes obvious when the solution is considered.)

This is the equation for **simple harmonic motion** and it incorporates the two conditions stated above. Mathematically it can be shown readily that a solution to the equation is

$$x = a \cos \omega t$$

where a is a constant representing the amplitude. It can be shown to be a solution by differentiating twice:

$$\frac{dx}{dt} = -a\omega \sin \omega t \qquad \left(\frac{dx}{dt} = \text{velocity of } x\right)$$

$$\frac{d^2x}{dt^2} = -a\omega^2 \cos \omega t$$

But $a \cos \omega t = x$

$$\therefore \quad \frac{d^2x}{dt^2} = -\omega^2 x$$

So $x = a \cos \omega t$ is a solution.

It is clear from the mathematics that a is a constant which can take any value. The maximum value that x can take (when $\cos \omega t = 1$) is a. Therefore, a is the amplitude of the oscillation. When $t = 0$, $x = a$, and this is the solution for the case where timing starts from a point of maximum displacement (fig. 64i).

Another solution is $x = a \sin \omega t$ and this can be shown to be a solution in the same way. Hence when $t = 0$, $x = 0$, and this is the solution for the case where timing starts when the body is at the centre of the oscillation (fig. 64ii).

In SHM, the maximum velocity is at the centre and is given by

$$v = a\omega \quad \text{since } v = \frac{dx}{dt} = a\omega \sin 90° \qquad \text{(from p. 112)}$$

The maximum acceleration is at maximum displacement and is given by

$$\text{acceleration} = -a\omega^2 \quad \text{since } \frac{d^2x}{dt^2} = -\omega^2 a$$

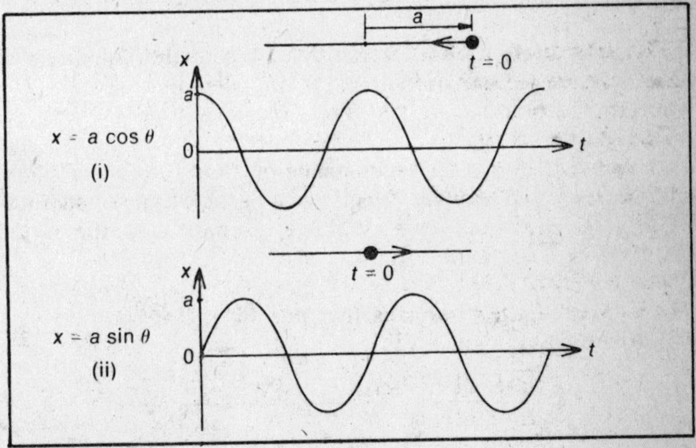

Figure 64. Sinusoidal waveforms

Circular motion analogy
Consider a particle moving round a circle of radius a, with constant angular velocity ω (fig. 65i). The projection of this particle onto a diameter will vary sinusoidally.

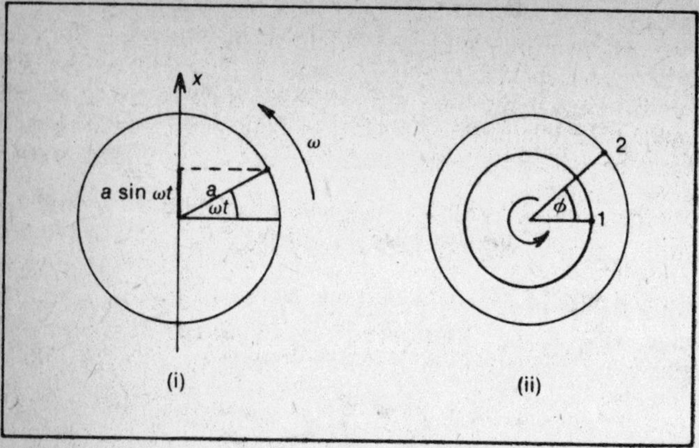

Figure 65. Circular motion analogy

If the time t is chosen so that the displacement is 0 when $t = 0$, then the angle turned through is ωt, and from the diagram

$$x = a \sin \omega t$$

This is the same as one of the solutions to the equation for SHM (the other solution can be obtained by making $t = 0$ when the particle has moved through a further 90°).

This solution shows the significance of ω and ωt in the SHM solution. ω is the angular velocity of a particle which generates SHM when projected onto a diameter. In particular, the period can now be calculated.

The period of the motion is the time taken for the radius to rotate once and is given by

$$T = \frac{\text{no. of radians rotated through}}{\text{angular velocity}} = \frac{2\pi}{\omega}$$

Applying this to find the period of the oscillating trolley.

$$\omega^2 = \frac{k}{m} \quad \therefore \quad \omega = \sqrt{\frac{k}{m}}$$

$$\therefore \quad T = \frac{2\pi}{\omega} = 2\pi \sqrt{\frac{m}{k}}$$

Phase
Two oscillators executing SHM of the same frequency are said to be in phase if they are at the same stage of their cycles at a certain time. If they are not in phase, then to return to the rotating particle analogy, the angle between the two vectors from the particles to the centre is called the **phase angle** ϕ (fig. 65ii).

Energy of a system executing SHM

Potential energy The energy of the system when at maximum displacement is the energy stored in the springs in the example discussed. From the earlier section (see p. 23) this is given by

$$W = \tfrac{1}{2}Fx = \tfrac{1}{2}kx^2$$
$$= \tfrac{1}{2}ka^2 \sin^2 \omega t$$

Since the maximum value of $\sin \omega t$ is 1 (at maximum displacement)

$$W_{max} = \tfrac{1}{2}ka^2$$

Kinetic energy The energy of the system when at zero displacement is the kinetic energy of the trolley. This is given by

$$W = \tfrac{1}{2}mv^2 \quad \text{but} \quad v = \frac{dx}{dt} = a\omega \cos \omega t$$

$$\therefore \quad W = \tfrac{1}{2}ma^2\omega^2 \cos^2 \omega t \quad \text{but} \quad \omega^2 = \frac{k}{m}$$

$$\therefore \quad W = \tfrac{1}{2}ka^2 \cos^2 \omega t$$

Since the maximum value of $\cos \omega t$ is 1 (when $\omega t = 0$ at the centre of the oscillation)

$$W_{max} = \tfrac{1}{2}ka^2$$

The **energy stored in the system** is thus proportional to the **square of the amplitude.** It can be all kinetic, all potential, or for most of the cycle partly kinetic and partly potential.

Example of SHM: Simple pendulum (fig. 66i). This consists of a mass m at the end of a cord of length l. Here the restoring force is the horizontal component of the tension T in the cord.

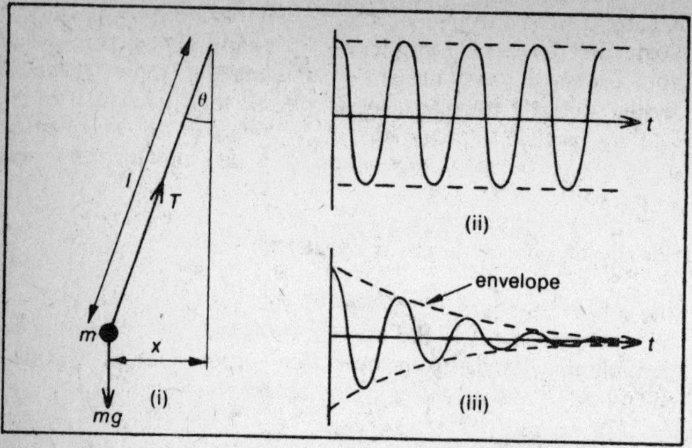

Figure 66. Simple pendulum; Damped oscillations

Resolving horizontally, $F_h = T \sin \theta$

Resolving vertically, $F_v = T \cos \theta = mg$

$$\therefore \quad T = \frac{mg}{\cos \theta}$$

and $$F_h = \frac{mg \sin \theta}{\cos \theta} = mg \tan \theta$$

Now F_h accelerates the mass horizontally

$$\therefore \quad F_h = -ma = -mg \tan \theta$$

where a is the acceleration and the minus sign indicates acceleration in the direction of decreasing θ.

$$\therefore \quad a = g \tan \theta$$

But for small angles, $\tan \theta = \sin \theta \quad \therefore \quad \tan \theta = \frac{x}{l}$

$$\therefore \quad a = \frac{d^2x}{dt^2} = -\frac{g}{l}x$$

Thus in this case $\omega = \frac{g}{l}$ and $T = \frac{2\pi}{\omega} = 2\pi\sqrt{\frac{l}{g}}$

Example 1 An oscillating trolley of mass 1 kg is held in a wide box by springs at each end of total spring constant of

$50\ \text{N m}^{-1}$. The trolley oscillates with amplitude 20 cm. Neglecting friction calculate (i) period (ii) velocity at 10 cm from centre of oscillation (iii) the velocity at the centre of oscillation (iv) energy stored in the system.

$$F = ma = -kx$$

$$\frac{d^2x}{dt^2} = -\frac{k}{m}x = -\omega^2 x \qquad \therefore \quad \omega = \sqrt{\frac{k}{m}} = \sqrt{\frac{50}{1}} = 7.07$$

(i) Period $= 2\pi/\omega = 0{\cdot}889$ second

(ii) If timing starts at $t = 0$ at the centre of oscillation, displacement is given by $x = a \sin \omega t$
At 10 cm,

$$0{\cdot}1 = 0{\cdot}2 \sin \omega t \qquad \therefore \quad \omega t = \sin^{-1}\tfrac{1}{2} = 30°$$

Velocity is given by

$$\frac{dx}{dt} = a\omega \cos \omega t$$

$$\therefore \quad \text{velocity at 10 cm} = 0{\cdot}2 \times 7{\cdot}07 \times \cos 30° = 1{\cdot}414 \times 0{\cdot}866 = 1{\cdot}22\ \text{m s}^{-1}$$

(iii) velocity at centre $= 1{\cdot}414 \times \cos 0° = 1{\cdot}414\ \text{m s}^{-1}$

(iv) energy stored $= \frac{1}{2}mv^2$ at centre (or $\frac{1}{2}ka^2$ at maximum displacement)

$$= \tfrac{1}{2} \times 1 \times 1{\cdot}414^2 \ (\text{or } \tfrac{1}{2} \times 50 \times (2 \times 10^{-1})^2) = 1\ \text{J}.$$

Example 2 Water in a U-tube is disturbed so that the level of liquid in one limb is above that in the other. If the total length of the liquid is 10 cm, calculate the period of the oscillation (neglect viscosity).

Let area of tube be A m^2, height in one tube above the other be x, and density be ρ.

When displaced, restoring force is the force on the extra x cm which one side is above the other.
Then restoring force $= x \times A \times \rho \times g$
This force accelerates all the liquid in the tube
$\therefore$ mass accelerated $= 10^{-1} \times A \times \rho$

By Newton's 2nd law $F = ma$

$$xA\rho g = 10^{-1}A\rho \frac{d^2x}{dt^2}$$

$$\therefore \frac{d^2x}{dt^2} = -\frac{9{\cdot}8}{10^{-1}}x \qquad \therefore \omega = \sqrt{\frac{9{\cdot}8}{10^{-1}}}$$

$$\text{period} = \frac{2\pi}{\omega} = 2\pi\sqrt{\frac{1}{98}} = 0{\cdot}635 \text{ s}$$

Free, damped and forced oscillations
So far, consideration has only been given to the oscillations which will occur if the system is given a displacement and then left to oscillate freely (fig. 66ii). These are known as free or natural oscillations. Under normal circumstances, however, frictional forces act. The energy of the oscillation is therefore continuously dissipated, and since energy $\propto$ amplitude^2, the amplitude decreases, but the frequency remains constant, or nearly so. The resultant variation of amplitude with time is shown in fig. 66iii. Mathematically the amplitude decays exponentially, i.e. the envelope in fig. 66iii is an exponential decay curve. These are called **damped oscillations**. A special case of damping is critical damping in which the system just fails to oscillate when disturbed.

If a system is subjected to a periodic driving force through some form of coupling then once the system has settled it will execute oscillations at the frequency (or very near the frequency) of the driving force. These are called forced oscillations.

Resonance
If the driving frequency is **equal** to the natural frequency of the system then resonance will occur. In this condition the amplitude of the oscillation reaches a maximum whose magnitude is determined by the condition that the energy lost per cycle by the oscillator is exactly made up by the driver each cycle.

A good example of resonance and forced oscillation is Barton's pendulums (fig. 67) in which a number of weighted paper cones are suspended from a string driven by a heavy pendulum (the driver). All the cords will oscillate at the frequency of the driver, but the one with the same natural period as the driver will have the greatest amplitude of forced oscillation.

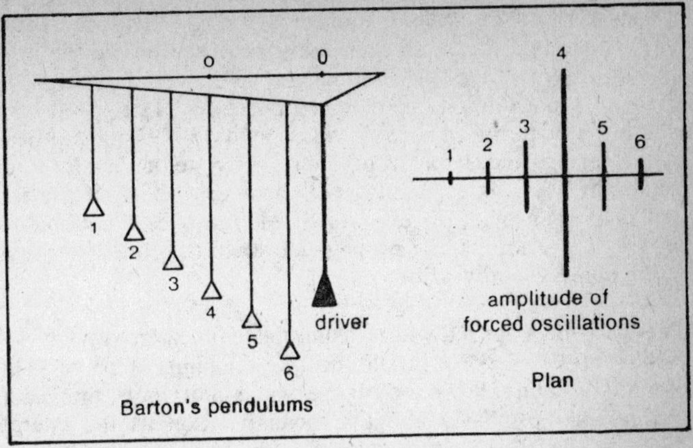

Figure 67. Barton's pendulums

Waves

Mechanical waves

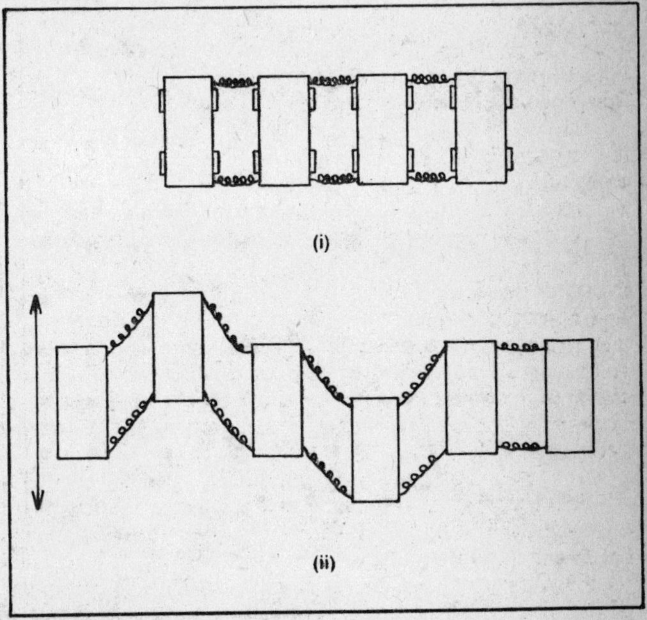

Figure 68. Transverse waves

Consider a row of trolleys connected laterally by springs (fig. 68i). If one end is moved then the springs will move the next one which will move the next one and so on, and a disturbance will be propogated down the row of trolleys. The speed with which the disturbance travels will depend on both the stiffness of the springs and the mass of each trolley, i.e. it travels faster with stiffer springs and slower with heavier trolleys. If the end trolley is then made to execute SHM (fig. 68ii) a continuous progressive wave will be propagated down the row of trolleys at the same velocity as before.

The wave thus caused will transmit mechanical energy and the trolley at the far end could do work against a force. The essential feature however of the wave motion is that each trolley only oscillates about a mean position as the energy passes it (fig. 68ii).

There are many kinds of mechanical wave motion, all of them involving media which possess both elasticity and inertia, and

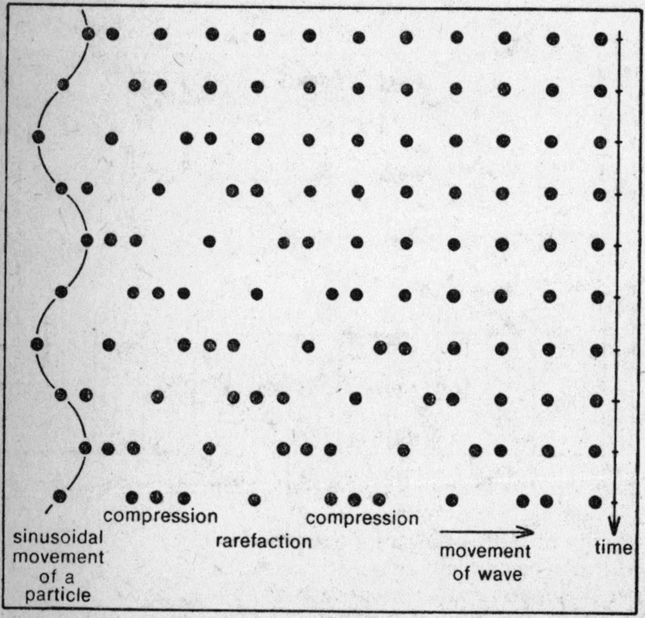

Figure 69. Longitudinal waves

in all cases the particles of the medium oscillate about a mean point.

In **transverse waves** the particles oscillate at right angles to the direction of propogation of the wave (fig. 68ii), e.g. waves on strings, water, etc.

In **longitudinal waves** the oscillation is in the same direction as the direction of propagation of the waves (fig. 69), e.g. sound waves in a gas or a rod.

A transverse wave can be represented by a sine wave (fig. 72i). Each particle will execute SHM laterally about the mean point. A longitudinal wave is more difficult to represent, as the motion of the particles results in compression and rarefaction progressing through the medium (fig. 69). Often a longitudinal wave is represented by a transverse wave in which the longitudinal displacement of the particle is represented by a lateral displacement, i.e. a sine wave (fig. 70). This is used particularly in discussing standing waves in air columns.

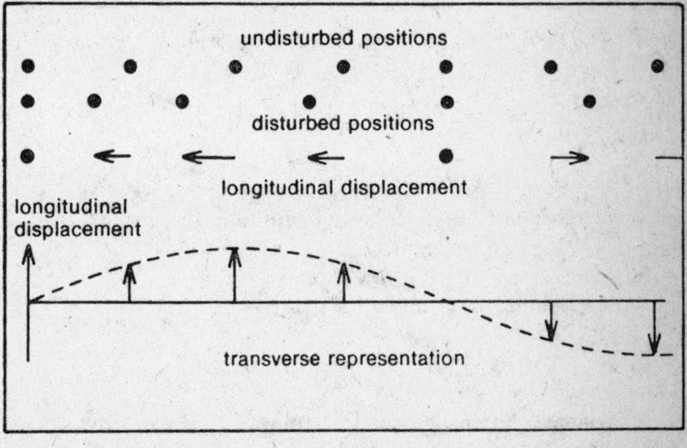

Figure 70. Transverse representation of longitudinal wave

Velocity of a longitudinal mechanical wave

The following is an argument which ignores transients but nevertheless gives the right answer and a feel for the situation. Consider a long row of frictionless trolleys connected end to end with springs (fig. 71). Let the first trolley be pushed with a force F and velocity u. After a time t all n trolleys will reach velocity u. Each trolley, once it has reached a final velocity u will experience no net force since the springs at each end will exert equal and opposite forces on it. It will therefore continue to move with velocity u and not accelerate.

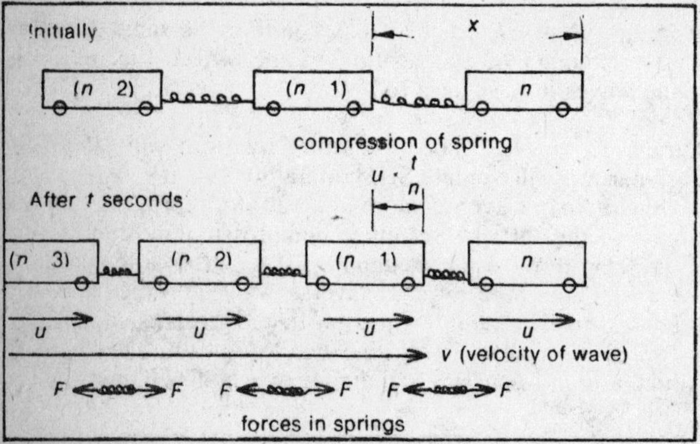

Figure 71. Longitudinal mechanical wave

Then the total change of momentum of the trolleys is given by

$$Ft = nmu \qquad \text{i.e. } F = \frac{nmu}{t} \qquad \text{(i)}$$

since n trolleys of mass m have been given a velocity u by a force F acting for t seconds.

The wave velocity v is given by

$$v = \frac{nx}{t}$$

since the wave has progressed n trolley lengths in time t.

Also, by Hooke's law, the force F in each spring (and also the force pushing the row of trolleys) is given by

$$F = k \times \frac{ut}{n} \qquad \text{(ii)}$$

where k is the spring constant and $\frac{ut}{n}$ is the compression of each spring since *ut* is the total compression of all *n* springs.

Thus from (i) and (ii)

$$F = \frac{nmu}{t}$$

$$= \frac{kut}{n}$$

$$\therefore \quad t^2 = n^2 \frac{m}{k}$$

$$t = n\sqrt{\frac{m}{k}}$$

But

$$v = \frac{nx}{t}$$

$$\therefore \quad v = x\sqrt{\frac{k}{m}}$$

i.e. the velocity depends on the ratio of the elasticity (restoring force) to the inertia (mass) – in this case the spring constant k to the mass m. All expressions for wave velocities involve a similar ratio.

String
(transverse)

$$v = \sqrt{\frac{T}{\mu}}$$

where T = tension (restoring force)
μ = mass per unit length (inertia)

Gas
(longitudinal)

$$v = \sqrt{\frac{\gamma p}{\rho}}$$

where γ = ratio of the specific heats of the gas
p = pressure (restoring force)
ρ = density (inertia)

Rod
(longitudinal)

$$v = \sqrt{\frac{E}{\rho}}$$

where E = Young modulus (restoring force)
ρ = density (inertia)

Relationship between velocity, wavelength and frequency
Velocity (v), wavelength (λ) and frequency (f) are related by a simple expression. Consider a point X past which waves are travelling (fig. 72i). In one second, f waves will pass X, each of length λ. The distance which the first wave past X has travelled in one second is thus $f \times \lambda$.

Therefore, $$v = f\lambda$$

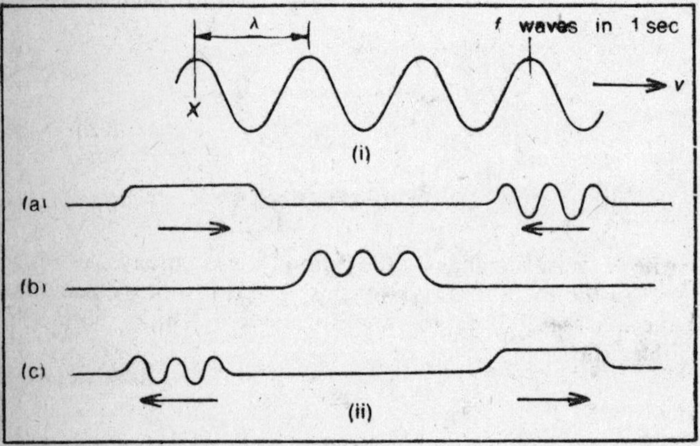

Figure 72. Superposition of waves

Phase The term phase can be used to relate the oscillation at one point on the wave to the oscillation at another point further down the wave. The phase angle between the oscillations at two points can be calculated from the distance between the two points and the wavelength. After a distance λ from a chosen reference position the motion of the particle is again in phase. Therefore a distance λ gives a phase difference of 2π. Therefore, phase angle ϕ after x metres is given by

$$\phi = 2\pi \frac{x}{\lambda}$$

Measurement of velocity of sound
The velocity of sound can readily be measured using the variation of phase along a wave (fig. 73). A loudspeaker is connected to a calibrated oscillator and the signal to the speaker is also fed to the X plates of a cathode ray oscillo-

scope. The Y plates are connected to a microphone. A Lissajous figure is seen whose shape depends on the phase difference between the X and Y signal (fig. 73ii). The microphone is moved from one point to the next where the shape of the trace is the same. The distance between the points is thus one wavelength. As the frequency of the oscillation is known, the velocity is given by

$$v = f\lambda$$

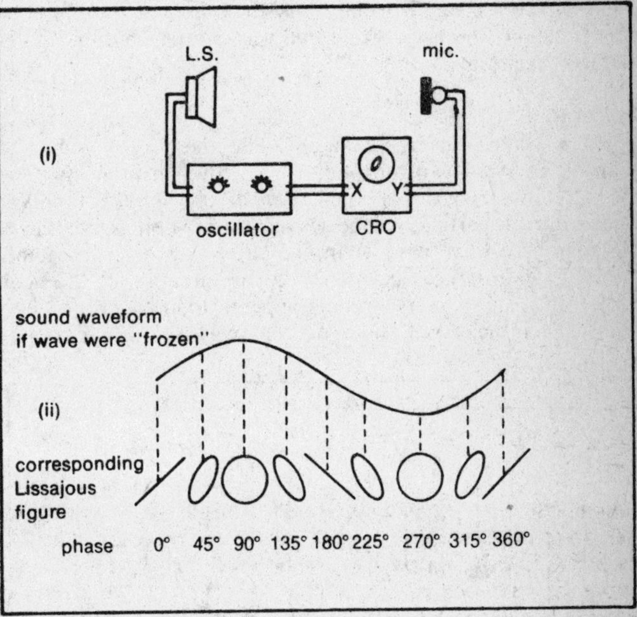

Figure 73. Velocity of sound

Intensity

The intensity of a wave, I, is the rate of transfer of energy by the wave. As each particle is executing SHM the energy of the wave is proportional to the square of the amplitude (see p. 115).

$$I \propto a^2$$

Superposition

One of the most important characteristics of wave motion is

superposition. This means that each wave motion in a medium proceeds as if no other wave motion were there. Thus at any point the resultant motion is due to a simple combination or superimposition of each independent wave motion, and there is **no mutual interaction**. **One wave motion can pass through or cross another and neither will be affected** by the process. An example is given in fig. 72ii. Because of this perhaps surprising property, the common effects of wave propagation – reflection and interference can be observed. This is particularly clear in ripple tank experiments. Interference effects can be observed where two waves cross, but the waves themselves are unaffected.

Diffraction

When a wavefront meets an obstacle the waves will bend round it or if a wavefront meets a narrow slit in an obstacle the wave will go through and spread out on the far side. Because each particle on the wavefront is itself oscillating at the edge of a wavefront (A in fig. 74i) waves must inevitably radiate outwards not necessarily in the direction of the main wavefront. The wavefront thus appears to travel round corners. The intensity of the diffracted waves falls off rapidly

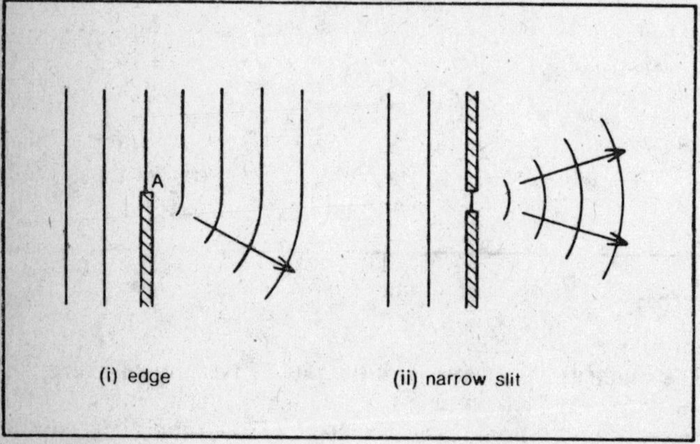

Figure 74. Diffraction

with angle from the main wavefront direction. The effect can be demonstrated with many types of wave motion, particularly light. The angle of spread is only significant however if the slit width is of the same order of magnitude as the wavelength.

Interference

Where two different wave motions of the same frequency cross each other interference will occur. This can be observed with several different types of wave motion.

Two source interference occurs when waves are travelling in the same general direction from two different sources of the same frequency and constant relative phase, e.g. dippers on a common vibrating beam in a ripple tank (fig. 75). In the diagram the circles represent wave crests. The troughs will of course be mid-way between the crests. At certain positions troughs of one wave motion will coincide with crests from the other. In these positions destructive interference occurs and the particles of the medium at these points do not move. By observing where crests and troughs occur, lines where no motion occurs can be drawn in (Y) (fig. 75). Similarly, in other positions the crests of one wave motion coincide with the crests of the other and constructive interference occurs (X). In these positions the waves will have twice the amplitude. They will be situated mid-way between the lines of destructive interference.

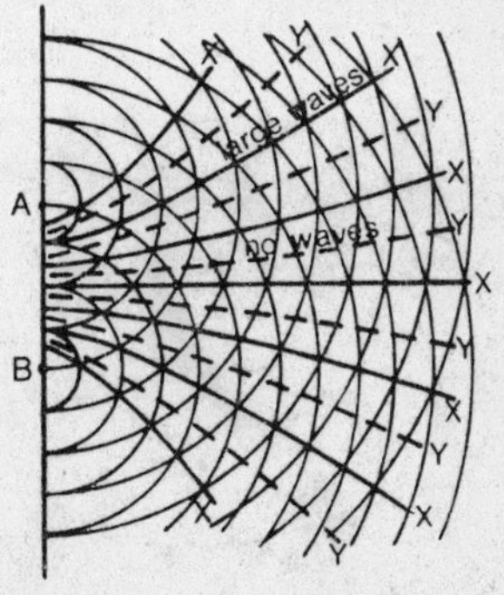

Interference of two sets of circular waves

Figure 75. Interference

This type of interference can be demonstrated with sound (two speakers), 3 cm waves (fig. 87iv) and light (Young's fringes).

Standing or stationary waves

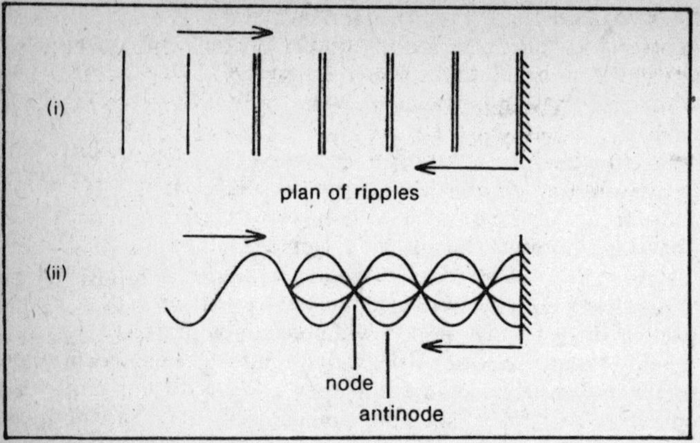

Figure 76. Standing waves

When two waves of the same frequency but travelling in opposite directions interfere, standing waves will occur. The usual situation is when the second wave is a reflection of the first – mostly of equal amplitude. By careful positioning of a reflector this can be observed in a ripple tank (fig. 76i). Again at certain positions no motion is observed (nodes) and at

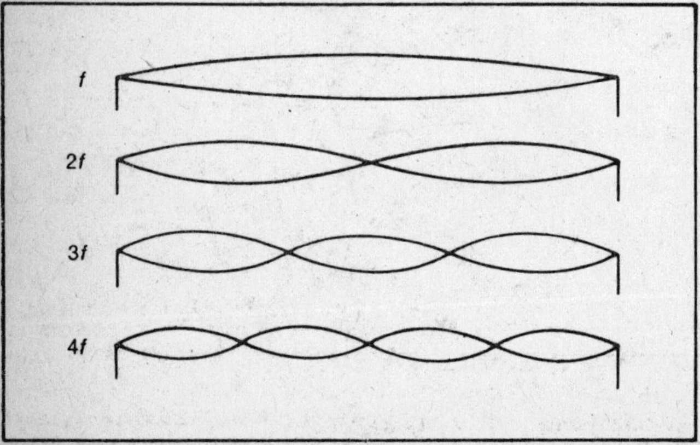

Figure 77. Standing wave modes

others the amplitude is doubled (antinodes) and the result is waves that do not move (fig. 76ii).

A more common example is the oscillation of a string fixed at both ends (fig. 77). Reflection occurs at both ends and a system of nodes and antinodes is set up provided the wavelength is suitable. The string therefore has a series of permitted modes at which it can vibrate at a natural frequency. If it is driven at any other frequency, then resonance will not occur and standing waves will not be observed to any great extent.

Polarization

Polarization occurs only with transverse wave motion because the oscillation of the particles must occur in some particular plane parallel to the direction of the wave motion. This plane is called the **plane of polarization**. For example, transverse waves on a rope will pass through a slot in a board if the plane of polarization is parallel to the slot (fig. 78). If the slot is rotated through 90° the wave motion cannot pass through because the oscillation of the rope in the slot is stopped. If a wave motion which could occur in any plane of polarization is restricted to one plane only, then it is said to be **plane polarized**. This is particularly relevant to light (see p. 145).

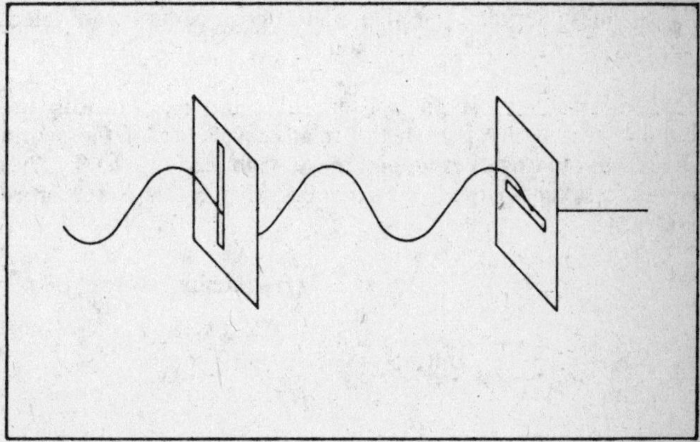

Figure 78. Polarization

A longitudinal wave motion cannot be polarized since the oscillation of the particles can take place in only one direction – that of the wave.

Resonance
As with simple oscillations, resonance can occur if the driving frequency is equal to the frequency of one mode of oscillation of a mechanical system, e.g. car door panel, chimney stack, bridge, machine, etc.

A classic example was the collapse of the Tacoma Narrows Bridge due to the wind causing a small vibration at one of the natural frequencies of the suspension bridge. The same process has caused collapse of cooling towers, and so on.

The frequency of a possible mode of oscillation depends both on the existence of boundaries which determine the positions of nodes and antinodes (and hence the wavelength), and on the velocity of the wave motion through the material since

$$f = \frac{v}{\lambda}$$

Doppler effect
The apparent change of frequency involved when there is relative motion between source and observer along a line joining them is called the Doppler effect. A good example is the change of observed pitch of a railway train whistle as it passes an observer. The Doppler effect occurs with electromagnetic waves as well as sound.

Moving observer If the observer is moving towards the sound at a velocity u then the relative velocity of the sound waves and the observer will increase from v to $(v + u)$ (fig. 79i). The time taken to receive two successive crests is therefore given by

$$t = \frac{\text{distance}}{\text{velocity}} = \frac{\lambda}{(v+u)} = \frac{1}{f'} \quad \left(\text{frequency} = \frac{1}{\text{period}}\right)$$

$$\therefore \quad f' = \frac{(v+u)}{\lambda} \qquad \text{But} \quad \lambda = \frac{v}{f}$$

$$\therefore \quad f' = \frac{(v+u)}{v} f$$

Similar reasoning for an observer moving away from the source leads to

$$f' = \frac{(v-u)}{v} f$$

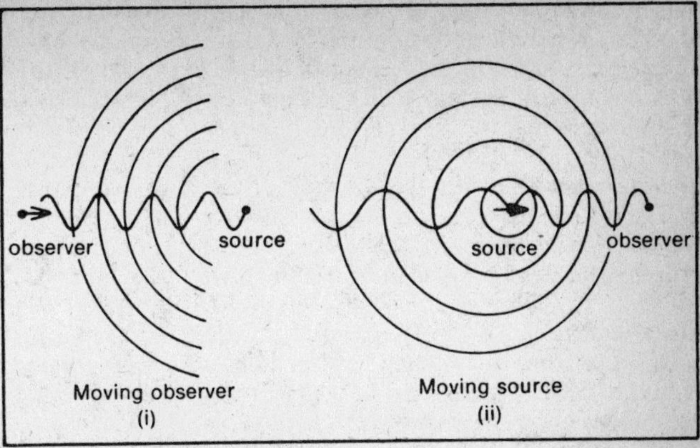

Figure 79. Doppler effect

Example
An observer on a train travelling at 30 m s^{-1} hears a track side bell of frequency 400 Hz. Calculate the observed change of pitch (speed of sound = 330 m s^{-1}).

$$\text{Frequency on approach} = \frac{v+u}{v} f = \frac{360}{330} \times 400 = 436 \text{ Hz}$$

$$\text{Frequency on recession} = \frac{v-u}{v} f = \frac{300}{330} \times 400 = 364 \text{ Hz}$$

Moving source If the source moves towards the observer then the distance between successive crests is reduced and the apparent wavelength is therefore less (fig. 79ii).

The distance the source moves per cycle is ut where t is the period $\left(\frac{1}{f}\right)$

$$\therefore \quad \lambda' = \lambda - ut$$

$$= \lambda - \frac{u}{f}$$

But the waves are moving through the air with a velocity v, i.e.

$$\lambda' = \frac{v}{f'} \qquad \lambda = \frac{v}{f}$$

$$\therefore \quad \frac{v}{f'} = \frac{v}{f} - \frac{u}{f} = \frac{(v-u)}{f}$$

$$\therefore \quad f' = \frac{v}{(v-u)} f$$

Similar reasoning for a source moving away from the observer leads to

$$f' = \frac{v}{(v+u)} f$$

In the case both of moving observer and moving sound, the pitch is always higher on approach, but not in the same ratio. In the examples quoted:

for moving observer approaching, $f' = \frac{330+30}{330} f = \frac{12}{11} f$

for moving source approaching, $f' = \frac{330}{330-30} f = \frac{11}{10} f$

(i.e. if the train was stationary and the moving bell was approaching it at 30 m s^{-1}).

For electromagnetic waves the Doppler expression is different because of the principle of relativity which states that the velocity of electromagnetic waves is the same for all observers. The relativistic Doppler effect produces changes of pitch given by

$$f' = \frac{(c-v)}{c} f \quad \text{approaching}$$

$$f' = \frac{(c+v)}{c} f \quad \text{receding}$$

Both of these expressions assume $v \ll c$.

A good example of the relativistic Doppler effect is the red shift, when characteristic lines in a star's spectrum are shifted towards the red end of the spectrum because of the recession of the star.

Sound

Sound is produced by vibrating bodies, e.g. a loudspeaker or tuning fork. It is transmitted through solids, liquids or gases by longitudinal vibration of particles of the medium. The ear can only hear those vibrations in the range of 30 Hz – 20 kHz.

Pitch is the frequency of a sound. The intervals between notes on a musical scale are determined by the ratios of the frequencies of the notes, e.g. an octave is 2:1.

Tone or quality of a sound depends on its harmonic content where a **harmonic** is a simple multiple of the fundamental, or lowest component frequency, of the sound. A typical waveform might be as shown in fig. 80, made up of a fundamental and third harmonic. Harmonics are named after their multiple of the fundamental frequency, e.g. third harmonic = 3 × fundamental frequency (fundamental and first harmonic are synonyms).

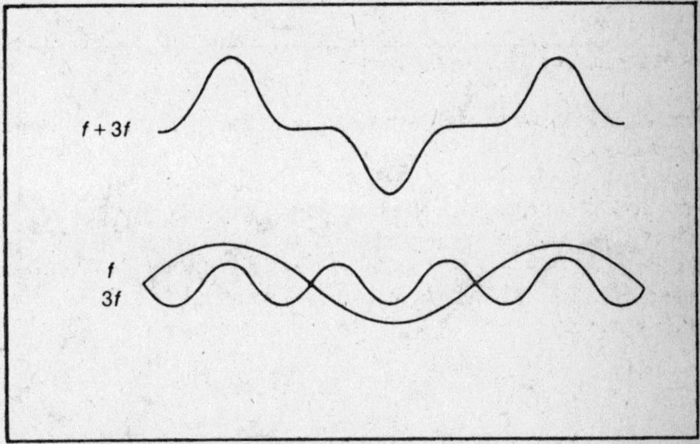

Figure 80. Addition of harmonics

The velocity of sound in various media is the velocity of longitudinal waves, the expressions for which were quoted on page 123. The velocity of sound in air thus depends on both the pressure and the density (though if the **temperature** is constant, the velocity is independent of pressure). The velocity of sound can be measured by several methods. One of the best is to use Lissajous's figures (see p. 125). Another method is to use the resonance of an air column. This method is discussed on p. 138.

Beats

If two sources of near equal frequency and amplitude are heard, then a periodic rise and fall of intensity is observed. The change of intensity is the beat frequency and is equal to the difference of the two frequencies being added.
Mathematically, if y_1 and y_2 are the displacements of air molecules due to two sinusoidal waves of frequency f_1 and f_2, and y is the resultant displacement, then

$$y = y_1 + y_2, \quad \text{where} \quad y_1 = a \cos \omega_1 t \qquad \omega_1 = 2\pi f_1$$

$$y_2 = a \cos \omega_2 t \qquad \omega_2 = 2\pi f_2$$

$$y = a\,(\cos \omega_1 t + \cos \omega_2 t) = 2a \cos\left(\frac{\omega_1 - \omega_2}{2}\right)t \cos\left(\frac{\omega_1 + \omega_2}{2}\right)t$$

i.e. a signal of frequency equal to the mean of the two, $(f_1 + f_1)/2$, whose amplitude varies with a frequency $(f_1 - f_2)/2$. An oscilloscope trace is shown in fig. 81.

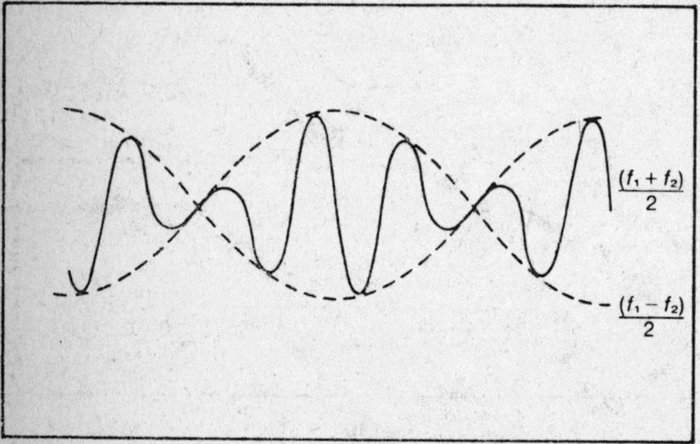

Figure 81. Beats

Since there are two beat maxima in each complete cycle, the beat frequency which is heard is given by

$$f = 2 \times \frac{(f_1 - f_2)}{2} = f_1 - f_2$$

Example An organ pipe sounds with a tuning fork of 440 Hz and 10 beats are heard in 5 seconds. When the pipe is made slightly longer, the beat frequency decreases. What was the original frequency of the pipe?

The beat frequency is $\frac{10}{5} = 2$ Hz. Since making the pipe longer makes its pitch lower and the beats less, the pipe frequency must have been above the fork frequency.
Therefore frequency of pipe = 442 Hz.

Vibration of strings
These have been discussed earlier in the section on standing waves (see p. 128).

The sonometer is a piece of equipment designed to investigate the fundamental mode of vibration (fig. 82i). The tension in the string can be altered by adding weights, and the length of the string can be altered by moving the bridges. The frequency of the note can be found by tuning for unison (same note) with the note produced by a calibrated oscillator with speaker or with tuning forks. It can be used to verify the expression for the velocity of sound in a string

$$v = \sqrt{\frac{T}{\mu}}$$

By measuring the length between the bridges ($\lambda/2$), and knowing f, v can be calculated from $v = f\lambda$.

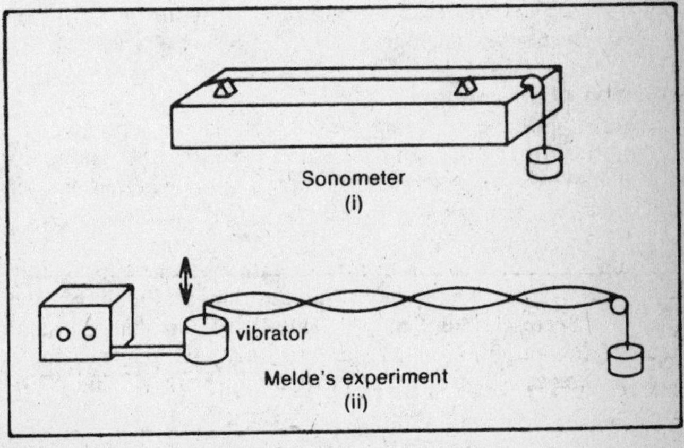

Figure 82. Sonometer and Melde's experiment

Melde's experiment is a demonstration of standing waves on a string (fig. 82ii). By adjusting the frequency of the oscillator, many different modes may be produced and again the expression for velocity of waves on a string may be verified since the distance between successive nodes is half a wavelength. It is interesting to illuminate the string with a stroboscope. The wave motion is frozen if the stroboscope frequency is the same as that of the oscillator.

Example In a version of Melde's experiment the tension was 10 N in a string of mass 1 gm m^{-1}. If the length of the string was 2 metres and 6 antinodes appeared what was the frequency of the vibration?
Each antinode corresponds to $\lambda/2$.

$$\text{Velocity of wave in string } v = \sqrt{\frac{T}{\mu}} = \sqrt{\frac{1}{10^{-3}}} = 31{\cdot}6\ \text{m s}^{-1}$$

$$\frac{\lambda}{2} = \frac{\text{length of string}}{\text{no. of antinodes}} = \frac{2}{6} \qquad \therefore \quad \lambda = \frac{4}{6} = \frac{2}{3}\,\text{m}$$

$$f = \frac{v}{\lambda} = \frac{31{\cdot}6}{2/3} = 47{\cdot}7\ \text{Hz}$$

Stringed instruments are bowed, struck or plucked, and the string will vibrate in its fundamental mode. However, depending on where it is excited, the string will vibrate in other modes as well, subject to the condition that there should be a node at both ends (fig. 77). Thus, harmonics are produced and these determine the resultant tone.

Vibration of air columns

These also involve standing waves, but now there are two possibilities – the end of an air column can either be a node (as with strings) or an antinode, depending upon whether the air molecules are free to move (open end) or not (closed end).

Consider a column of air in a tube with one end closed (fig. 83i). The air at the top is free to vibrate longitudinally but the air at the bottom cannot move because it is against the solid surface. The amplitude of the longitudinal wave is represented by a transverse waveform as discussed on page 137 (fig. 83ii).

Thus the fundamental mode of vibration is such that

$$\lambda = 4l$$

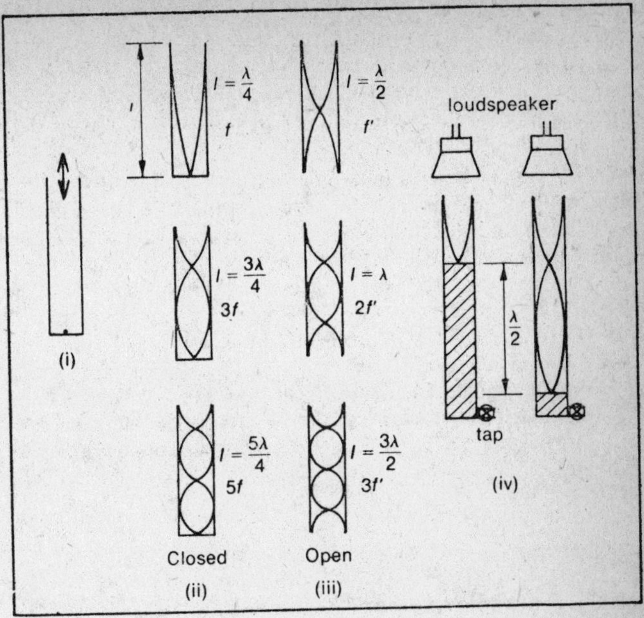

Figure 83. Standing waves in air columns

since the length of the tube is $\lambda/4$. The frequency is therefore given by

$$f = \frac{v}{\lambda} = \frac{v}{4l}$$

Other modes of oscillation are possible, as long as there is an antinode at the open end and a node at the closed end (fig. 83ii). It will be seen that as a result only certain modes are possible and hence the only harmonics at which it can vibrate naturally are $3f$, $5f$ etc. These are called **overtones.**

A pipe open at both ends will vibrate with antinodes at both ends (fig. 83iii). The fundamental mode is such that $\lambda = 2l$. The harmonics will be due to the modes shown, and can be seen to be the same as those on a string, i.e. $2f$, $3f$, $4f$ etc.

Wind instruments are excited by the vibration of lips (trumpet, etc.) or reeds (clarinet, etc.) or by edge tones produced by blowing air at a thin wedge (organ, flute, etc.). The air columns resonate at their natural frequency when excited at the correct frequency – which may be one of many edge tones produced by the edge. Again the tone will depend on the nature of the excitation, and also on the frequency range produced by the lips, reed, etc. as well as where the excitation takes place.

The velocity of sound in a gas can also be found from the resonance of an air column. One method is to mount a loudspeaker or hold a tuning fork above a tube containing water which can be run out (fig. 83iv). Because of end effects, the antinode at the top does not coincide with the end of the tube, but by obtaining resonance with the same frequency at two different lengths, the problem can be avoided by measuring the distance between the two nodes. From the figure it can be seen that the distance between the nodes is $\lambda/2$. Hence λ can be calculated. The frequency of the note from the loudspeaker or tuning fork is known. Hence the velocity of the sound is given by

$$v = f\lambda$$

Key terms

Simple harmonic motion The periodic motion of a body subjected to a restoring force proportional to displacement from the centre, in which the period of the oscillation is independent of amplitude and the displacement varies sinusoidally with time.
Period Time taken for one complete oscillation or cycle.
Amplitude Maximum displacement either side of the centre of oscillation
Phase The fraction of the period that has elapsed measured from a fixed starting point. It is usually measured as an angle, the angle corresponding to one complete period being 2π or 360°.
Free oscillation The oscillation of a system at its natural frequency, without any periodic supply of energy to the system.
Damped oscillation An oscillation which progressively dies away due to expenditure of energy by friction, viscosity, etc.
Critical damping Damping such that a system just fails to oscillate when disturbed.
Forced oscillations Oscillations produced by an external driving force.
Resonance A condition of maximum response which occurs

when the driving frequency is equal to the natural frequency of the system.

Transverse wave A wave in which the particles oscillate at right angles to the direction of wave propagation.

Longitudinal wave A wave in which the particles oscillate in the direction of wave propagation.

Progressive wave A wave which progresses through a medium; neighbouring particles are not in phase.

Standing (or stationary) wave The wave caused by a reflected wave being superimposed on an incident wave and thereby creating an interference pattern of nodes and antinodes which do not move.

Node A point in an interference pattern at which particle displacement is minimum or zero.

Antinode A point in an interference pattern at which particle displacement is a maximum.

Intensity The rate of transfer of energy by a wave.

Superposition The phenomenon of two or more waves being superimposed on each other to give a complex wave but without mutual interaction. Interference effects are observed where two waves cross but the waves themselves are unaffected.

Diffraction The phenomenon of waves appearing to 'travel round corners'. It occurs when a wavefront meets a 'narrow' slit or an obstacle.

Interference The phenomenon occurring when two coherent waves interact to produce points of maximum and minimum particle displacement.

Polarization The restriction of particle displacement to a single plane. It can only occur in transverse waves.

Doppler effect The apparent change of frequency when there is relative motion along the line between source and observer.

Pitch Frequency of a sound.

Tone or quality The 'colour' of a musical sound caused by the presence of harmonics.

Harmonic A simple multiple of the fundamental frequency.

Fundamental Lowest component frequency of a sound.

Lissajous's figures The patterns produced by two oscillations at right angles to each other, e.g. sinusoidal signals applied to X and Y plates of an oscilloscope.

Beats The periodic rise and fall of intensity when two sound waves of near equal frequency and amplitude are heard together.

Overtones The only harmonics possible from a pipe.

Chapter 5
Electromagnetic Waves and Optics

Electromagnetic waves

An immensely important class of waves, requires no medium for transmission and propagates readily through a vacuum. These are the electromagnetic waves which consist of mutually perpendicular time varying electric and magnetic fields (fig. 84). The changing magnetic field produces an electric field, and the changing electric field produces a magnetic field. The direction of propagation of the wave is perpendicular to both fields.

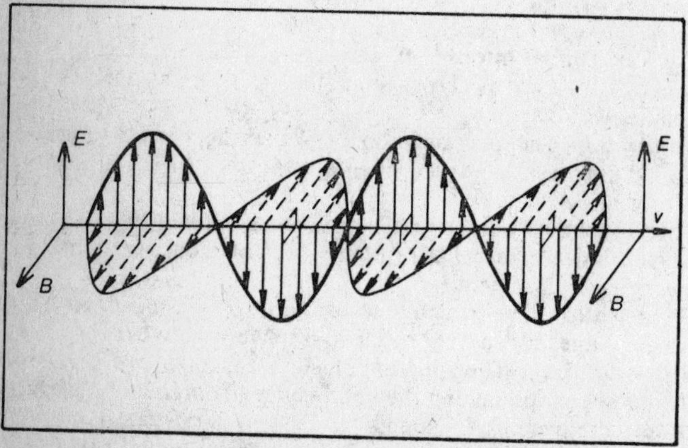

Figure 84. Electromagnetic wave

The electromagnetic spectrum is the full range of electromagnetic waves, from the shortest wavelengths to the longest. Although they all travel at the same velocity, the methods of production and detection vary widely, as do their properties and uses. The electromagnetic spectrum is summarized in fig. 85. There is a degree of overlap in the frequencies which can be ascribed to particular types of radiation.

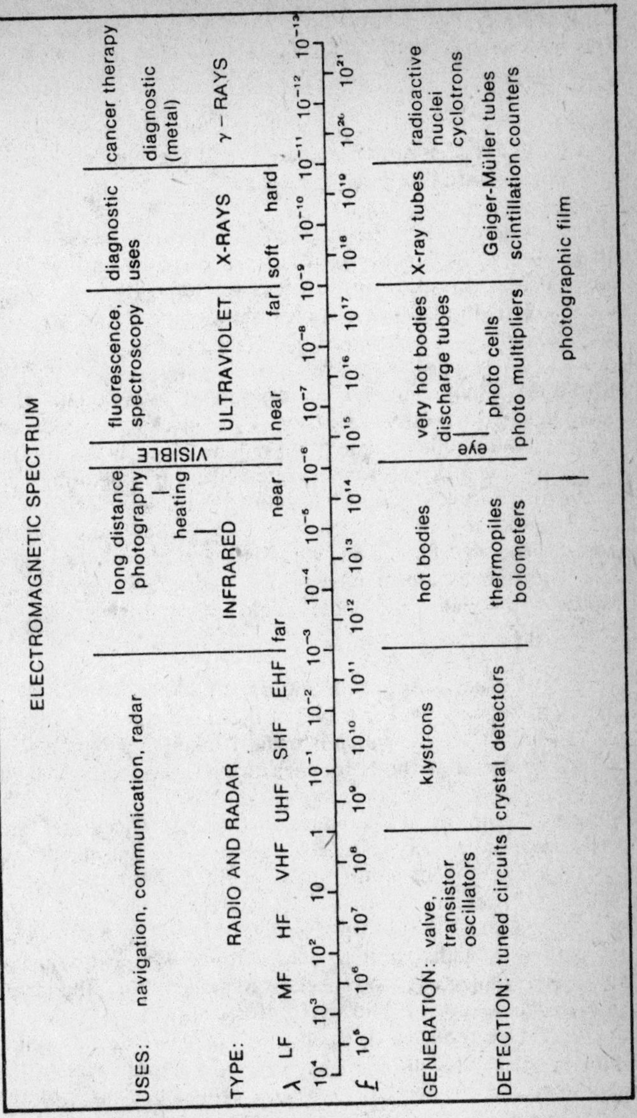

Figure 85. Electromagnetic spectrum

Several types of radiation are discussed elsewhere. Before considering light for the rest of this chapter, the two near visible regions should be mentioned.

Infrared (i.r.) radiation is produced by hot bodies but cannot be seen. Glass absorbs i.r. radiation and the problems of i.r. spectrometers are discussed on page 103.

Infrared is detected by thermopiles and bolometers (see p. 103) and photography can be used for wavelengths shorter than about 10^{-6} m. Infrared rays are less scattered by fog or haze than visible light and long distance photographs in i.r. are very much clearer.

Ultraviolet (u.v.) radiation is of shorter wavelength than visible light. It is produced mainly by gas discharge in mercury vapour within a tube opaque to all radiation except u.v. It may also be produced by arcs. It is detected by photographic film (colour film mistakes it for blue, so an ultraviolet filter must be used at altitude), by fluorescence (see p. 309) and by the photoelectric effects (see p. 296). Glass and many other transparent substances are opaque to u.v. and atmospheric ozone absorbs it. Incandescent bodies yield only a very small proportion of u.v.

Velocity of electromagnetic waves (c)

All electromagnetic waves travel at the same velocity – that of light ($2{\cdot}997 \times 10^8$ m s^{-1}, which is usually taken as 3×10^8 m s^{-1}). There are several methods for measuring the velocity of light.

Michelson's method was one of the most accurate, and consisted in timing the passage of light to a distant mirror and back (fig. 86). Rays of light from a slit S fell on one side of an eight sided rotating mirror M. It was then reflected by the concave mirror C to another concave mirror D 1·6 km away, returning by a similar route to reflect from the opposite face of M into the eyepiece As the speed of M was built up, the image in the eyepiece moved. The speed of the mirror was increased until the image returned to the eyepiece cross-wires, at which time M had rotated through exactly $\frac{1}{8}$ revolution. Hence the time taken for the light to travel to D and back is $\frac{1}{8}$ of the period of revolution of M, i.e. $\frac{1}{8n}$ where n is the number of revolutions per second of the mirror.

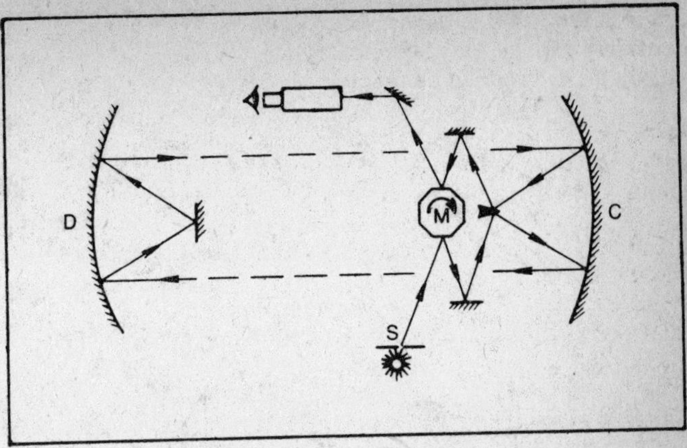

Figure 86. Michelson's method for velocity of light

Thus if the return distance to D is d, then,

$$\text{velocity of light} = \frac{\text{distance}}{\text{time}} = \frac{d}{\frac{1}{8n}}$$
$$= 8nd$$

The velocity of electromagnetic radiation can be shown theoretically to be given by

$$c = \frac{1}{\sqrt{\epsilon_0 \mu_0}}$$

where ϵ_0 and μ_0 are the permittivity and permeability of free space respectively. ϵ_0 and μ_0 can be measured by various electrical methods and hence c can be calculated.

Microwaves

Most schools now have 3 cm microwave demonstration equipment. Using these waves many interference, diffraction and polarization effects are readily demonstrated as well as reflection and refraction. Figure 87 illustrates some of the experiments. The polarization effects (fig. 87vi) occur because the electric field of the wave sets up an oscillating electric current in the metal bars, and the energy of the wave is dissipated as heat. The wave is thus destroyed when the grid is in the direction of the electric vector.

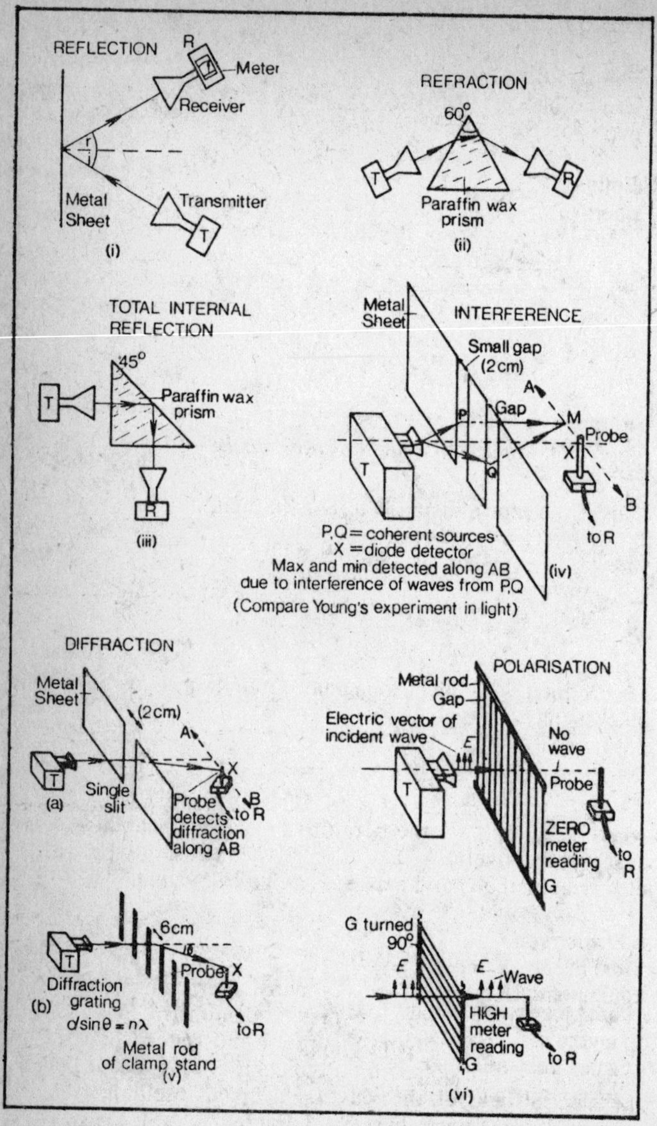

Figure 87. Experiments with microwaves

Optics

The nature of light

Visible light is an extremely small section of the electromagnetic spectrum already discussed.

Emission of light Hot bodies, gas discharge tubes, phosphors, etc. emit light in random trains of waves of length about 30 cm, the duration of which is of the order of 10^{-9} s. The phases and planes of polarization of each of these trains of waves are random and the resultant light is said to be unpolarized (fig. 88i). Different parts of a source will be emitting individually so that there is no correlation either in phase or plane of polarization

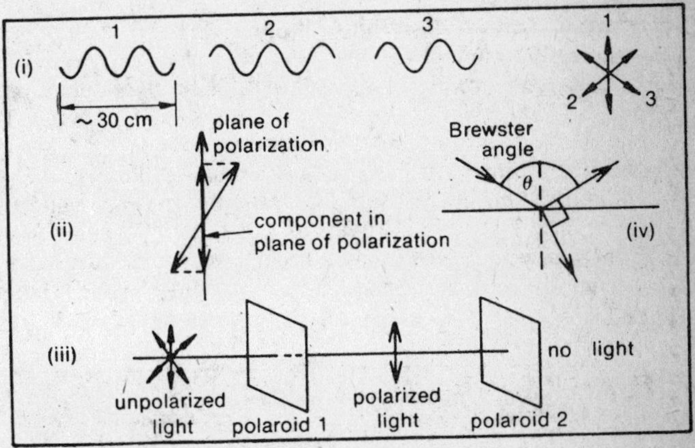

Figure 88. Polarization

between the waves from the different parts. Two light sources are said to be **coherent** if light from one is of the same frequency and phase as light from the other. Two coherent light sources are best produced by a laser illuminating a double slit. Alternatively, a very narrow slit is placed in front of the source to select light from only one tiny part of it, in which case the two slits are receiving only light produced by that small part of the source.

Plane polarized light can be produced by passing unpolarized light through a sheet of Polaroid which allows only light of one plane of polarization to pass through. Thus only the components of the unpolarized light in the plane of polarization will be transmitted (fig. 88ii). If another sheet of Polaroid is placed in the path of the polarized light but with its plane of polarization perpendicular to that of the first, no light will be transmitted (fig. 88iii).

Light reflected from a polished surface such as glass is partially plane polarized. It can be shown that when the reflected ray is perpendicular to the refracted ray then the reflected ray is completely plane polarized in the plane parallel to the reflected ray and perpendicular to the refracted ray (fig. 88iv). For glass, $n = 1{\cdot}5$, the angle of incidence is 57°. This is known as the **Brewster** angle.

Interference and diffraction of light

The interference of waves has been discussed on page 127. For interference to be observed with light two conditions have to be met;

(i) the two light sources must be coherent.

(ii) the two beams must be of roughly equal amplitude.

The first arises because observable static interference patterns can only occur between waves of the same frequency and constant phase difference. Light from lasers, can be used to illuminate two slits, or a small slit or hole in front of a lamp can be used.

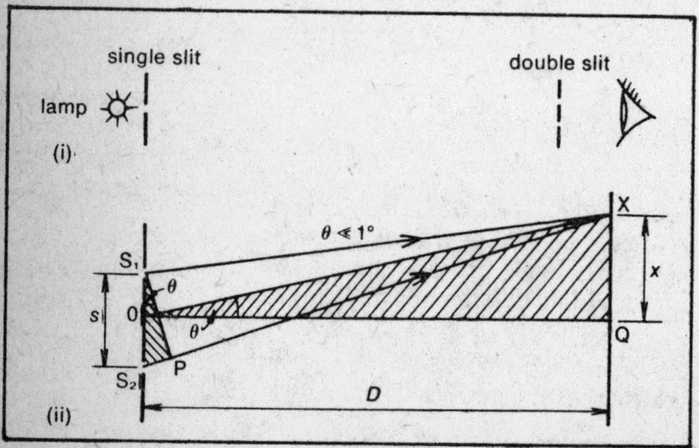

Figure 89. Young's fringes

Young's fringes are due to interference between rays from two fine parallel slits about a third of a millimetre apart (fig. 89). The fringes are best seen by holding the double slit close to the eye and observing a parallel illuminated slit about a metre away. For measurement, the fringes can be observed on a ground glass screen with a travelling microscope.

A diagram in which the angles are grossly exaggerated is shown in fig. 89ii. For a **bright** fringe at X the path difference SP_2 must be an **integral number of wavelengths**. If the angles are very small indeed triangles S_1PS_2 and OQX are very nearly similar.

Hence $\frac{XQ}{OQ} = \frac{S_2P}{S_1S_2}$ (since $\tan\theta \doteq \sin\theta$ for small angles)

i.e. $$\frac{x_m}{D} = \frac{m\lambda}{s} \text{ (for the } m\text{th bright fringe)} \quad \text{(i)}$$

also $$\frac{x_{m+1}}{D} = \frac{(m+1)\lambda}{s} \text{ (for the } (m+1)\text{th bright fringe)} \quad \text{(ii)}$$

Hence subtracting (i) from (ii) and rearranging $\lambda = sy/D$ where $y = x_{m+1} - x_m$ (the spacing between two adjacent fringes). This also shows that the fringes are equally spaced.

The first dark fringe occurs when the path difference S_2P equals $\lambda/2$. Therefore for the mth dark fringe

$$\frac{x_m}{D} = \frac{(m - \frac{1}{2})\lambda}{s}$$

The experiment can also be performed using a single slit and forming the second one by using glancing reflections from a mirror (Lloyd's mirror) (fig. 90i). This is readily demonstrated with 3 cm radio waves using a sheet of metal as the mirror.

Thin film interference occurs when a ray of light can take two paths on reflection at a thin film of air or oil etc. (fig. 90ii). It must be noted that there is a phase change of π (equivalent to a path difference of $\lambda/2$) when light is reflected at an optically denser medium. Thus for normal incidence, there will be **destructive** interference (dark fringe) when

$$2d = n\lambda$$

because of the phase change at the air–glass interface.

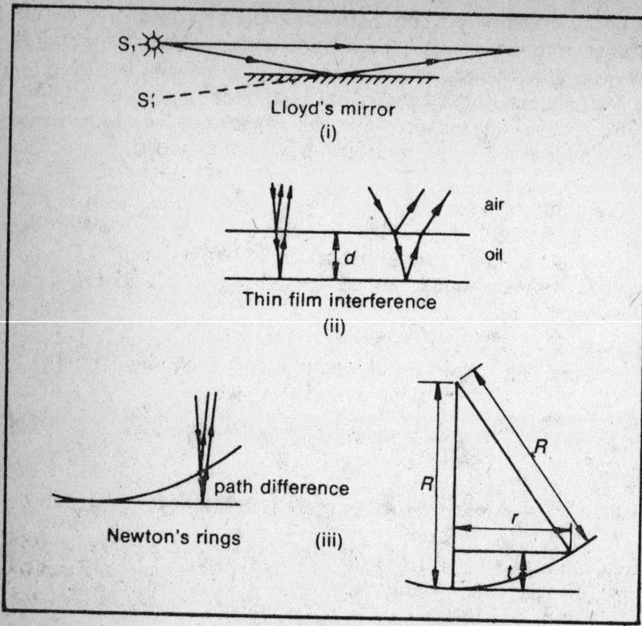

Figure 90. Thin film interference

This result can be used to measure the thickness of a wedge between two microscope slides, for example. Each dark fringe from the end (which is dark with zero path difference) represents a path difference of λ, i.e. a film thickness of λ/2. Thus, if a thin film is illuminated with white light, at particular film thicknesses certain colours will be removed by destructive interference, leaving fringes in the complementary colours.

Example Two glass plates in contact at one edge are separated by a metal foil 15 m from the edge. If 100 dark fringes are counted while it is illuminated by sodium light ($\lambda = 589$ nm) calculate the thickness of the foil.

Extra path between each successive fringe is given by

$$2t = \lambda \quad \text{where } t = \text{thickness of film}$$

$$t = \frac{\lambda}{2}$$

$\therefore$ thickness of foil $= 100t = 50\lambda = 29.4\ \mu\text{m}$

Newton's rings between a lens and a plane glass surface are formed in this way (fig. 90iii). If R = radius of lens, r = radius of ring and t = thickness of air:
By Pythagoras, (fig. 90iii) $R^2 = (R - t)^2 + r^2$

$$R^2 = R^2 - 2Rt + t^2 + r^2$$

$$\therefore \quad 2Rt = r^2 \quad \text{since } t^2 \text{ is very small}$$

$$2t = \frac{r^2}{R}$$

Hence for the nth **dark** fringe $\frac{r^2}{R} = n\lambda$
because of the phase change of π at the air–glass interface,

$$\therefore \quad r = \sqrt{nR\lambda}$$

i.e. the radii of the rings are proportional to the square roots of integers.

Diffraction

The diffraction of waves in general has already been discussed on p. 126. Light, too, 'travels round corners' to form diffraction patterns which are readily observed at narrow slits or obstructions, provided the light is parallel.

Diffraction at a slit can be analyzed for the case when the light leaving the slit is parallel and forms an image with a focusing lens, e.g. the cornea focusing onto the retina of the eye (fig. 91i). This is called Fraunhofer diffraction.

If the angle θ (fig. 91ii) is such that the path difference AX between AB and CD is $\lambda/2$ then AB and CD will interfere destructively. By the same argument A'B' and C'D' will also interfere destructively and so on with the result that all the waves between A and C will cancel with those between C and P. Consequently no light will be seen in the direction θ.

Since in triangle AXC, $\sin\theta = \frac{\lambda/2}{d/2}$

For a dark fringe $\frac{d}{2}\sin\theta = \frac{\lambda}{2}$, i.e. $\sin\theta = \frac{\lambda}{d}$

or since θ is very small, $\quad \theta = \frac{\lambda}{d}$

If θ is now increased so that the path difference between AB

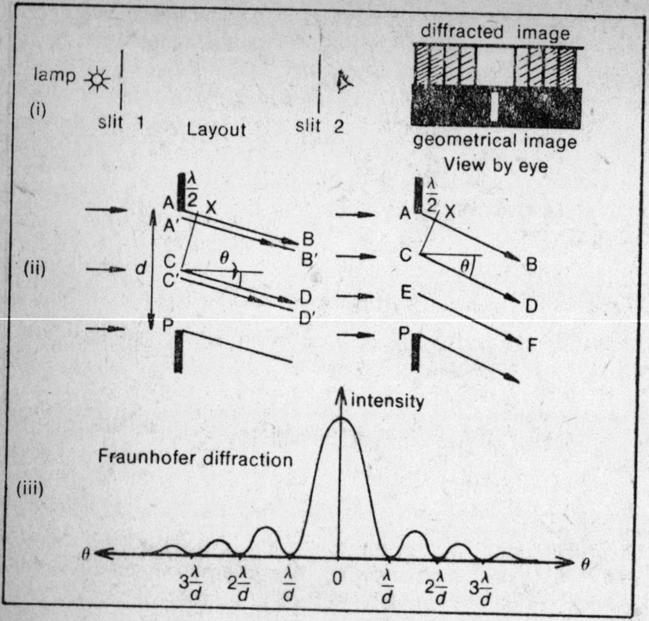

Figure 91. Fraunhofer diffraction

and CD is still $\lambda/2$, but now C is only $\frac{1}{3}$ the way across the slit, then again AB and CD, A′B′ and C′D′ will cancel and so on, and all the waves between AC will cancel those between CE, leaving however those between E and P uncancelled. As a result light will be seen in this direction. Continuing this argument for $AC = \frac{1}{4}AP$ and so on, the resultant diffraction pattern can be shown to be that of fig. 91iii, and the familiar Fraunhofer fringes, equally spaced about the centre but of decreasing intensity, will be observed.

Resolving power The ability of an optical instrument or the eye to separate two images which are very close together is called **resolving power.** For example, each image of a star in a telescope should be a point, but, in practice, it will be a Fraunhofer diffraction pattern. What is actually seen will be the resultant of the two diffraction patterns overlapping. Whether the images are resolved or not depends on whether two separate maxima can be distinguished (fig. 92).

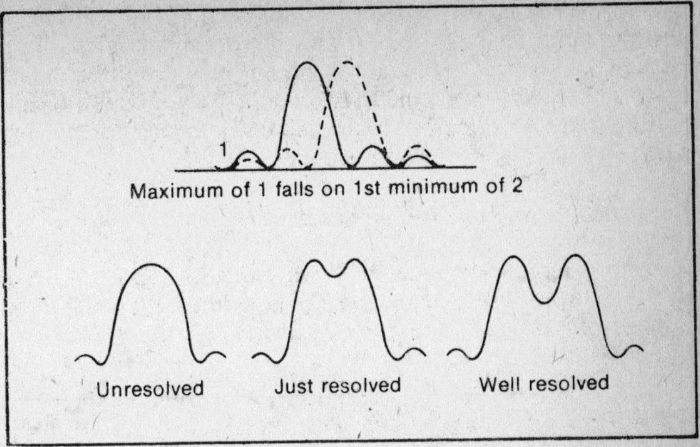

Figure 92. Resolution

Rayleigh's criterion states that the limit of resolution is when the central maximum of intensity of one pattern falls on the first minimum of intensity of the other. The minimum angular separation for resolution is therefore given by

$$\theta = \frac{\lambda}{d} \text{ for a slit}$$

For a circular aperture (telescope, microscope or the eye) the condition is given by

$$\theta = \frac{1 \cdot 22\lambda}{d}$$

Thus for the human eye with a pupil diameter of 2 mm, the minimum angular separation of two points of light of mean wavelength 500 nm will be given by

$$\theta = \frac{1 \cdot 22 \times 5 \times 10^{-7}}{2 \times 10^{-3}} \approx 3 \times 10^{-4} \text{ radian}$$

This is equivalent to a separation of the two points of 1 mm at a distance of about 3 metres.

Diffraction gratings

A diffraction grating consists of a transparent surface with a large number of lines ruled across it. If parallel light falls on it the result is that the wavefront is split up into many separate coherent sources. In certain directions, the path difference between adjacent sources is λ and so the waves from all the sources across the grating are in phase. In these directions, a bright image will be formed. The condition for two adjacent (and hence all) sources to be in phase and hence for a bright image is that

$$\sin\theta = \frac{n\lambda}{d} \quad \text{i.e. } d\sin\theta = n\lambda$$

where n is an integral number of wavelengths (fig. 93ii). n also gives the order of the image (fig. 93iii). White light splits into a number of spectra, since each colour leaves the grating at a different angle.

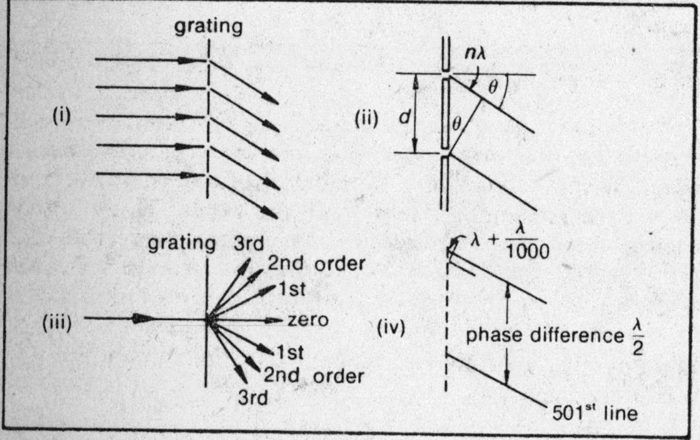

Figure 93. Diffraction gratings

The images from a diffraction grating are in fact extremely sharp. The sharpness can be deduced by considering a small departure from a whole wavelength path difference between adjacent sources; say $\lambda/1000$ (fig. 93iv). The path difference between the first wave and the five hundred and first will therefore be given by

$$500 \times \left(\lambda + \frac{\lambda}{1000}\right) = 500\,\lambda + \frac{\lambda}{2}$$

and thus the two waves will cancel. The same process will occur for adjacent rays right across the grating only leaving a few waves uncancelled. Thus the brightness of the image falls off very sharply with angle from the calculated maximum.

Example A diffraction grating of 9000 lines per centimetre is used with white light. How many orders of spectra will be seen?

$$\text{No. of lines per metre} = 9 \times 10^5$$

$$\text{spacing } d = \frac{1}{9 \times 10^5} = 1{\cdot}11 \times 10^{-6}$$

for the *n*th order $d \sin \theta = n\lambda$

$$\text{max. value of } \theta = 90°$$

$$\text{max. value of } n = \frac{d \sin 90°}{\lambda} = \frac{1{\cdot}11 \times 10^{-6} \times 1}{5 \times 10^{-7}} = 2{\cdot}22$$

∴ 2 complete orders are seen.

X-ray diffraction

The diffraction of X-rays is widely used for analysis of the structure of materials. X-rays (see p. 303) are used because their wavelengths are short (typically 0.1 nm) and they can penetrate many atomic layers. The interference in this case is between the X-ray beams reflected from successive layers in the material (fig. 94i). Although the proportion of the X-ray beam reflected at each layer is minute, many layers contribute (more than 10^6 per mm). From the diagram it can be seen that rays from adjacent layers (and hence from all layers) are in phase when the path difference BCD $= n\lambda$. But $\sin \theta = BC/d$. Therefore rays are in phase and an image is formed when

$$2d \sin \theta = n\lambda, \quad \text{where } n = 0, 1, 2, \text{etc.}$$

This is known as **Bragg's law**. Note that the angle θ is with the **plane** and not the normal to the plane as for diffraction gratings. The angle θ at which the image is formed is called the **Bragg angle** and the total deflection of the beam for an image is twice the Bragg angle (fig. 94ii).

Example The spacing between 2 layers in a calcite crystal is $3{\cdot}03 \times 10^{-10}$ m. The minimum angle with the crystal plane at which the reflection of X-rays occurs is 15° 30′. Calculate the wavelength of the X-rays.

Bragg's law states $2d \sin \theta = n\lambda$
for minimum θ, n is a minimum, i.e. 1

$$\therefore \quad 2 \times 3{\cdot}03 \times 10^{-10} \times \sin 15° 30' = \lambda$$

i.e. $\lambda = 1{\cdot}62 \times 10^{-10} = 162$ pm

Powder photographs are taken using the specimen in the form of powder stuck onto an amorphous fibre. Minute crystallites of the material will be presented to the X-ray beam at all possible orientations. Thus the single diffracted beam at angle 2θ of fig. 94ii will become a cone of diffraction at half angle 2θ (fig. 94iii), and will form a circle on a photographic film as shown. In practice, only a narrow strip of film is used and it is placed inside a circular camera round the specimen to give the photograph as shown (fig. 94iv). Information on the structure and atomic spacing of the material can be found from the pattern and the spacing of the rings. Electrons and neutrons can also be used for the determination of structure by this method because of their wave properties (see p. 310).

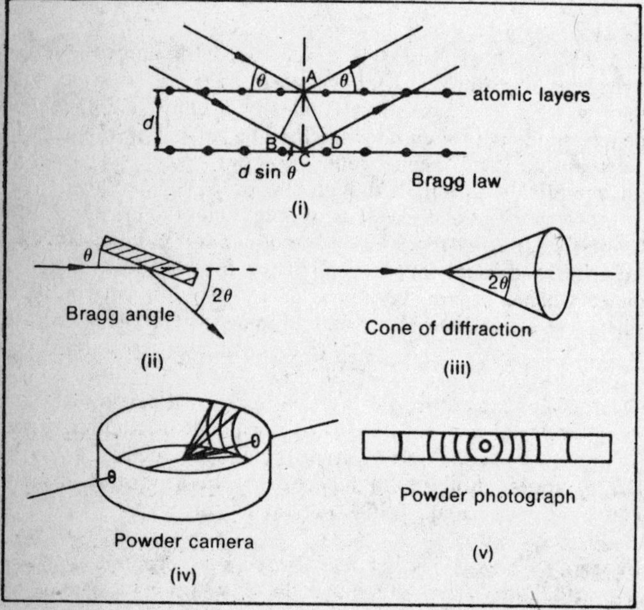

Figure 94. X-ray diffraction

Geometrical optics

This section is concerned with the passage of light through systems of mirrors, lenses and prisms. The subject was introduced originally as an example of applied physics.

Huygens' construction

Huygens postulated that every point on a wave front becomes a secondary centre of disturbance. Thus when light from a source forms the wave front ABC (fig. 95i) each point on the wave front A, B, C, for example, emits wavelets. The new wave front is the surface XY which touches all the wavelets from the secondary sources, and so the process repeats.

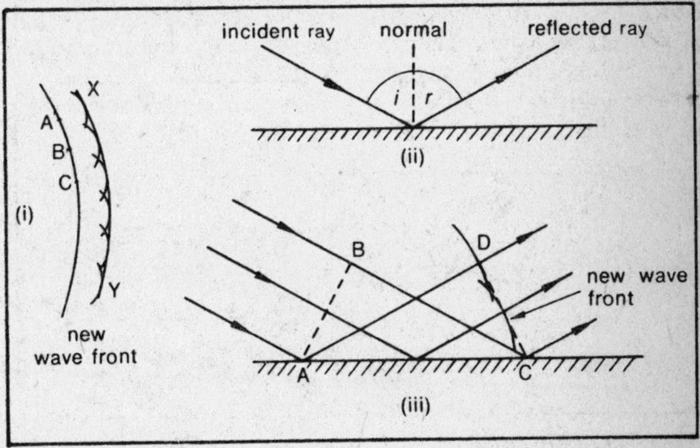

Figure 95. Huygens' construction

Reflection

Light is reflected from smooth polished surfaces (fig. 95ii).

The laws of reflection are

(i) the incident ray, the reflected ray and the normal are all in the same plane.

(ii) the angle of incidence is equal to the angle of reflection.

The second law can readily be proved by Huygens' construction (fig. 95iii). Consider a plane wave front AB incident on a reflecting surface AC. A emits a wavelet which reaches D during the time that the wavelet from B reaches C. Each secondary source between A and B will also emit wavelets, and the surface normal to all the resultant wavelets of the reflection will be CD, which is the reflected wave front. Therefore since BC equals AD and the wave fronts are perpendicular to the rays, triangles ABC and ADC are identical, and in particular the angles which BC and AD make with the surface are the same. Consequently

angle of incidence = angle of reflection

Refraction

Light passing from air into a more dense medium is refracted towards the normal (fig. 96i).

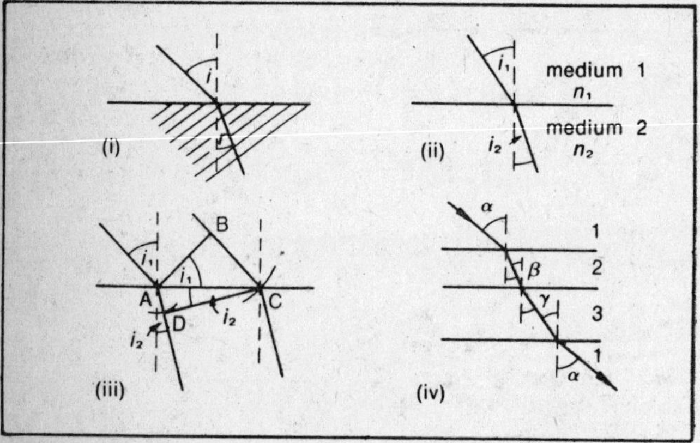

Figure 96. Refraction

The laws of refraction are

(i) the incident ray, the refracted ray and the normal are in the same plane.

(ii) the ratio of the sine of the angle of incidence to the sine of the angle of refraction is constant for a given pair of media and wavelength of light. This is **Snell's law,** i.e.

$$\frac{\sin i}{\sin r} = \text{constant}$$

The refractive index, *n*, is the constant given by

$$n = \frac{\sin i}{\sin r}$$

In this case the refractive index is that for the boundary between air and glass. The absolute refractive index n_1 is the refractive index between a vacuum and a medium 1.

It is more general, however, to use two subscripts when

representing two media and then the two angles are written i_1 and i_2 since light could be travelling in either direction across the boundary, and either angle could be an angle of incidence. In this case (fig. 96ii)

$$_1n_2 = \frac{\sin i_1}{\sin i_2}$$

Refractive indices for several media

Consider two parallel-sided layers, of medium 2 and medium 3 (fig. 96iv). The incident and emergent rays will be parallel.

Hence

$$_1n_2 = \frac{\sin \alpha}{\sin \beta}, \quad _2n_3 = \frac{\sin \beta}{\sin \gamma}, \quad _3n_1 = \frac{\sin \gamma}{\sin \alpha} \quad \text{and} \quad _1n_3 = \frac{\sin \alpha}{\sin \gamma}$$

Multiplying: $$\frac{\sin \alpha}{\sin \beta} \times \frac{\sin \beta}{\sin \gamma} = \frac{\sin \alpha}{\sin \gamma}$$

i.e. $$_1n_2 \times {_2n_3} = {_1n_3}$$

and $$_1n_3 = {_1n_2} \times {_2n_3} \quad \text{in general}$$

If medium 1 is a vacuum then

$$_2n_3 = {_2n_1} \times {_1n_3}$$

$$= {_1n_3} \times \frac{1}{_1n_2}$$

But for a vacuum $_1n_2$ is written simply n_2, etc.

$$\therefore \quad _2n_3 = \frac{n_3}{n_2} \quad \text{or generally} \quad _an_b = \frac{n_b}{n_a}$$

Applying this to the result above

$$_1n_2 = \frac{n_2}{n_1} = \frac{\sin i_1}{\sin i_2} \quad \text{(fig. 96ii)}$$

$$\therefore \quad n_1 \sin i_1 = n_2 \sin i_2$$

Again, the second law of refraction can be proved by Huygens' construction which also throws further light on the meaning of refractive index (fig. 96iii). The wavelet from A will take the same time to travel to D as the wavelet from B takes to travel to C. Let this time be t.

Then $$\sin i_1 = \frac{BC}{AC} \qquad \sin i_2 = \frac{AD}{AC}$$

and $$_1n_2 = \frac{\sin i_1}{\sin i_2} = \frac{BC}{AC} \times \frac{AC}{AD} = \frac{BC}{AD} = \frac{v_1 t}{v_2 t} = \frac{v_1}{v_2}$$

i.e. the refractive index from medium 1 to medium 2 is the ratio of the velocity in medium 1 to that in medium 2. Since this ratio is constant, Snell's law is proven.

Commonly the term refractive index means the value for sodium yellow ($\lambda = 589{\cdot}3$ nm) and relative to air whose absolute refractive index is 1·00029.

Real and apparent depth A ray leaving a submerged object will be refracted on leaving a liquid (fig. 97i). The real depth is OR, but because the eye imagines light to travel in straight lines, the apparent depth is OA.

$$n = \frac{\sin i}{\sin r} \quad \text{but since angles are small } \sin\theta = \tan\theta$$

$$\therefore \quad n = \frac{\tan i}{\tan r}$$

$$= \frac{\frac{OP}{OA}}{\frac{OP}{OR}} = \frac{OR}{OA} = \frac{\text{real depth}}{\text{apparent depth}}$$

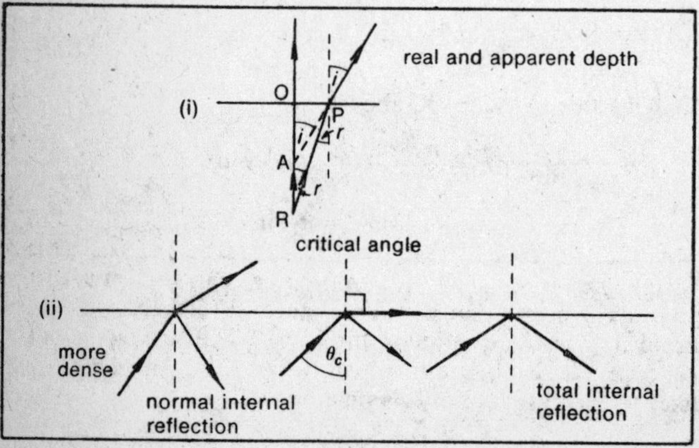

Figure 97. Apparent depth and critical angle

Total internal reflection can occur when a ray travels from a more dense to a less dense medium (fig. 97ii). In the critical condition, the angle of incidence within the medium is called the **critical angle, θ_c.**

Thus
$$\frac{\sin 90°}{\sin \theta_c} = n$$

Since $\sin 90° = 1$, $\sin \theta_c = \dfrac{1}{n}$

Typically, for water, $n = 1{\cdot}33$

$$\therefore \quad \sin \theta_c = \frac{1}{1{\cdot}33} = 0{\cdot}75, \qquad \theta_c = 48{\cdot}6°$$

Refraction at prisms

There is in general no simple relationship between the angle of a prism A, the refractive index n and the deviation D of a ray of light passing through it, (fig. 98i). There are, however, two special cases where there is a straightforward expression linking them.

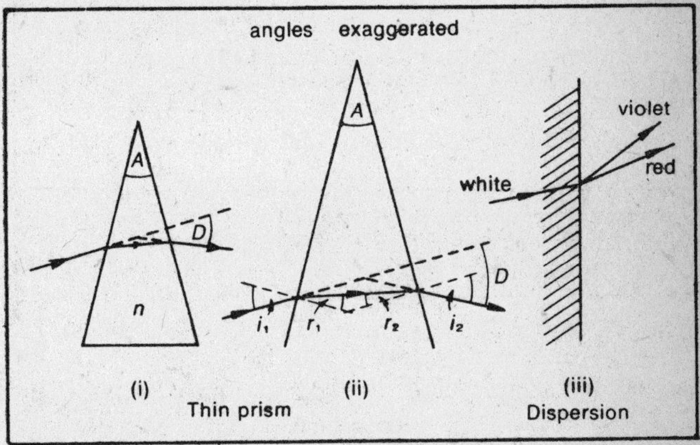

Figure 98. Thin prism deviation and dispersion

Small angle prism at near normal incidence

By geometry (fig. 98ii)

$$A = r_1 + r_2 \qquad D = (i_1 - r_1) + (i_2 - r_2)$$
$$= (i_1 + i_2) - (r_1 + r_2)$$

Since angles are small, $\sin i_1 \to i_1$ etc., so

$$\frac{i_1}{r_1} = n = \frac{i_2}{r_2}$$

$$\therefore \quad i_1 = nr_1, \qquad i_2 = nr_2$$

$$D = (nr_1 + nr_2) - (r_1 + r_2)$$

$$= (n-1)(r_1 + r_2)$$

$$\therefore \quad D = (n-1)A$$

i.e. independent of i, provided i is small.

Minimum deviation It can be shown that if a ray passes symmetrically through a prism then the deviation is a minimum (fig. 99i).

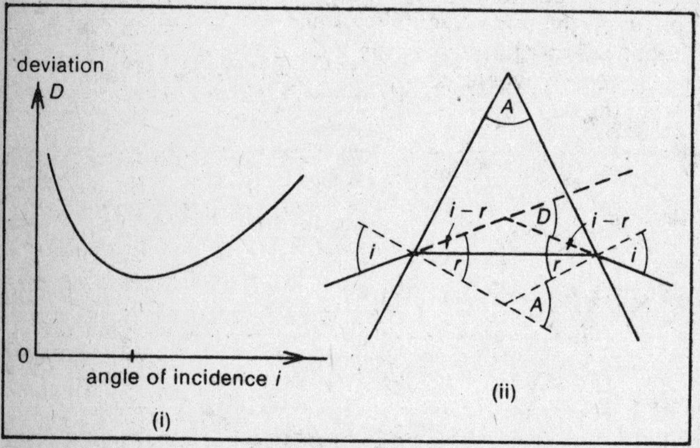

Figure 99. Minimum deviation

Because the ray is symmetrical (fig. 99ii), from equations above

$$i_1 = i_2 \qquad \text{and} \qquad r_1 = r_2$$

$$\therefore \quad D = 2(i - r); \qquad A = 2r$$

$$i = \frac{(D + 2r)}{2}; \qquad \therefore \quad 2r = A \quad \text{and} \quad r = \frac{A}{2}$$

$$\therefore \quad i = \frac{(D + A)}{2}$$

$$\therefore \quad n = \frac{\sin i}{\sin r} = \frac{\sin \frac{(A+D)}{2}}{\sin A/2}$$

Dispersion

The splitting up of white light into its components is called **dispersion**. It occurs at refracting surfaces because the refractive index of red light is less than the refractive index for blue light (fig. 98iii). For example, for crown glass $n_{red} = 1{\cdot}5146$, $n_{blue} = 1{\cdot}5233$. The dispersion of a prism was used for the production of spectra before the development of diffraction gratings, and dispersion accounts for the chromatic aberration of lenses.

Example Calculate the dispersion for a thin prism of angle 10° ($n_{red} = 1{\cdot}512$, $n_{blue} = 1{\cdot}524$)

Deviation is given by $D = (n-1)A$

$$\therefore \quad D_{red} = (1{\cdot}512 - 1)A \quad \text{and} \quad D_{blue} = (1{\cdot}524 - 1)A$$

$$\text{Dispersion} = D_{blue} - D_{red} = (1{\cdot}524 - 1{\cdot}512)A$$

$$= 0{\cdot}012 \times 10 = 0{\cdot}12°$$

Lenses and spherical mirrors

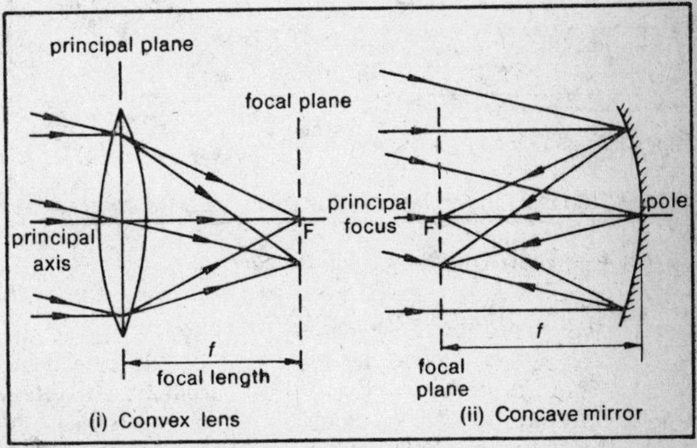

Figure 100 Focal lengths

The main property of lenses and spherical mirrors is that they bring parallel light to a focus. If the light is parallel to the principal axis, then it comes to focus at the **principal focus**, otherwise the focus for parallel light is in the **focal plane** (fig. 100i). The distance from the focal plane to the principal plane of the lens is the **focal length**. The **principal plane** is a plane in the lens at which for convenience the rays are imagined to be deviated once only (in fact rays are deviated twice, once at each surface). The slight inaccuracies which result are ignored.

Spherical aberration In practice lenses and spherical mirrors are not perfect. Most lens and mirror surfaces are spherical, and this causes rays at different distances from the principal axis to come to different foci (fig. 101i). As a result when the entire lens or mirror is used, the image will be slightly blurred. Spherical aberration can be reduced by stopping down, i.e.only using the inner section. More expensive lenses and mirrors overcome the problem by changing the shape of the lens.

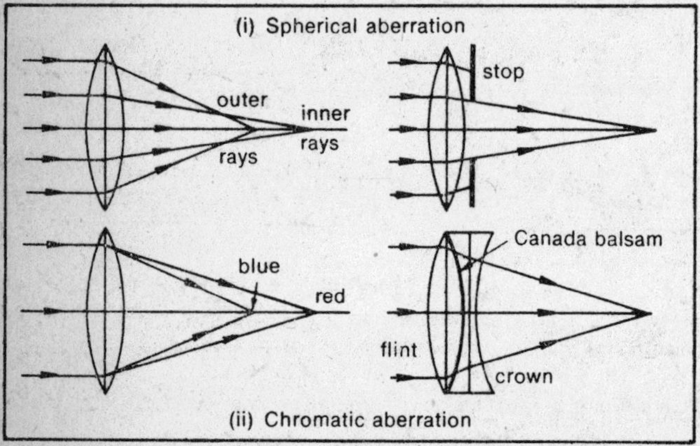

Figure 101. Spherical and chromatic aberration

Chromatic aberration Because lenses rely on refraction, different colours will come to different foci, the blue being deviated more than the red (fig. 101ii). Chromatic aberration can be removed by using a doublet of two lenses made of materials of different refractive indices. Mirrors, of course, are not subject to chromatic aberration.

Ray diagrams

The positions of the object and image can readily be found by drawing ray diagrams in which construction lines are used which may, or may not, be actual rays. In practice, only two such rays or construction lines are needed and the path of these is known accurately (fig. 102i).

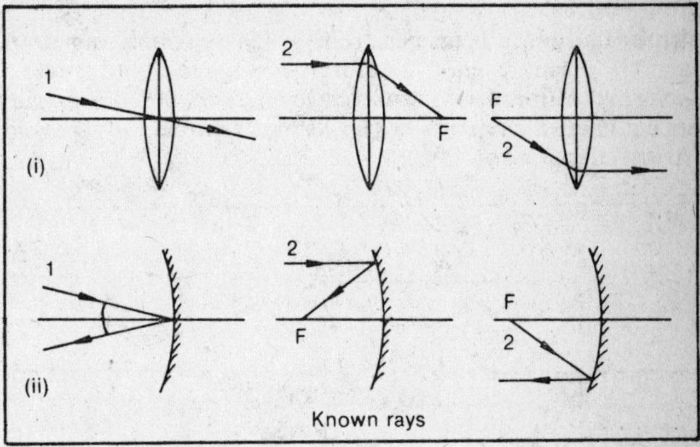

Figure 102. Known rays

Ray 1 passes through the centre of the lens where there is no deviation because the faces of the lens are parallel at that point.

Ray 2 passes through the principal focus and must therefore be parallel to the axis on the other side of the lens. As can be seen from the diagram, there are two possibilities.

For spherical mirrors, the same rays can be used (fig. 102ii).

Ray 1 is reflected back at the same angle to the principal axis. This is the same as if the right hand of the lens diagram had been folded back onto the left.

Ray 2 passes through the principal focus and must therefore be parallel to the axis either before or after reflection at the mirror. This again is the same as if the lens diagram had been folded back on itself. This equivalence of the lens and mirror diagrams is illustrated in fig. 103i.

Images
Images are formed at points from which the eye (which assumes that light always travels in straight lines) imagines the rays to be radiating.

Real images are formed by rays actually passing through a point, and they can therefore be projected onto a screen.

Virtual images are images from which rays only appear to have come, and cannot therefore be projected onto a screen (fig. 103ii). Virtual rays and images are always drawn with dashed lines. Since no light travels along virtual rays they are drawn without arrows.

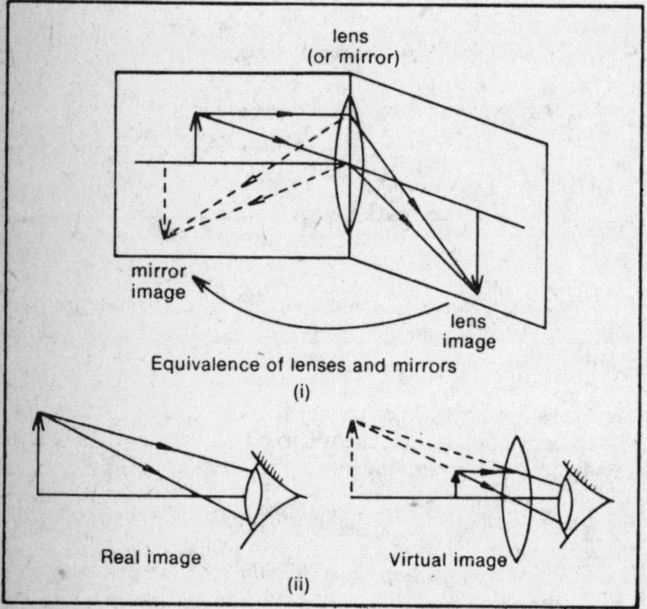

Figure 103. Ray diagrams

Focal length of a spherical mirror
From the diagram of fig. 104

$$\tan \theta = \frac{OP}{OC} \qquad \tan 2\theta = \frac{OP}{OF}$$

But since angles are small

$$\tan\theta = \theta;$$

$$\tan 2\theta = 2\theta$$

so $2\tan\theta = \tan 2\theta$

$$\therefore \quad 2\times\frac{OP}{OC} = \frac{OP}{OF}$$

i.e.
$$\frac{2}{r} = \frac{1}{f}$$

$$\therefore \quad f = \frac{r}{2}$$

i.e. the focal length is half the radius of curvature.

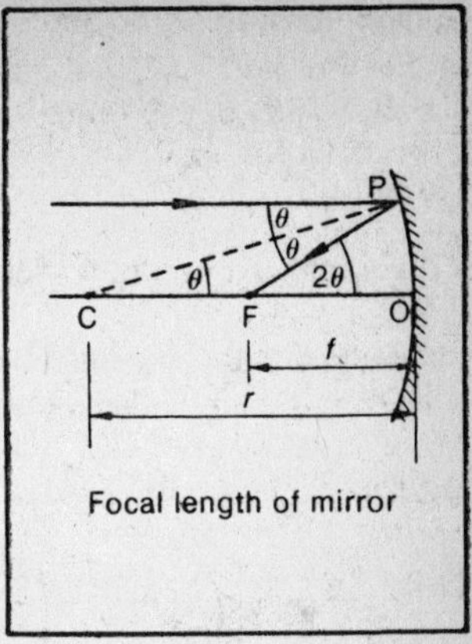

Figure 104. Focal length of mirror

Formation of images by a convex lens

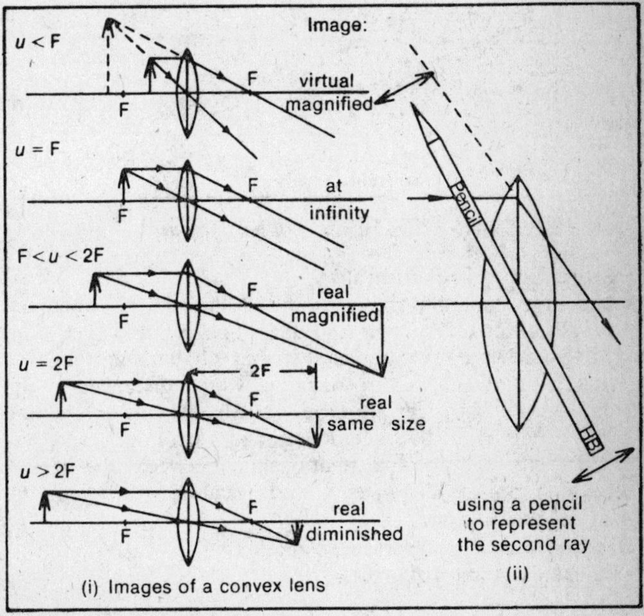

Figure 105. Convex lens images

For a convex lens, the type and size of the image depends on the object distance (fig. 105i). Note that ray 2 remains the same but the angle of ray 1 varies with object distance. This can be seen by drawing ray 2 and using a pencil to represent ray 1 as shown in fig. 105ii.

Similar diagrams can be drawn for a concave mirror.

For a concave lens the size of the image again depends on the object distance but the image is always diminished and virtual (fig. 106i).

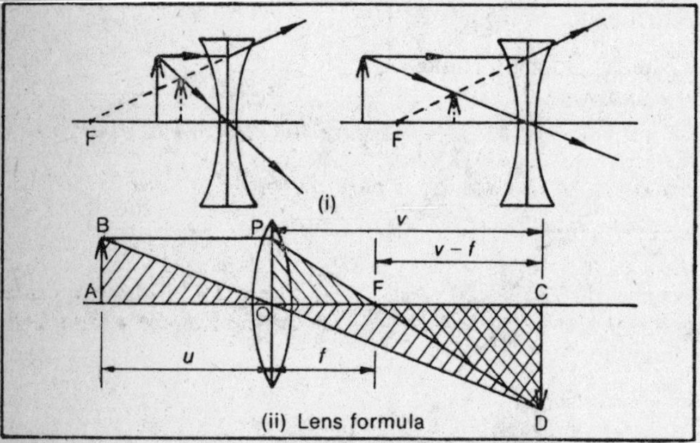

Figure 106. Concave lens image and lens formula

The lens and mirror formula
By choosing a suitable sign convention, the same formula can cover all cases of mirror and lens image formation. The **real-is-positive** convention states that all distances to real objects, or real images, are positive, whilst distances to the virtual objects or images are negative. Also by this convention the focal lengths of diverging lenses and mirrors are negative. Referring to fig. 106ii a relationship between the object distance u, image distance v and focal length f can be established as follows:

In similar triangles ABO and CDO

$$\frac{AB}{u}=\frac{CD}{v} \qquad \therefore \quad \frac{CD}{AB}=\frac{v}{u}\ (= \text{magnification } m)$$

In similar triangles OPF and CDF

$$\frac{OP}{f} = \frac{CD}{(v-f)} \quad \therefore \quad \frac{CD}{OP} = \frac{(v-f)}{f}$$

$$\text{But OP = AB} \quad \therefore \quad \frac{v}{u} = \frac{(v-f)}{f} \qquad vf = uv - uf$$

$$\text{Dividing by } uvf\text{:} \quad \frac{1}{u} = \frac{1}{f} - \frac{1}{v} \quad \text{or} \quad \frac{1}{u} + \frac{1}{v} = \frac{1}{f}$$

The **New Cartesian** convention takes distances in the direction of the incident rays as positive, and distances against the incident rays as negative.

Convex lenses and mirrors have positive focal lengths.

Concave lenses and mirrors have negative focal lengths. The lens and mirror formula which is used is

$$\frac{1}{v} - \frac{1}{u} = \frac{1}{f}$$

Examples Find the image distances in the following cases where the object distance is 10 cm (using real-is-positive convention).
The solutions are drawn out in fig. 107.

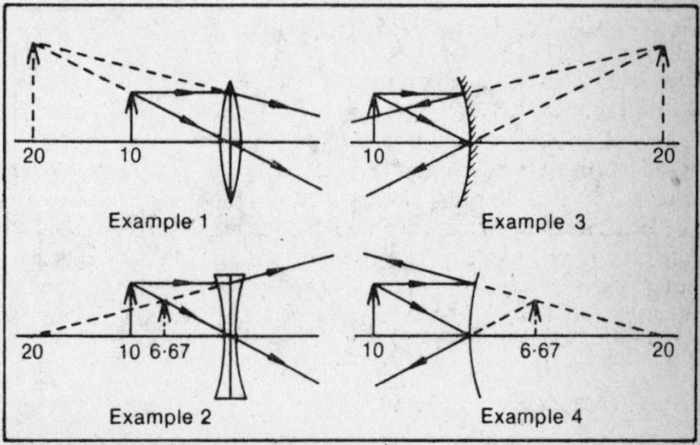

Figure 107. Ray diagrams of examples

1. Convex lens of focal length 20 cm ($f = +20$)

$$\frac{1}{10}+\frac{1}{v}=\frac{1}{20} \quad \therefore \quad \frac{1}{v}=\frac{1}{20}-\frac{1}{10}=-\frac{1}{20} \quad \therefore \quad v=-20$$

2. Concave lens of focal length 20 cm ($f = -20$)

$$\frac{1}{10}+\frac{1}{v}=\frac{1}{-20}-\frac{1}{v}=\frac{1}{-20}-\frac{1}{10}=-\frac{3}{20} \quad \therefore \quad v=-6{\cdot}67$$

3. Concave mirror of focal length 20 cm ($f = +20$)
   Same calculation as example 1.
4. Convex mirror of focal length 20 cm ($f = -20$)
   Same calculation as example 2.

Linear magnification (m) is the ratio of the height of the image to the height of the object.

$$m = \frac{\text{size of image}}{\text{size of object}} = \frac{CD}{AB} = \frac{v}{u}$$ (p. 166)

Thin lenses in contact can be regarded as a single lens whose focal length is given by $1/f = 1/f_1 + 1/f_2$ where f_1 and f_2 are the focal lengths of the two lenses.

Power of a lens is the reciprocal of its focal length in metres. Power = $1/f$. The unit is the Dioptre.

Methods for measuring focal lengths

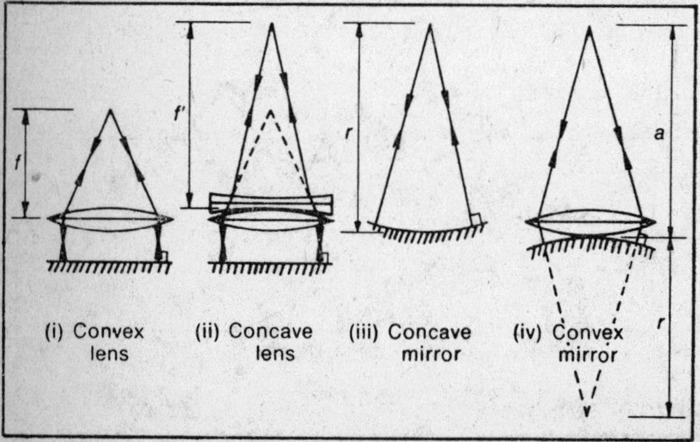

Figure 108. Methods for focal length

There are many methods available, but only one representative method will be given for each type of lens and mirror. In all of the methods the position of coincidence of object and image can be found either by using a search pin and the method of no parallax, or by using an illuminated slit in a white screen where the image of the slit can be focused onto the screen beside the slit.

Convex lens (fig. 108i). Using a plane mirror the point is found at which the object and image coincide. Since the light to and from the mirror must be parallel, the distance from the point to the lens must be the focal length.

Concave lens (fig. 108ii). Using an auxilliary convex lens of greater power the focal length of the combination can be found by the method above, then

$$\frac{1}{f}=\frac{1}{f_1}-\frac{1}{f_2}$$

where f_1 and f_2 are the focal lengths of the convex lens and concave lens respectively.

Concave mirror (fig. 108iii). Again the point is found where object and image coincide. This point must be the centre of curvature since the rays then strike the mirror at right angles. The focal length is given by $f = r/2$.

Convex mirror (fig. 108iv). Again using a convex lens of known greater power in contact the point is found where object and image coincide.

For the convex lens $$\frac{1}{u}+\frac{1}{v}=\frac{1}{f}$$

i.e. $$\frac{1}{a}+\frac{1}{r}=\frac{1}{f_1}$$

where f_1 = focal length of convex lens, from which the radius of curvature r of the mirror can be found,

and $$f_2 = r/2$$

where f_2 = focal length of convex mirror.

Magnifying power

The purpose of an optical instrument is to enable an object to be seen more clearly. This involves using a greater area of the retina of the eye, and hence the angle subtended by the image at the eye must be increased (fig. 109i). The magnification which matters therefore is the angular magnification or magnifying power of the instrument.

The magnifying power of a single lens is the ratio of the angle subtended by the image β at the eye to the angle subtended by the object α at the eye when it is at the Least Distance of Distinct Vision (LDDV), i.e. the closest it can be placed to the eye and still be in focus (fig. 109ii).

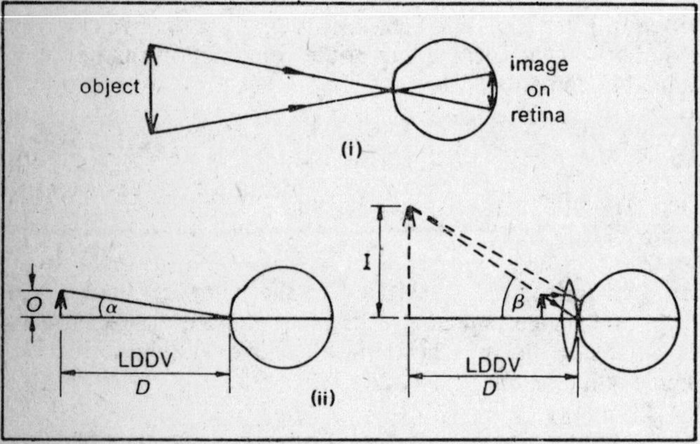

Figure 109. Angular magnification

∴ Magnifying power in this adjustment is given by

$$M = \frac{\beta}{\alpha} = \frac{I}{D} \div \frac{D}{O} = \frac{I}{O}$$

But linear magnification also $= \dfrac{I}{O} = m$

∴ **In this adjustment only** linear magnification = angular magnification.

Example A manufacturer trying a new product uses a large lens as a magnifier for old people to read. The lens of focal length 25 cm is held 15 cm from a book which is held 40 cm from the reader's eyes. An old lady says that it is no help to her. Why?

Linear magnification $= \frac{v}{u}$ Let height of object $= x$

$$\frac{1}{u}+\frac{1}{v}=\frac{1}{f} \qquad \therefore \quad \frac{1}{v}=\frac{1}{25}-\frac{1}{15}=\frac{3-5}{75}=\frac{2}{75} \qquad \therefore \quad v=\frac{75}{2}$$

$\therefore$ **Linear** magnification $= \frac{v}{u} = \frac{75}{2 \times 15} = 2\frac{1}{2}$ times

and angle subtended by image $2{\cdot}5x/40 = x/16$ rad

The manufacturer noticed that without the lens the old lady held the book at a distance of 16 cm from her eyes. At that distance, the angle subtended by the object is then $x/16$

$\therefore$ **Angular** magnification is $\frac{\beta}{\alpha} = \frac{x}{16} \Big/ \frac{x}{16} = 1$

i.e. the lens was of no value to her despite its linear magnification.

Telescopes and microscopes

Both of these instruments work in the same way. An objective lens forms a real image of the object which is then examined by a

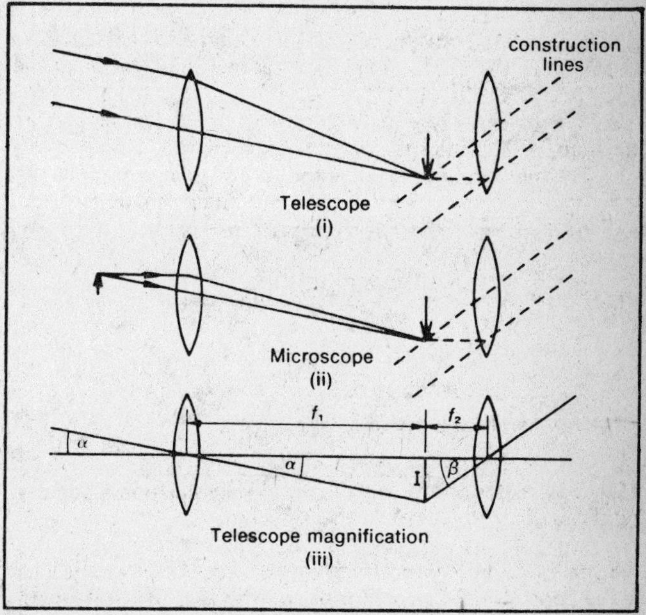

Figure 110. Telescope and microscope

magnifying glass (the eyepiece). The only difference between the two instruments is that in the telescope the incident light is from infinity, and hence rays from a point on the object are roughly parallel, whereas in the microscope it comes from an object very close to the objective (fig. 110i,ii). Therefore the telescope objective lens will be of long focal length whilst that of the microscope will be of very short focal length. In both simple instruments the final image is inverted. In figure 110i,ii, dashed construction lines only are used for clarity to indicate the position of the final image. The full ray diagram for a telescope is shown in fig. 112i.

Astronomical telescope In normal adjustment of the instrument the image is formed at infinity (fig. 110iii). The first image is naturally at the focus of the objective since the light is coming from infinity, and is then arranged to be at the focus of the eyepiece to give a final image at infinity.

Thus $$M = \frac{\beta}{\alpha} = \frac{I}{f_2} \div \frac{I}{f_1} = \frac{f_1}{f_2}$$

Therefore, the objective needs to have as large a focal length as possible, and the eyepiece as short as possible, to make the magnifying power large.

Microscope The microscope can be used in several adjustments in which the image can be formed anywhere from infinity to the Least Distance of Distinct Vision. In normal adjustment,

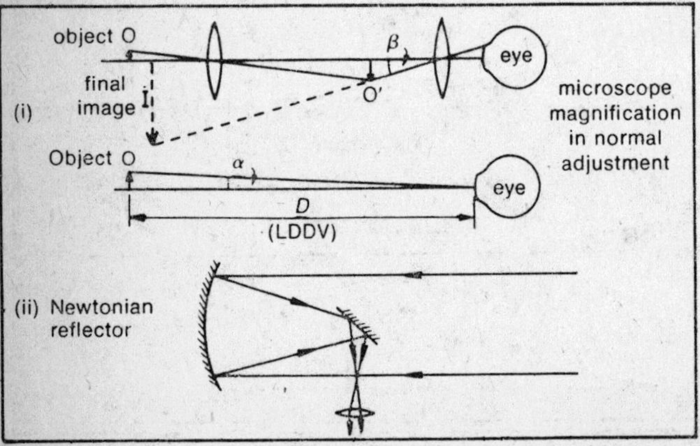

Figure 111. Microscope magnification and reflecting telescope

however, the final image is formed at infinity as drawn in fig. 110ii. To find the magnifying power the angle subtended at the eye by the image of the instrument must be compared with the angle subtended by the object if it were placed at the LDDV (fig. 111i which is drawn for image at LDDV).

Thus **if image at LDDV,** i.e. **not** normal adjustment

Angular magnification $$M = \frac{\beta}{\alpha} = \frac{I}{D} \div \frac{O}{D} = \frac{I}{O}$$

But calculating the linear magnification of each lens

$$\frac{O'}{O} = \frac{v}{u} = m_1; \qquad \frac{I}{O'} = \frac{D}{u} = m_2 \qquad \therefore \quad M = \frac{I}{O} = \frac{I}{O'} \times \frac{O'}{O} = \frac{Dv_1}{u_2 u_1}$$

or $M = m_1 m_2$ where m_1 and m_2 are the linear magnifications of the objective and eyepiece. If the image is at infinity (normal adjustment) then M is more complicated.

Reflecting telescope The Newtonian reflecting telescope shown in fig. 111ii uses a spherical mirror instead of a convex lens for the objective. A small plane mirror is used to project the image out of the side of the instrument, where it is viewed with a normal eyepiece. Calculations of magnifying power are exactly the same as for a refracting telescope.

The eye ring is the position at which the eye should be placed

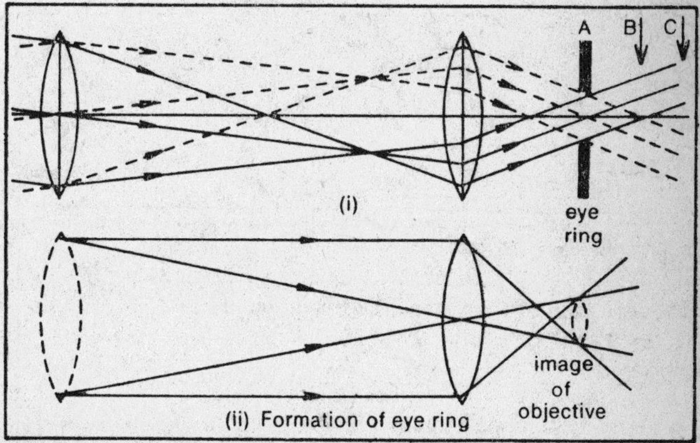

Figure 112. The eye ring

for maximum brightness and field of view (fig. 112i). It is in fact the position of the image of the objective lens formed by the eyepiece and hence all rays which go through the objective must go through the eye ring. Placing the eye on the axis at B will mean that some rays from the outer parts of the object will not enter the eye, i.e. the outer parts will appear dimmer, and at C no rays from the outer parts are seen at all, i.e. field of view is reduced.

The spectrometer

The spectrometer is an instrument for accurate measurement of angles of deviation from prisms and diffraction gratings (fig. 113). For both prisms and diffraction gratings it is essential that all rays should be incident at the same angle, i.e. that the incident light should be accurately parallel. The spectrometer consists of a collimator to produce parallel light and a telescope to receive it. The collimator is simply an adjustable slit in the focal plane of a lens, and the telescope forms a sharp image of the collimator slit on the cross-wires in its focal plane.

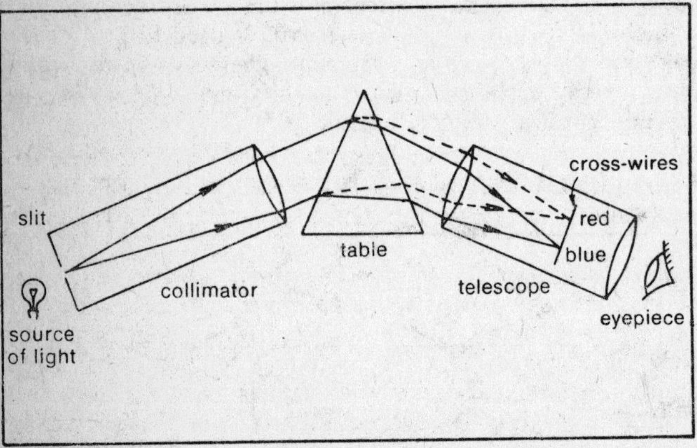

Figure 113. Spectrometer

The sequence of alignment is as follows

(i) the eyepiece is adjusted so that the cross-wires are clearly in focus.

(ii) the telescope is focused on a distant object so that there is no parallax between image and cross-wires.

(iii) the collimator is lined up with the telescope, and then adjusted by altering the position of the slit so that a sharp image of the slit appears in no parallax with the telescope cross-wires.

Key terms

Electromagnetic spectrum The full range of electromagnetic waves.
Infrared Electromagnetic radiation of wavelength longer than visible light.
Ultraviolet radiation Electromagnetic radiation of shorter wavelength than visible light.
Michelson's method One of the most accurate methods for measuring velocity of light.
Coherent light sources Light sources from which the light waves are of the same frequency, phase and plane of polarization.
Plane polarized light Light having a single plane of polarization. It is produced by passing light through Polaroid, for example.
Young's fringes Interference fringes produced by light illuminating two closely spaced parallel narrow slits.
Thin film interference Interference occurring when a ray of light can take two paths on reflection at the top and bottom surfaces of a thin film of air, oil, etc.
Newton's rings Pattern of circular interference fringes produced when a lens is placed on a plane glass surface.
Fraunhofer diffraction Diffraction of light by a single slit, obstacle, or edge.
Resolving power The ability of an optical instrument or the eye to separate two images which are very close together.
Rayleigh's criterion The limit of resolution occurs when the central maximum of intensity of one Fraunhofer diffraction pattern falls on the first minimum of the other.
Diffraction grating Transparent surface with a large number of lines ruled across it (which for example splits light up into its component colours).
Bragg's law The law that governs formation of an image in X-ray diffraction. $2d \sin \theta = n\lambda$ where θ is the angle between atomic plane and incident X-ray beam.
Huygens' construction A construction for drawing an advancing wave front based on the idea that every point on a wave front becomes a secondary centre of disturbance.
Snell's law The ratio of sine of angle of incidence to sine of angle of refraction is a constant.

Refractive index The constant in Snell's law.
Total internal reflection The phenomenon of light being completely reflected at a boundary between a more dense and a less dense medium when incident at more than the critical angle in the denser medium.
Critical angle The angle at or beyond which total internal reflection will occur.
Minimum deviation Deviation through a prism is a minimum when a ray of light passes symmetrically through it.
Dispersion The splitting up of white light into its component colours.
Principal focus The point at which light parallel and near to the principal axis of a lens is brought to a focus.
Focal plane The plane normal to the principal axis at which parallel light is brought to a focus by the lens.
Spherical aberration A lens imperfection in which light from the outer zone of the lens comes to a focus at a different point to light from the inner zone.
Chromatic aberration A lens imperfection in which blue light and red light from the same source come to focus at different points.
Real image An image formed when rays actually pass through it. It can be projected onto a screen.
Virtual image An image from which rays only appear to have come. It cannot be projected onto a screen.
Convex lens A converging lens; thicker at the middle.
Concave lens A diverging lens; thinner at the middle.
Convex mirror A diverging lens; curving outwards towards the observer.
Concave mirror A converging mirror; curving away from the observer.
Linear magnification Ratio of height of image to height of object.
Power of a lens Reciprocal of focal length in metres.
Magnifying power Ratio of angle subtended at the eye by the image to that subtended by the object when, in the case of a microscope, at the least distance of distinct vision, or in the case of a telescope, at infinity (or wherever it is).
Eye ring Position at which the eye should be placed for maximum brightness and field of view.
Spectrometer An instrument for accurate measurement of angles of deviation. It consists of a collimator for producing parallel light, a table for holding a prism or diffraction grating, and a movable telescope for receiving parallel light.

Chapter 6
Electricity and Electrostatics

Electrostatics

The study of electric charges at rest is called electrostatics. The sparks one produces when stroking a cat, and the current to the starter motor of a car, may seem very different, but in both cases the movement of electrons is responsible. The difference lies in the 'pressure' and the 'rate of flow'. The sparks on the cat involve minute quantities of charge, but at very high 'pressure.' The current to the starter motor involves very large quantities of charge, but at very low 'pressure'.

Elementary electrostatic phenomena

Many materials become electrified when rubbed. The process involves the moving of electrons from one object to another leaving both objects charged electrically – one positively (deficiency of electrons) and one negatively (excess of electrons). It can be shown that like charges repel but unlike charges attract.

Gold leaf electroscope

The oldest of electric instruments is the gold leaf electroscope (fig. 114i) which consists of a gold leaf L fitted to an insulated metal stem suspended in an earthed metal case C with two glass sides. If the electroscope is charged then the leaf will be repelled from the stem by an amount which is the measure of the charge, or of the potential difference between L and C since the potential difference will determine the charge on L.

Electrostatic induction

If a charged object is brought up to a conductor then the charges within the conductor are redistributed with the positive charge nearest to the inducing charge and some of the negatively charged electrons repelled to the far end (fig. 114ii). If part of the conductor is earthed, the far charges are neutralized (or seem to 'run to earth'), leaving the conductor with an overall

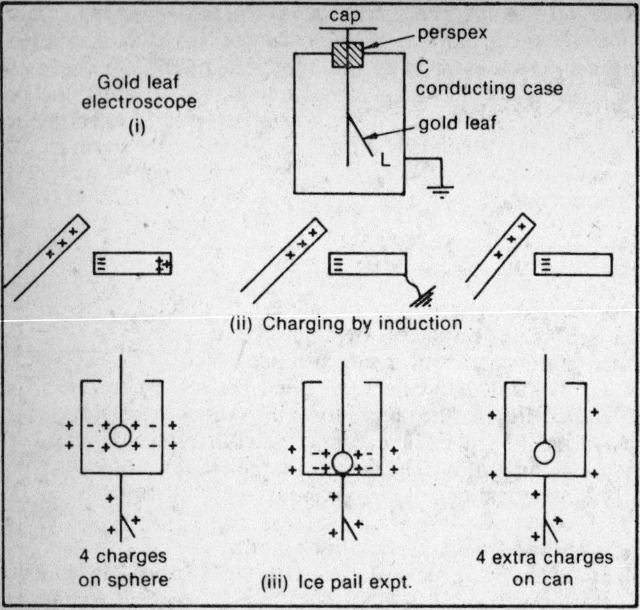

Figure 114. Electrostatics

charge. If the earth connection is removed and then the inducing charge removed, the conductor is left with this charge. This is known as charging by induction.

Faraday's ice-pail experiment
A deep hollow conductor placed on an electroscope has a charged sphere lowered into it. The leaves of the electroscope open and remain at the same deflection when the sphere is touched and then removed. The sphere is subsequently found to be uncharged.

This experiment shows (fig. 114iii)
(i) equal and opposite quantities of charge are produced by induction.
(ii) charge cannot reside on the inside of a hollow conductor.

Charge distribution on a conductor
If a wire connected to an electroscope is moved over a charged pear shape conductor, the deflection remains the

same, showing that the potential is constant over it. If a 'proof plane' (a small metal disc fitted to an insulated handle) is placed on various parts of the conductor (fig. 115i) and then touched on the inside of an 'ice-pail' on an electroscope (thereby transferring its acquired charge), it is found that the charge density depends inversely on the radius of curvature of the conductor, i.e. the charge density is high on a pointed part of the conductor.

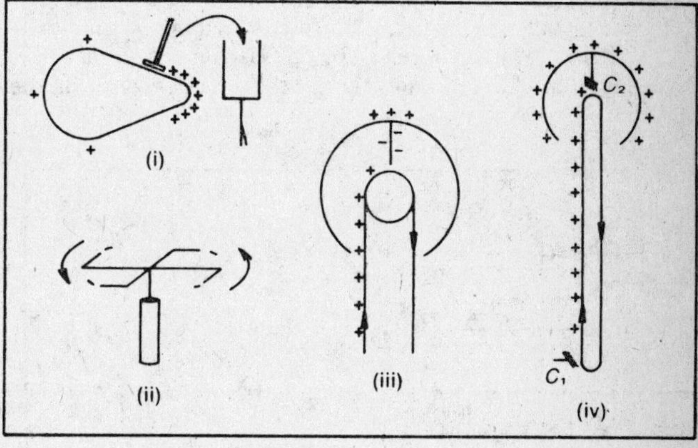

Figure 115. Action of points

This can also be demonstrated by connecting an 'electric windmill' to a source of high potential (fig. 115ii). The very large charge density on the sharp points of the windmill causes ionization of the air and the 'wind' of ions of the same sign as the charge on the point will be repelled away, causing the windmill to rotate. The mechanism of production of a stream of ions is known as **action of points** or **corona discharge**. Lightning conductors depend on the action of points 'to attract lightning' by producing a lower resistance path of ionized air.

Van de Graaff generator

In this electrostatic generator (fig. 115iv) the action of points from the comb C1 is used to transfer charge to a fast moving insulating belt which conveys it to the smooth sphere at the top which is supported by an insulating support column. At the top a similar comb C2 inside the sphere discharges the belt by the action of points, transferring a charge of the same sign as that on the belt to the outside of the sphere. In this way the sphere can be charged up to very high potentials. The energy for the charging comes from the motor driving the belt which is propelling charge up the column against the repulsive force of the like charges on the sphere.

Electrostatic voltmeter

This instrument (fig. 116i) depends on the attraction between opposite charges on the fixed and moving vanes. The torque produced is balanced by the restoring couple of the hair-springs. It is, however, a high voltage instrument suitable for measuring hundreds of volts since the charges need to be large.

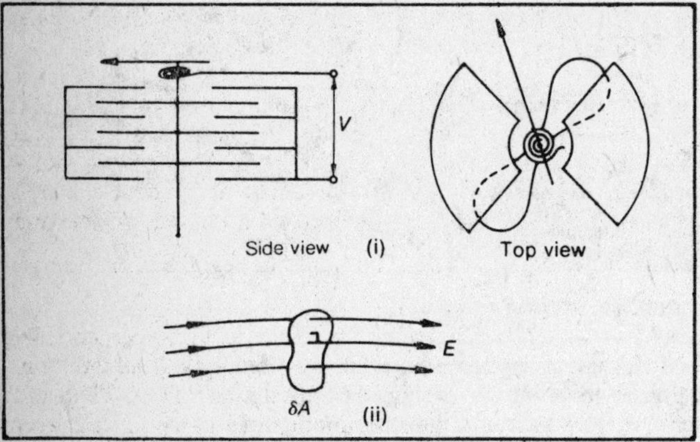

Figure 116. Electrostatic voltmeter and lines of force

Electric field and potential

To analyze quantitatively the forces acting between charges and the energies involved the concept of electric field and electric potential must be introduced.

An electric field is a region of space in which electric forces act on an electric charge.

Electric charge The basic unit of charge is the coulomb (which is defined in terms of the amp). This is discussed on page 204.

Electric field strength or intensity
As with gravitational and magnetic fields the electric field strength is measured in terms of the force on a 'unit detector' – in this case a unit positive charge.

Electric field strength *E* at a point is defined as the force acting on one coulomb of positive charge at that point. This is represented theoretically in fig. 15ii. It would, of course, be impossible to get one coulomb of charge to reside on a practical conductor. The potential of the conductor would need to be of the order of 10^{11} volts!

The direction of the field is the direction in which a positive charge would move.

The units of electric field strength can be newtons per coulomb, but volts per metre are used in practice (see p. 184).

Breakdown field strength is the field strength which will cause an insulator to break down. Air, for instance, will become ionized as the electric force rips electrons from molecules. The breakdown field strength for air is 3×10^6 V m^{-1}, and this limits the maximum potential of a conductor. Beyond this point corona discharge occurs.

Lines of electric force
It is easier to visualize an electric field in terms of lines of force. These represent the field in both strength and direction. The lines are imagined such that they are parallel to the field and that the number of lines per unit area over an infinitely small area perpendicular to the field is equal to the field strength *E* (fig. 116ii).

Electrical potential difference
In a gravitational field a mass lifted against the gravitational force is given potential energy. In the same way a charge can be given electrical potential energy by being moved against the force exerted on it in an electric field.

The electrical potential difference between two points is the work done in taking a coulomb of positive charge from one point to the other. The p.d. is measured in volts.

The volt is defined as the p.d. between two points such that one joule of work is done if a coulomb of charge is moved from one point to the other.

Thus the change in electrical energy W of a charge q when it is moved through a p.d. of V volts is given by

$$W = qV$$

Electric potential

Instead of referring to potential differences between pairs of points it is convenient to measure potential difference relative to a single agreed reference point. This is chosen to be infinity, since the field at this distance due to a system of charges will be zero. A similar choice is made in the gravitational case. The electric potential at a point is defined as the work done in bringing up unit positive charge from infinity to the point.

Equipotential surfaces are surfaces of equal potential and are always normal to the field lines.

This can be understood from the following argument. If field lines were not normal to an equipotential (fig. 117i), then in moving a charge along the surface work would be done against the component of E parallel to the surface and hence the surface would not be an equipotential because work has been done in moving the charge along it. Hence equipotentials must be normal to field lines.

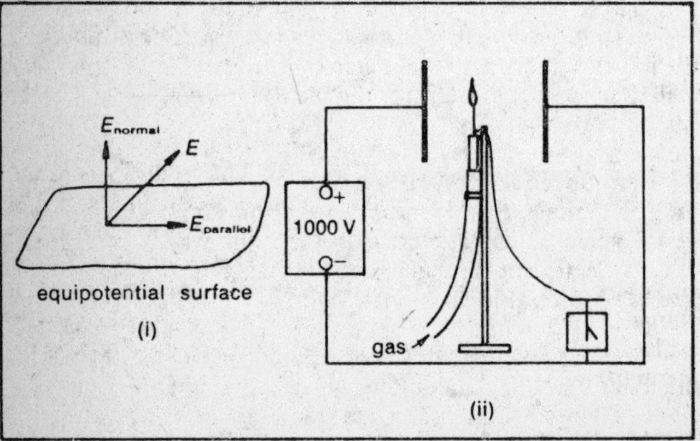

Figure 117. Equipotentials and flame probe

Electric field strength, being a force per unit charge, is a vector quantity, and electric field strengths can only be added vectorially. Electric potential, being the work per unit charge, is a scalar quantity, and therefore potentials can be added arithmetically.

Measurement of potential difference and charge

Potential differences can be measured with a calibrated gold leaf electroscope, a high resistance voltmeter, an electrostatic voltmeter (see p. 180) or an electrometer. An electrometer is a very high input impedance electronic voltmeter which will draw as little as 10^{-12} amp. Oscilloscopes can also be used as they have high input impedances (1 M), and can be calibrated so that the movement of the spot in the Y-direction corresponds to a known p.d.

Potentials in an electric field can be measured using a flame probe (fig. 117ii), attached to a calibrated gold leaf electroscope. The principle of the flame probe is to bring it and the electroscope to which it is attached, to the potential of the point in the field. Ions are produced by a tiny gas flame on the end of a hypodermic needle, and the ions charge the needle, wire and electroscope. The process continues until the potential of the needle is the same as that in the field at the point. Thus the electroscope will indicate the potential of the point.

Charge can be measured with a ballistic galvanometer (see p. 247) or with an electrometer. The principle of the electrometer method is to charge up a calibrated capacitor connected across the electrometer which measures the p.d. across it (see p. 196).

The field inside a conductor is zero. This follows because the existence of a field inside a conductor will cause the charges to move. The charges will thus redistribute themselves until the resultant field is zero. The same applies if the conductor is a hollow shell. Because the field is zero the potential is constant since no work is done in moving charge against zero field. The whole of the metal is therefore equipotential.

Uniform fields

The field between two infinite, oppositely charged parallel plates

is uniform. In practice if the dimensions of the plates are large compared with their spacing the field is effectively uniform except near the edges. Since the field is uniform the density of lines of force is uniform and the field is shown in fig. 118i.
The potential difference between two points A and B is the

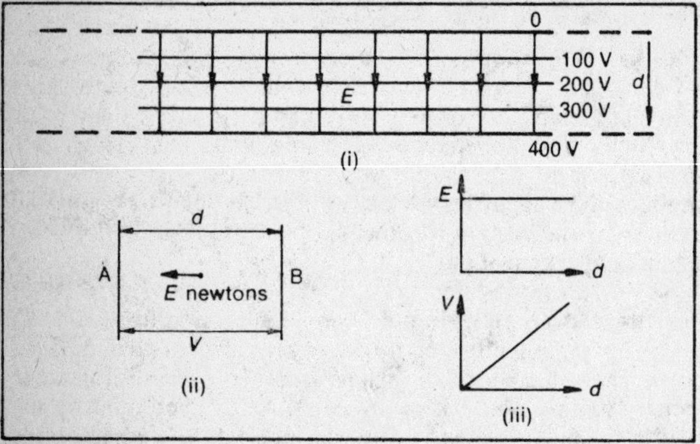

Figure 118. Field and equipotentials

work done in moving unit positive charge against the force acting on it (fig. 118ii).

Since work done = force × distance

$$V = (E \times 1) \times d \quad \text{since } F = Eq \quad \text{and} \quad q = 1$$

$$\therefore \quad E = \frac{V}{d}$$

This is an important relationship between field and potential. It shows that the units of field strength can also be **volts per metre**. These are the units actually used because volts per metre are far easier to measure in practice than newtons per coulomb. This relationship also shows that the equipotentials will be equally spaced in a uniform field (fig. 118i). The variation of field strength and potential with distance between the two plates is shown in fig. 118iii.

Field strength between parallel plates
By measurement, the charge on parallel plates can be shown to

be given by

$$Q \propto \frac{AV}{d}$$

where Q = charge on plates (the positive charge on one plate or, equally the negative charge on the other), A = area of plates, V = p.d. between plates, d = spacing of plates.

If the plates are in vacuo (or, to a good approximation in air) this can be written

$$Q = \epsilon_0 \frac{AV}{d}$$

where ϵ_0 is a constant of proportionality called the **permittivity of free space** (or **electric constant**). Its value is $8{\cdot}84 \times 10^{-12}$ F m^{-1}.

Rearranging this equation

$$\frac{Q}{A} = \epsilon_0 \frac{V}{d}$$

i.e.

$$\sigma = \epsilon_0 E \quad \text{or} \quad E = \frac{\sigma}{\epsilon_0}$$

where σ = charge per unit area.

This relationship shows that E is independent of d and therefore uniform. This result can also be obtained by summing the field contributions due to single charges, or by the use of Gauss's theorem.

Example Two parallel plates separated by 1 millimetre are charged to a p.d. of 1000 volts. What is the field strength between them. What is the charge on each plate if the area of the plate is 500 sq. centimetres?

$$E = \frac{V}{d}$$

$$= \frac{1000}{10^{-3}} = 10^6 \text{ V m}^{-1}$$

$$E = \frac{\sigma}{\epsilon_0}$$

$$\therefore \quad \sigma = \epsilon_0 E = 8{\cdot}84 \times 10^{-12} \times 10^6 = 8{\cdot}84\ \mu\text{C m}^{-2}$$

$$\text{Area of plate } A = 500 \times 10^{-4} = 5 \times 10^{-2}\ \text{m}^2$$

$$\text{Charge} = \sigma A = 8{\cdot}84 \times 10^{-6} \times 5 \times 10^{-2} = 442\ \text{nC}$$

(Note how small the charge is).

Inverse square law field

Coulomb's law states that the force between two isolated charges Q_1 and Q_2 a distance r apart in vacuo is given by

$$F = \frac{1}{4\pi\epsilon_0} \cdot \frac{Q_1 Q_2}{r^2} \qquad \left(\frac{1}{4\pi\epsilon_0} \approx 9 \times 10^9\ \text{N m}^2\ \text{C}^{-2}\right)$$

The electric field strength a distance r from a charge Q in vacuo is therefore given by

$$E = \frac{1}{4\pi\epsilon_0} \cdot \frac{Q}{r^2} \quad \text{since } Q_2 \text{ is unit charge.}$$

If the charge is isolated, the field lines will radiate symmetrically from the charge to infinity.

Gauss's theorem

The total number of field lines crossing a concentric spherical surface round a charge is independent of the distance from the charge. This implies that the field lines are continuous (fig. 119i). This can readily be established by considering the field

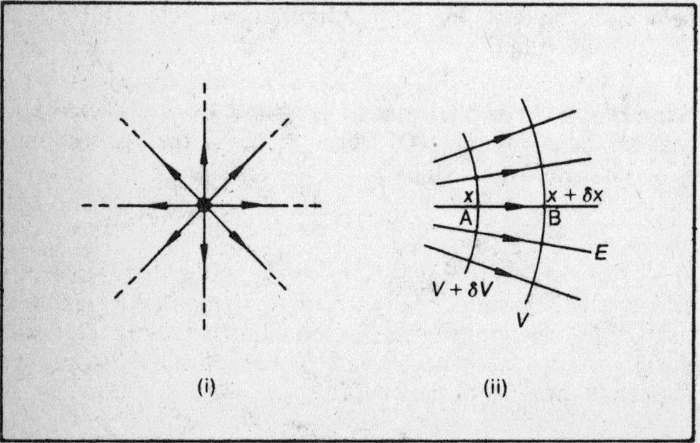

Figure 119. Electric fields

lines through the surface of a concentric sphere round the charge. From the definition of field lines:

Number of lines of force = field strength × area of sphere

$$= \frac{1}{4\pi\epsilon_0} \cdot \frac{Q}{r^2} \times 4\pi r^2 = \frac{Q}{\epsilon_0}$$

i.e. the total number of field lines passing through a closed surface enclosing a charge is constant and independent of the radius of the surface chosen and equals Q/ϵ_0. The number of lines remains constant because the area of the sphere is increasing with $(\text{distance})^2$ whilst the field strength is decreasing as $\left(\frac{1}{\text{distance}^2}\right)$. This expression for the total number of lines of force leaving a charge Q is Gauss's theorem and is perfectly general – it can be established for any closed surface containing a charge Q.

Potential in an inverse square law field

As the field strength varies with distance, calculus must be used. Consider the situation in fig. 119ii. From the definition of potential difference as the work done per unit charge,

$$\delta V = F\delta s$$

where F is the force on unit charge (i.e. field strength E in this case), δs is the distance moved and δV is an infinitesimal change of potential corresponding to the infinitesimal distance δs moved from A to B over which the field strength E is assumed to be constant.

$\therefore$ $\delta V = E(-\delta x)$ (the minus sign is because E and δx are in opposite directions and hence V decreases as x increases).

Hence in the limit as $\delta x \to 0$

$$E = -\frac{dV}{dx}$$

This is an important relationship which states that the electric field strength is numerically equal to the potential gradient. Using this relationship the potential distribution around a charge can be calculated, i.e. how the potential varies with distance r away from the charge Q.

$$dV = -E dx$$

Integrating between limits r and ∞, where the potential is V,

$$\int_0^V dV = \int_\infty^r -\frac{Q}{4\pi\epsilon_0} \cdot \frac{dx}{x^2}$$

$$[V]_0^V = -\frac{Q}{4\pi\epsilon_0}\left[-\frac{1}{x}\right]_\infty^r$$

$$V = \frac{Q}{4\pi\epsilon_0 r} \quad \left(\text{i.e. } 9 \times 10^9 \times \frac{Q}{r}\right)$$

This relationship can be established experimentally using a flame probe connected to an electroscope to investigate the potential around a charged sphere (fig. 120i), and plotting V against $1/r$. The resultant plot should be a straight line (fig. 120ii). This is the most satisfactory way of establishing the inverse square variation of field around a charge. Direct measurement of the forces on charges is extremely difficult due to the small forces involved, and the leakage of charge

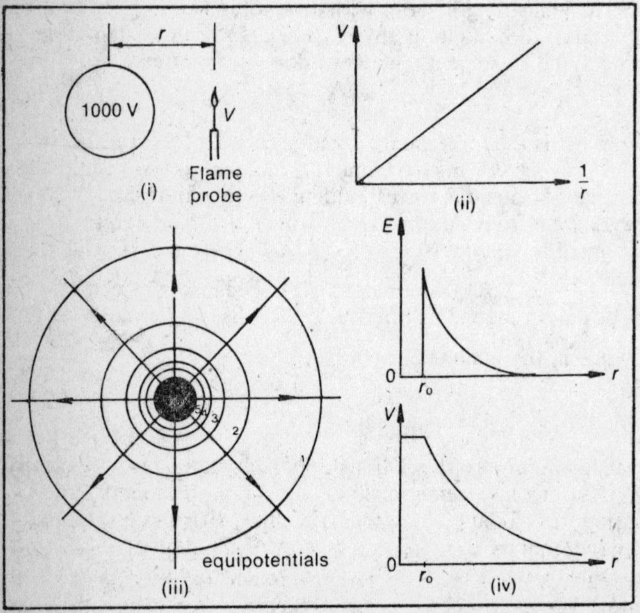

Figure 120. Field and potential round a sphere

The distribution of electric field lines and equipotentials around an isolated sphere is shown in fig. 120iii. It can be seen that as with the gravitational field, the charge behaves as if it were concentrated at the centre. The resultant plots of the variation of electric field strength and potential difference are given in fig. 120iv. It can be seen that inside the conductor the field strength is zero and the potential is constant.

Example Calculate the maximum potential to which a sphere of radius 10 centimetres can be charged if the breakdown field strength of air is 3×10^6 V m^{-1}.

Charge behaves as if it were concentrated at the centre of the sphere, therefore field strength at a distance of r metres is given by

$$E = \frac{1}{4\pi\epsilon_0} \cdot \frac{q}{r^2}$$

So for the maximum possible field strength of 3×10^6 V m^{-1}

$$q = 4\pi\epsilon_0 E r^2 = 4\pi\epsilon_0 \times 3 \times 10^6 \times (10^{-1})^2 = 12\pi\epsilon_0 \times 10^4 \text{ C}$$

Potential at surface of sphere is given by

$$\frac{1}{4\pi\epsilon_0} \cdot \frac{q}{r} = \frac{1}{4\pi\epsilon_0} \cdot \frac{12\pi\epsilon_0 \times 10^4}{10^{-1}} = 3 \times 10^5 \text{ V}$$

Capacitance

An important property of a conductor is the ratio between the charge on the conductor and its resultant potential. It is called the capacitance of the conductor.

$$C = \frac{Q}{V}$$

The unit of capacitance is the farad.

The **farad** is defined as the capacitance of a conductor such that one coulomb of charge would raise its potential by one volt. The farad is impracticably large and the microfarad ($1\,\mu\text{F} = 10^{-6}$ F) and the picofarad ($1\,\text{pF} = 10^{-12}$ F) are used instead. A good analogy of capacitance is a compressed air tank. There is clearly a fixed ratio between the charge of compressed air which is pumped into it and the resultant pressure inside it. This ratio is proportional to the capacity of the tank – a large tank will take a large charge of air whereas a small tank will only take a small charge to produce the same pressure, i.e.

$$\text{capacity} \propto \frac{\text{charge}}{\text{pressure}}$$

Capacity of an isolated sphere
If the conductor is a sphere of radius r_0 in vacuo then its capacitance can be calculated easily.

$$C = \frac{Q}{V} \quad \text{and} \quad V = \frac{1}{4\pi\epsilon_0} \cdot \frac{Q}{r_0}$$

$$\therefore \quad C = \frac{Q}{Q/4\pi\epsilon_0 r_0} = 4\pi\epsilon_0 r_0$$

Example Calculate the capacitance of the moon. (Radius of moon is 1740 km)

$$C = 4\pi\epsilon_0 r \qquad \left(\frac{1}{4\pi\epsilon_0} = 9 \times 10^9\right)$$

$$\frac{1{\cdot}740 \times 10^6}{9 \times 10^9} = 193\ \mu\text{F}$$

This illustrates how large a unit the farad is!

Capacitance of parallel plates
More commonly, however, the term capacitance is applied to a capacitor consisting of two plates. In this case the capacitance is the ratio between the charge on either plate and the potential difference between the plates.

Again $$C = \frac{Q}{V}$$

where $$V = \text{p.d.}$$

For a parallel plate capacitor of area A and distance between plates d in vacuo the capacity can be calculated as follows:

The field between the plates is given by

$$E = \frac{\sigma}{\epsilon_0} \quad (\sigma = \text{charge per unit area})$$ (p. 185)

But $$V = E \times d = \frac{\sigma d}{\epsilon_0} \quad \text{and} \quad Q = \sigma \times A$$

$$\therefore \quad C = \frac{Q}{V} = \frac{\sigma A}{\sigma d/\epsilon_0} = \frac{\epsilon_0 A}{d}$$

Dielectrics and permittivity

Usually capacitors have an insulating material between their plates. Many materials have the property of increasing the capacitance, and they are called **dielectrics**. The reason for this is that such materials become '**polarized**' by the electric field (fig. 121i). Each molecule of the material becomes an electric dipole (two equal and opposite charges situated a very short distance apart) as the positive and negative regions of the molecule separate slightly. As a result there is an apparent layer of charge on the top and bottom of the dielectric. These layers of charge produce a field e in the opposite direction to the original field E, and the resultant field in the dielectric E' is therefore less than it was before.

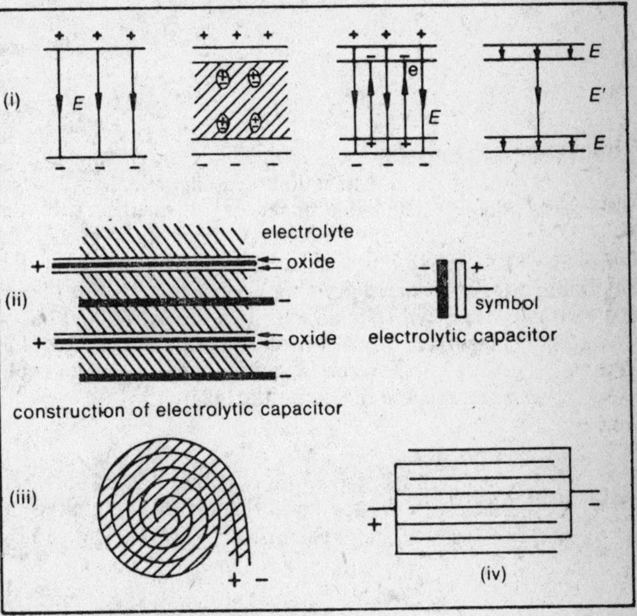

Figure 121. Dielectric and capacitors

As $V = Ed$, V is reduced, and so since $C = Q/V$, C is increased.

The ratio of the capacitance with dielectric to that without is called the **relative permittivity** ϵ_r of the material.

Thus
$$C = \frac{\epsilon_r \epsilon_0 A}{d}$$

The product $\epsilon_r \epsilon_0$ is called the **absolute permittivity** ϵ of the medium, i.e. $\epsilon = \epsilon_r \epsilon_0$. Thus the expression for electric field strength around a point charge if the space is filled with dielectric of absolute permittivity ϵ is

$$E = \frac{1}{4\pi\epsilon} \cdot \frac{Q}{r^2}$$

Example Calculate the capacitance of a capacitor with plates of dimension 5 centimetres by 1 metre, with waxed paper dielectric 5×10^{-4} m thick and relative permittivity 6.

$$C = \frac{\epsilon_0 \epsilon_r A}{d} \qquad \text{Area} = 5 \times 10^{-2} \times 1 \text{ m}^2$$

$$= \frac{8{\cdot}84 \times 10^{-12} \times 6 \times 5 \times 10^{-2} \times 1}{5 \times 10^{-4}} = 5{\cdot}3 \text{ nF}$$

Construction of capacitors

The usual form of the construction of a capacitor is a 'swiss-roll' of aluminium with wax paper or other dielectric (fig. 121iii). For large values of capacitance, **electrolytic** capacitors are used. The construction is similar but one side of the aluminium foil is anodized forming a very thin (10^{-7} m) layer of aluminium oxide which is an excellent dielectric, and paper soaked in electrolyte which forms the other 'plate' of the capacitor (fig. 121ii). In smaller capacitors there is just a simple interleaving of plates and dielectric (fig. 121iv).

Capacitors in parallel

Consider the capacitors shown in fig. 122i. The potential difference across both capacitors is the same. The charge on the capacitor C, which is equivalent to C_1 and C_2, is given by

$$Q = Q_1 + Q_2$$

But
$$Q = CV, \; Q_1 = C_1 V \quad \text{and} \quad Q_2 = C_2 V$$

$$\therefore \quad CV = C_1 V + C_2 V$$

i.e.
$$C = C_1 + C_2$$

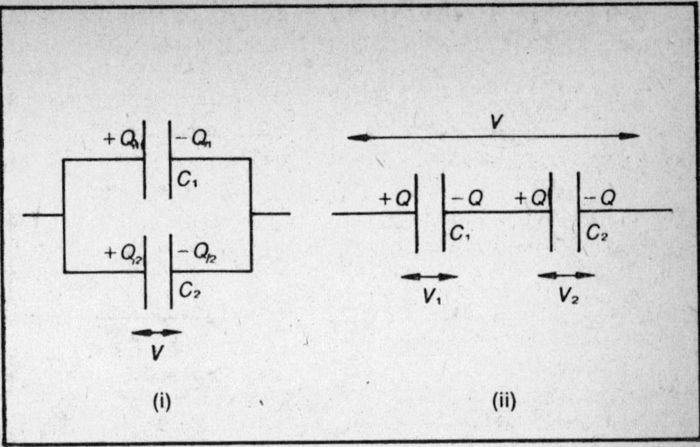

Figure 122. Capacitors in parallel and series

Capacitors in series

Consider the capacitors in fig. 122ii. In this case, the charge is the same on both capacitors (this must be so since if Q_1 were not equal to Q_2 the central section consisting of one plate of C_1 the connecting wire and one plate of C_2 would become charged by $Q_1 - Q_2$. But this is impossible since the section is isolated.) The p.d. across the equivalent single capacitor C is given by

$$V = V_1 + V_2$$

But $$V = \frac{Q}{C}, \quad V_1 = \frac{Q}{C_1} \quad \text{and} \quad V_2 = \frac{Q}{C_2}$$

$$\therefore \quad \frac{Q}{C} = \frac{Q}{C_1} + \frac{Q}{C_2}$$

i.e. $$\frac{1}{C} = \frac{1}{C_1} + \frac{1}{C_2}$$

Energy stored in a charged capacitor

The graph of potential across a capacitor on one of its plates against charge is shown in fig. 123. The reciprocal of its slope equals the capacitance.

Since V = joules per coulomb, the work done δW in increasing the charge by δQ against the p.d. V is given by

$$\delta W = V\delta Q$$

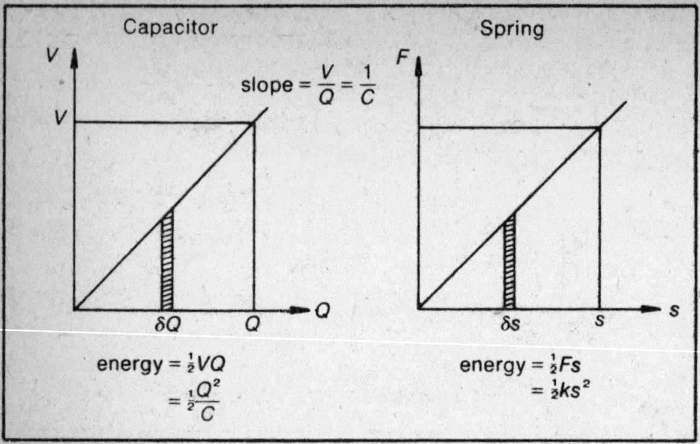

Figure 123. Energy in a capacitor and a spring

This is the shaded area beneath the graph. Thus the total work done in charging the capacitor is the total area beneath the graph. Since it is a straight line

$$W = \tfrac{1}{2}\text{height} \times \text{base}$$
$$= \tfrac{1}{2}VQ$$

Since $C = \dfrac{Q}{V}$ this can also be written

$$W = \frac{1}{2}\frac{Q^2}{C}$$

or

$$W = \tfrac{1}{2}CV^2$$

The same result can be obtained by integration, substituting $V = \dfrac{Q}{C}$

$$\int_0^W \mathrm{d}W = \int_0^Q \frac{Q}{C}\,\mathrm{d}Q$$

$$\therefore \quad W = \frac{1}{2}\frac{Q^2}{C}$$

This expression is very similar to that for the energy stored in a spring (see p. 23).

$$W = \tfrac{1}{2}ks^2$$

Example Two capacitors of 1 μF and 2 μF, are connected in series across a 100 V supply. Calculate the energy stored in the 1 μF capacitor.

Total capacitance is given by

$$\frac{1}{C}=\frac{1}{1\times 10^{-6}}+\frac{1}{2\times 10^{-6}}=\frac{3}{2\times 10^{-6}}$$

$$C=\tfrac{2}{3}\,\mu F$$

Charge on each plate (fig. 122ii) is given by

$$Q=CV$$

$$=\tfrac{2}{3}\times 10^{-6}\times 100=66{\cdot}7\,\mu C$$

$$\text{Energy in } 1\,\mu F \text{ capacitor}=\frac{1}{2}\cdot\frac{Q^2}{C}$$

$$=\frac{1}{2}\frac{(6{\cdot}67\times 10^{-5})^2}{10^{-6}}$$

$$=2{\cdot}22\text{ mJ}$$

Measurement of capacitance

Capacitance can be measured absolutely (rather than by comparison with a standard capacitor) by charging a capacitor to a known p.d. and measuring the resultant charge.

Then $$C=\frac{Q}{V}$$

Several methods are available.

(i) **Reed switch** The principle of this method is repeatedly to charge a capacitor and discharge it through a microammeter. By measuring the current and knowing the repeat rate the charge can be calculated. The circuit is shown in fig. 124i. The reed switch consists of two magnetic reeds which touch when the switch is placed in a magnetic field. The field is provided by a coil connected to a suitable source of a.c., the frequency of which must not be higher than that for which the switch is designed (typically 400 Hz). When the switch is in position 1 the capacitor charges. When the switch is in position 2 it discharges completely through the meter. As this is repeated at regular intervals, the discharge constitutes a current, which is measured.

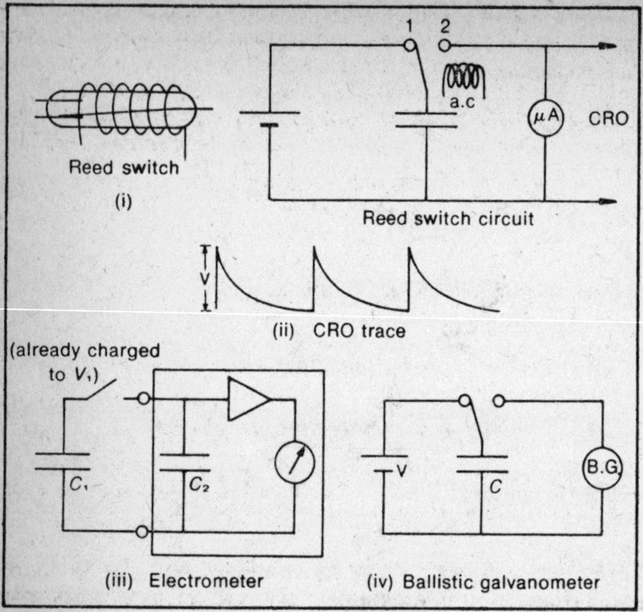

Figure 124. Measurement of capacitance

If the charge is Q and the frequency is f, then the current is given by

$$I = \text{charge per second} = Qf$$

Hence $$Q = \frac{I}{f} \quad \text{and} \quad C = \frac{Q}{V} = \frac{I}{Vf}$$

Care must be taken that the capacitor fully discharges on each cycle (which depends on the time taken to discharge through the resistance of the meter and is best checked by observing the wave form of the voltage across the capacitor using an oscilloscope) (fig. 124ii).

Example In a reed switch experiment the frequency of the switch was 400 Hz and the current measured was 5 mA when the capacitor was charged to 12 V. What was its capacitance?

$$C = \frac{Q}{V} = \frac{I}{fV} = \frac{5 \times 10^{-3}}{400 \times 12} = 1{\cdot}04\ \mu\text{F}$$

(ii) **Electrometer** The principle of this method is to measure the p.d. across a known large capacitor which effectively takes all the charge when a small charged capacitor is placed in parallel with it (fig. 124iii). The electrometer measures p.d. of up to a volt, but draws virtually no current. Usually the calibrated capacitor is built in as part of the electrometer. The sharing of charge can be proved as follows:

$$V = \frac{Q_1}{C_1} = \frac{Q_2}{C_2} \quad \text{i.e. } Q_2 = \frac{C_2}{C_1} Q_1$$

If $C_2 = 0{\cdot}1$ F and $C_1 = 10\ \mu$F, for instance

$$\frac{C_2}{C_1} = 10^4$$

$$\therefore \quad Q_2 = 10^4\, Q_1$$

i.e. the majority of the charge is now in C_2 and the charge left in C_1 is negligible. The charge involved is C_2V_2 where V_2 is the electrometer measurement of p.d. across C_2.

(iii) **Ballistic galvanometer** As mentioned on p. 247 the throw of a ballistic galvanometer is proportional to the charge flowing through it. The capacitor is charged to a known p.d. (fig. 124iv) and then discharged. Thus, if the galvanometer has previously been calibrated, Q is measured directly, and then

$$C = \frac{Q}{V}$$

(iv) **a.c. methods** The capacitance can also be found by measuring its reactance in an a.c. circuit (see p. 268).

Factors affecting capacitance

Using any of the above methods to measure the capacitance of two large flat metal plates it can be shown by varying the overlapping areas that $C \propto A$ and by varying the spacing by using small spacers at the corners it can be shown that

$$C \propto \frac{1}{d}$$

i.e.

$$C \propto \frac{A}{d}$$

Comparison of capacitors Any of these methods can be used to compare capacitors by comparing readings with those obtained with a standard capacitor charged to the same p.d.

Millikan's experiment

All charges, however produced, are positive or negative integer multiples of the charge on the electron *e*. Millikan's experiment (fig. 125) is the only direct method for determining the value of *e*. The principle of the experiment is to measure the force acting on a charged droplet of oil in an electric field. This is done by measuring terminal velocities with and without the electric field.

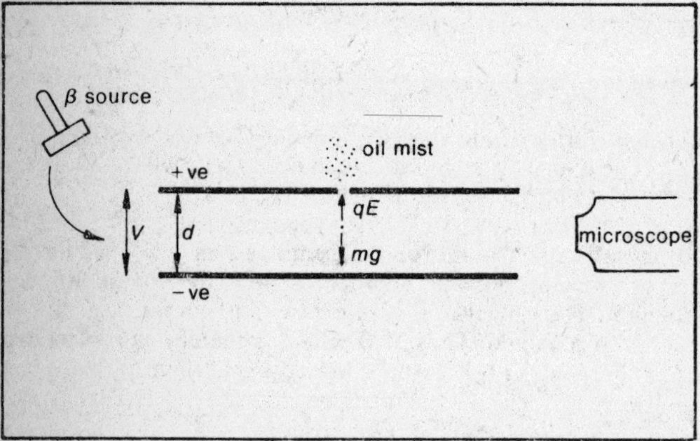

Figure 125. Millikan's experiment

The apparatus consists of two parallel plates connected to a variable p.d. supply. Oil can be sprayed so that a few droplets fall through the hole in the top plate. The oil droplets are charged by friction as they are formed, but the charge can be changed with ionizing radiation (see p. 280). A powerful lateral beam of light enables a droplet to be seen in a low power microscope as a point of light. The microscope has a scale so that the distance moved by a droplet can be measured. The terminal velocity of one droplet is determined with the plates uncharged, and the experiment is then repeated with the electric field switched on causing the droplets to rise. The second experiment is repeated many times, each time the charge on the droplet is changed with the ionizing radiation. Finally the values of charge on the droplet are analyzed to find the highest common factor which must then be a single electronic charge e.

The calculation is as follows. Stoke's law states that at the terminal velocity v the viscous drag F on a sphere of radius r is given by

$$F = 6\pi r\eta v$$

where η is the viscosity

When falling at velocity v_1 without the field

$$\text{Viscous drag} = \text{weight} - \text{upthrust of air}$$

$$6\pi r\eta v_1 = \tfrac{4}{3}\pi r^3\rho g - \tfrac{4}{3}\pi r^3\rho_A g$$

where ρ and ρ_A are densities of oil and air respectively

$$\therefore \quad r^2 = \frac{9\eta v_1}{2g(\rho - \rho_A)}$$

Hence r and apparent weight of oil drop W can be found.

When rising at velocity v_2 with field switched on

$$\text{Drag} = \text{electric force} - \text{apparent weight}$$

$$6\pi r\eta v_2 = qE - W \quad \text{when } E = \frac{V}{d}$$

(where V = voltage across plates)

Hence q can be found.

e = highest common factor of all values of q.

In a simpler version of the experiment (but difficult to perform) the droplet can be made stationary.

Then $$qE = W$$

Current electricity

Electrical conduction

An electric current is a flow of mobile charge carriers. These carriers can take several forms but always carry simple multiples of the charge on the electron.

In metals, the charge carriers are outer electrons of the metal atoms. They can wander freely about the lattice, not belonging to any particular atom, and form what is sometimes referred to as an 'electron gas' (fig. 126i).

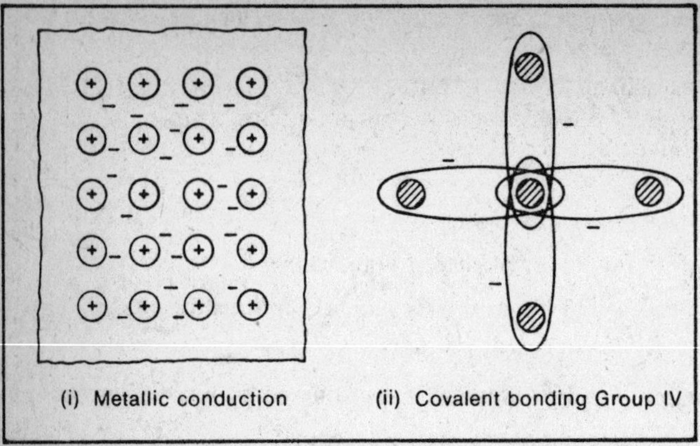

Figure 126. Metallic and covalent bonding

In insulators, the outer electrons are tightly bound to the atoms, and are therefore no longer free to carry charge through the lattice.

In intrinsic semiconductors, the outer electrons form covalent bonds and are loosely bound (fig. 126ii). They can be released by receiving relatively little energy and thus the number of charge carriers can be increased by heating. A free electron leaves behind an atom short of an electron, and this 'hole' may be filled by another electron. Thus, a 'hole' moves from atom to atom, and therefore constitutes a positive charge carrier. The combination is known as a hole-electron pair. The resistance of a sample drops as its temperature rises because of the production of extra charge carriers.

In extrinsic semiconductors, small traces of impurities are added – a process called doping. If the impurity is group V (e.g. antimony or arsenic) then one electron is left over after the valence bonds have been satisfied and becomes free. Conduction is therefore mostly due to negative charge carriers provided by the donor impurity, and the semiconductor is known as n-type. A p-type semiconductor is made by adding a group III acceptor impurity (e.g. indium or gallium). In this case there are only three electrons available to satisfy the four valence bonds, and an electron is 'robbed' from a neighbouring atom which thus becomes a 'hole'. Conduction is then mostly

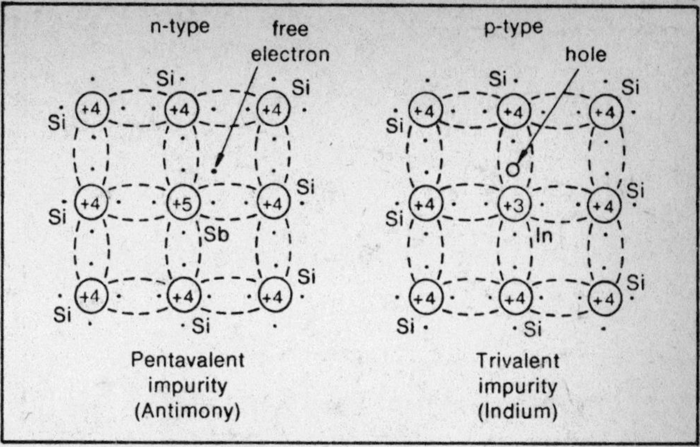

Figure 127. Extrinsic semiconductors

due to positive charge carriers (fig. 127).

In ionized gases, the charge carriers are ions and electrons. The ions are atoms or molecules which have had outer electrons knocked off by fast moving electrons and other ions accelerated by an electric field.

In electrolytes, the charge carriers are positive and negative ions in the electrolyte. The positive ions have lost one or more electrons but the negative ions have gained electrons.

Current

Current is the rate of flow of charge. Consider a section of a conductor containing n per unit volume carriers of charge e moving with velocity v (fig. 128). A 'slug' of charge of length v passes point X in one second. Since current I is charge passing per second

$$\begin{aligned} I &= \text{volume} \times \text{charge per unit volume} \\ &= Av \times ne = Avne \end{aligned}$$

Example Typical values for copper are: $n = 8{\cdot}5 \times 10^{28}\ \text{m}^{-3}$; $e = 1{\cdot}6 \times 10^{-19}$ C; $I = 10$ amps; $A = 10^{-6}\ \text{m}^2$ say. Find the velocity of the charges.

$$v = \frac{I}{Ane} = \frac{10}{10^{-6} \times 8{\cdot}5 \times 10^{28} \times 1{\cdot}6 \times 10^{-19}} \approx 7{\cdot}3 \times 10^{-3}\ \text{m s}^{-1}$$

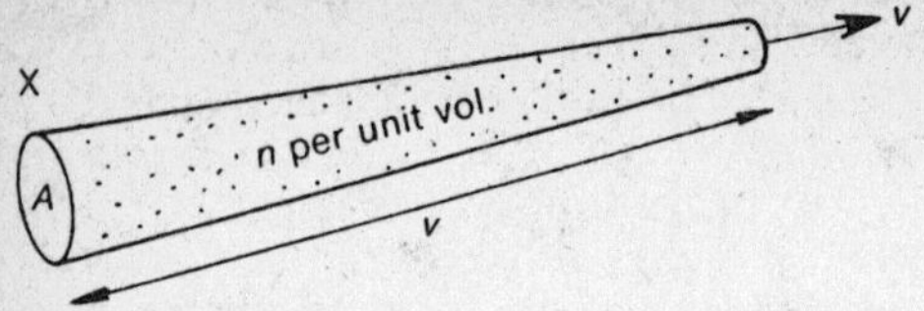

Figure 128. Current calculation

This is very slow, and is called the **drift velocity**. It is an overall drift of charge over and above the random thermal velocities of electrons (about 10^5 m s^{-1} at room temperature). The random velocities of the electrons do not constitute a current since on average as many electrons will be moving in one direction as in the opposite direction.

The charge carriers move because of the electric field in the wire due to the p.d. across its ends. They only attain a steady drift velocity instead of accelerating continuously because they make inelastic collisions with atoms. The energy given to the atoms by collisions increases their vibrational energy. Therefore the temperature of the conductor increases. In this way electrical energy is converted into thermal energy in a resistor.

The unit of current is the ampere which is defined in terms of the force between two currents and is discussed in the chapter on Electromagnetism (see p. 237).

Potential difference

A current will only flow between two points if there is a potential difference between them. The conventional current or positive charge carriers flow from a higher potential to a lower potential. It is sometimes helpful to think of potential difference as a difference of 'electrical pressure' forcing a current through a load. The potential difference between two points is defined in the section on Electrostatics (see p. 181).

Electromotive force (EMF)

In a complete circuit there may be at some point a source of 'electrical force' which acts on the charge carriers giving rise to current. This could be a battery, dynamo, etc. which produces an electromotive force. The e.m.f. is defined as the energy given to the complete circuit in electrical form per coulomb passing through the source. The units are also volts.

Usually, when the source is providing a current in a circuit some of the electrical energy given to the charges is lost in the internal resistance of the source itself, so that the potential difference across its terminals is not equal to the e.m.f. The e.m.f. of a source can therefore only be measured directly when it is not delivering a current, or indirectly when it is.

Water analogy

A helpful analogy can be drawn between the flow of electricity in a circuit and the flow of water round a system of pipes. **Charge** is equivalent to the quantity of water (litres). **Current** is equivalent to the rate of flow of water (litres per second). If we have a complete series circuit, the flow of water is the same at all points round the circuit otherwise water would be stored at some point (or be compressed!).

Potential difference is equivalent to pressure difference between two points which is pushing the water through the pipes. Apart from causing a flow, however, the pressure difference is also responsible for the power that a flow of water can deliver. The pressure acting over the area of the pipe exerts a force and because the water is moving this force is acting through a distance each second, and is thus delivering power. In the electrical case, the unit of 'pressure difference' is the volt, which is defined in terms of the energy that each coulomb would deliver if moving across that potential difference.

Electromotive force is equivalent to the total pressure difference which a pump could introduce to propel the water round a circuit (including that needed to propel the water through the pump itself).

Resistance is equivalent to the resistance to water flow, i.e.

the ratio of the pressure difference to the resultant rate of flow. Higher resistance means that a higher pressure is needed to force the same quantity of water through the resistor each second. Two pipes, one after the other, clearly present more resistance to flow, and two pipes side by side present less.

Summary of electrical units

1 coulomb is the charge which passes when 1 amp flows for 1 second.

1 ampere is the unit of current and is defined on page 237.

1 volt is the p.d. such that 1 joule of work is done when 1 coulomb passes.

I–V relationships (characteristic curves)

The relationship between *I* and *V* varies widely for different devices (fig. 129). Metallic conduction is a special case in which the relationship is linear.

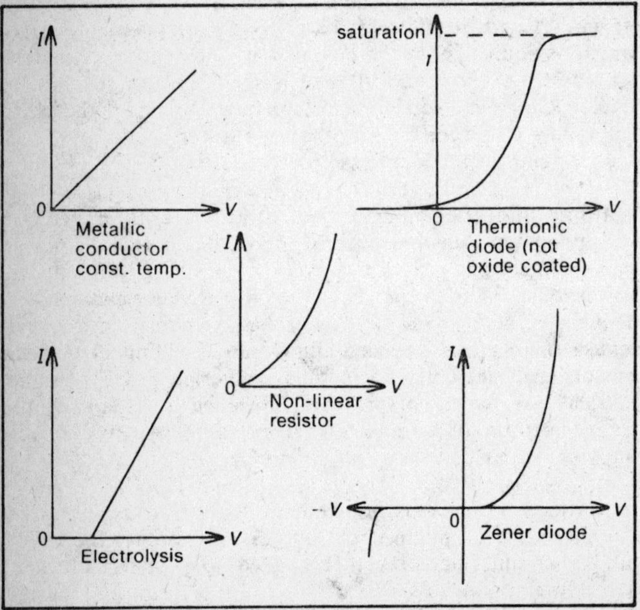

Figure 129. I–V curves

Ohm's law
Ohm's law states that the current flowing through a metallic conductor is directly proportional to the voltage, provided the physical conditions (e.g. temperature) remain constant.

Resistance, R, is the ratio between the potential difference across a resistor and the current through it, and its unit is the ohm (Ω).

$$R = \frac{V}{I}\,\Omega$$

Conductance, G, is the reciprocal of resistance. The unit is the siemens (S).

$$G = \frac{I}{V}\,\text{S}$$

Resistors in series and parallel
Several resistors can be combined into one equivalent resistor.

Series The same current flows through both resistors (fig. 130i).

Let p.d.'s V_1 and V_2 exist across R_1 and R_2, and let V be the p.d. across the equivalent resistor of resistance R.

Then $$V = V_1 + V_2$$

By Ohm's Law $V = IR$, $$V_1 = IR_1 \quad \text{and} \quad V_2 = IR_2$$

$$\therefore \quad IR = IR_1 + IR_2$$

i.e. $$R = R_1 + R_2$$

Parallel The same potential difference is applied to both resistors (fig. 130ii).

$$I = I_1 + I_2$$

By Ohm's Law $I = \frac{V}{R}$, $I_1 = \frac{V}{R_1}$ and $I_2 = \frac{V}{R_2}$

$$\therefore \quad \frac{V}{R} = \frac{V}{R_1} + \frac{V}{R_2}$$

i.e. $$\frac{1}{R} = \frac{1}{R_1} + \frac{1}{R_2}$$

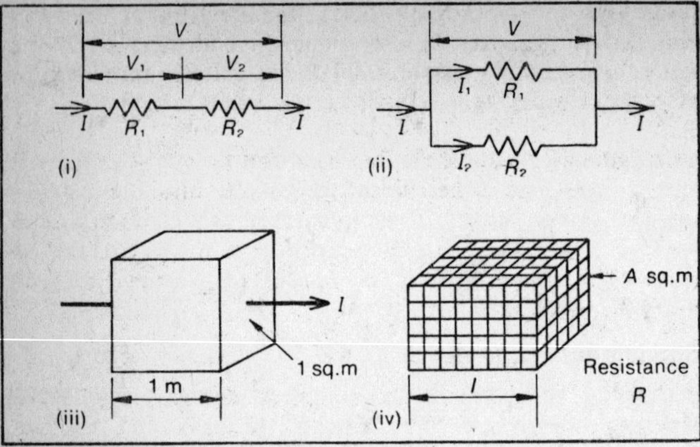

Figure 130. Resistors and resistivity

Resistivity

Resistivity ρ is a measure of the resistance of a material rather than of a particular resistor. It is the resistance of unit length of a material of unit cross-sectional area (fig. 130iii). Thus a length of l metres increases the resistance l times, and an area of A square metres decreases the resistance A times.

The resistance of the sample in fig. 130iv will thus be given by

$$R = \frac{\rho l}{A}$$

Hence

$$\rho = \frac{RA}{l}$$

The units of resistivity, from the equation, are ohm metres (Ω m).

Typical values are: for a good conductor 10^{-8} Ω m
for a semiconductor 10 Ω m
for a good insulator 10^{14} Ω m

Temperature dependence of resistance

The resistance of metals increases with temperature. This is due to increased interaction between the free electrons and the lattice ('friction') which requires more power to make a given current flow. The resistance of semiconductors decreases with temperature because, although the electron–lattice interaction is still present, there is a more rapid increase in the number of charge carriers due to the increased production of hole-electron pairs.

The temperature coefficient of resistance (α) is a measure of the change of resistance with temperature. It is the increase in resistance per unit rise in temperature per unit resistance at 0°C. Over a limited range of temperature, α is constant, so change of resistance $= R_0\alpha t$ and hence the resistance at temperature t°C is given by

$$R = R_0 + R_0\alpha t = R_0(1 + \alpha t)$$

Example A Wheatstone bridge circuit is used to find the temperature coefficient of resistance of a coil. The coil was found to have a resistance of 5 Ω at 0°C. When heated to 100°C it was found that a 200 Ω resistor had to be added parallel with the coil to restore the bridge balance. Calculate the temperature coefficient of resistance.

The bridge always balances at 5 Ω

So at 0°C $\qquad R_0 = 5\ \Omega$

at 100°C $\qquad \dfrac{1}{R_{100}} + \dfrac{1}{200} = \dfrac{1}{5}$

$$\frac{1}{R_{100}} = \frac{1}{5} - \frac{1}{200} = \frac{40-1}{200} = \frac{39}{200}$$

$$\therefore \quad R_{100} = \frac{200}{39} = 5{\cdot}1282\ \Omega$$

$$R_{100} = R_0\ (1 + \alpha t)$$

$$\alpha t = \frac{R_{100}}{R_0} - 1 = \frac{5{\cdot}1282}{5} - 1 = 0{\cdot}0256$$

$$\therefore \quad \alpha = \frac{0{\cdot}0256}{100} = 2{\cdot}56 \times 10^{-4}\ \mathrm{K}^{-1}$$

Conductivity

Conductivity, σ, is the reciprocal of resistivity.

$$\sigma = \frac{1}{\rho}$$

Units are siemens per metre ($\mathrm{S\,m^{-1}}$). Conductivity increases directly as the number of charge carriers increases and in particular the conductivity of semiconductors increases with temperature due to the rapid increase in the number of hole-electron pairs.

Internal resistance

All practical sources of electric current have internal resistance. The origin of the resistance varies, but cannot be removed in practice. In a generator, it is the resistance of the copper of the windings. The result of internal resistance r is that the p.d. V between the terminals of a source is not equal to its e.m.f. E when it is delivering current. The difference between the two is sometimes referred to as 'lost volts' (fig. 131i). The 'lost volts' are $E - V = Ir$. If a source is on open circuit then the p.d. between the terminals is the e.m.f. since there are no lost volts ($I = 0$ so $E - V = 0$ i.e. $V = E$). One way of determining the internal resistance if the e.m.f. is known is to vary the load until the p.d. falls to half the e.m.f. The load resistance then equals the internal resistance (fig. 131i). Alternatively any method of measuring e.m.f. and p.d. when delivering a current will enable r to be calculated.

Example A circuit is shown in fig. 131ii. Calculate (i) the p.d. across R_3 (ii) the current through R_1 and (iii) 'the lost volts'.

Combine R_1 and R_2 to give equivalent resistor R_a

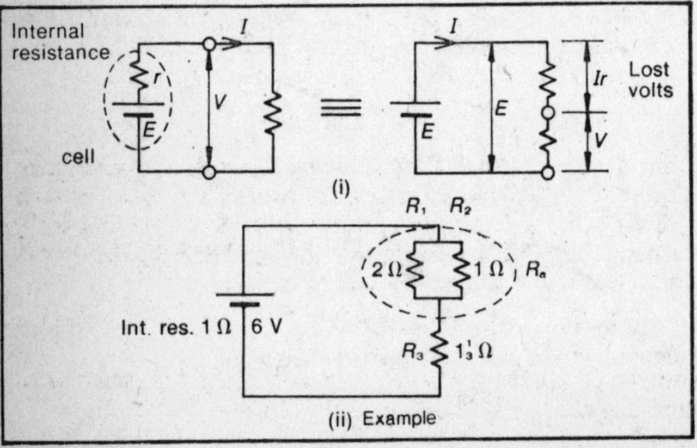

Figure 131. Lost volts and example

$$\frac{1}{R_a}=\frac{1}{R_1}+\frac{1}{R_2}=\frac{1}{2}+\frac{1}{1}=\frac{3}{2} \quad \therefore \quad R_a=\frac{2}{3}\,\Omega$$

Let internal resistance be r

Total resistance $= r + R_a + R_3$

$= 1 + \frac{2}{3} + 1\frac{1}{3} = 3\,\Omega$

$\therefore$ Current from cell $= \frac{V}{R} = \frac{6}{3} = 2$ amps

(i) p.d. across $R_3 = IR_3 = 2 \times 1\frac{1}{3} = 2\frac{2}{3}$ V

(ii) p.d. across $R_a = IR_a = 2 \times \frac{2}{3} = 1\frac{1}{3}$ V

$\therefore$ Current through $R_1 = \frac{V}{R_1} = \frac{1\frac{1}{3}}{2} = \frac{2}{3}$A

(iii) lost volts $= Ir = 2 \times 1 = 2$ V

Finally check round the circuit to make sure that all p.d.'s add up to the e.m.f.

$$E = V_r + V_{R_a} + V_{R_3}$$

$$6 = 2 + 1\tfrac{1}{3} + 2\tfrac{2}{3} = 6$$

Kirchhoff's laws

When dealing with more complex circuits two important general laws are used, known as Kirchhoff's laws. These state that, when steady currents flow in a network of conductors:

(i) the algebraic sum of the currents entering any point in the network is zero. This implies that charge cannot accumulate at a point and therefore current in equals current out.

$$\Sigma I = 0$$

(ii) the algebraic sum of the products of current and resistance taken round any closed path in a network must equal the sum of the e.m.f.s acting in the same direction round that path. This is simply a statement that the sum of the p.d.s across resistors round a loop is equal to the total e.m.f.

$$\Sigma IR = \Sigma E$$

Example The example above can be used to illustrate Kirchhoff's laws.

(i) Use Kirchhoff's 1st law to find I_2. Consider the point where

R_1, R_2 and R_3 meet. Let I_1, I_2, and I_3 be the currents in R_1, R_2, and R_3 respectively, all flowing in the same direction. $\Sigma I = 0 = I_1 + I_2 + I_3$ (if all currents are flowing to the point).

$$\therefore \quad I_1 + I_2 = -I_3$$

i.e. I_1 and I_2 flow into the point (+ve) and I_3 flows out (−ve).

From above

$$I_1 = \tfrac{2}{3}, \quad I_3 = -2$$

$$\therefore \quad 0 = \tfrac{2}{3} + I_2 - 2$$

$$\therefore \quad I_2 = 1\tfrac{1}{3}\ \text{A}$$

(ii) Use Kirchhoff's 2nd law to check the circuit (which has just been done).

$$\Sigma E = \Sigma Ir$$

$$E = Ir + IR_a + IR_3$$

$$6 = 2 + 1\tfrac{1}{3} + 2\tfrac{2}{3}$$

Ammeters and voltmeters

Both of these instruments are based on the moving coil galvanometer (see p. 239) which responds to very small currents.

An ammeter consists of a galvanometer with a shunt resistor to channel off the majority of the current. Note that an ammeter is always used **in series** with a circuit element.

Example What shunt resistor is needed to convert a 1 mA f.s.d. (full scale deflection) meter of resistance 100 Ω into an ammeter to read 1 A f.s.d. (fig. 132i)?

By Ohm's Law, p.d. across meter = $IR = 10^{-3} \times 100 = 0{\cdot}1$ volts.

This p.d. is common to both meter and shunt.

Current through shunt = $1 - 0{\cdot}001 = 0{\cdot}999$ A

$$\therefore \text{Resistance of shunt} = \frac{V}{I} = \frac{0{\cdot}1}{0{\cdot}999} = 0{\cdot}1001\ \Omega$$

A voltmeter consists of a galvanometer with a series resistor to limit the current through the meter. Although a voltmeter measures p.d. it must in fact draw a small current to operate the galvanometer.

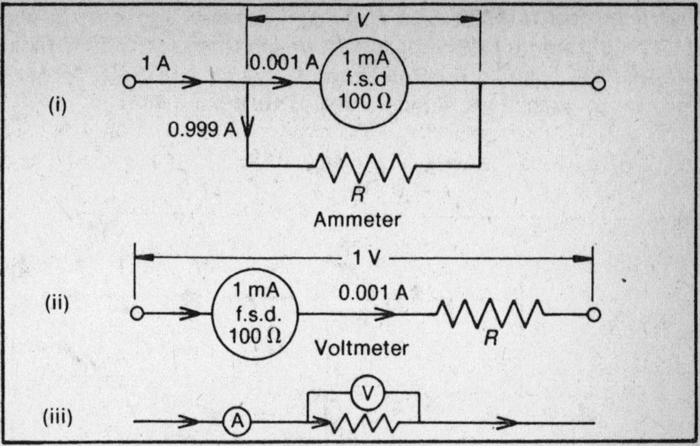

Figure 132. Ammeter and voltmeter

Example What series resistor is needed to convert the same meter into a voltmeter to read 1 volt f.s.d. (fig. 132ii)?

Current through meter = 1 mA

The current is common to both meter and series resistor.

p.d. across meter and series resistor = 1 volt

Resistance of meter and series resistor $= \frac{V}{I} = \frac{1}{10^{-3}} = 1000\ \Omega$

Series resistor = total resistance − meter resistance

$= 1000 - 100$

$= 900\ \Omega$

The resistance of a voltmeter is usually quoted as ohms per volt of f.s.d. For example, for the meter just quoted this would be given by:

$$\frac{\text{total resistance}}{\text{volts f.s.d.}} = \frac{1000}{1} = 1000\ \Omega/\text{V}$$

Note that a voltmeter is always used **across** (or in parallel with) a circuit element. The main current never flows through it (fig. 132iii). Be particularly careful **not** to use loose terminology, for instance, 'the voltage through resistor is . . .'.

The potentiometer

The potentiometer is an accurate method for comparing potential differences. In this sense it is a sort of voltmeter. It depends on passing a steady current through a uniform resistance wire AB to provide a p.d. which is proportional to the length of wire (fig. 133i).

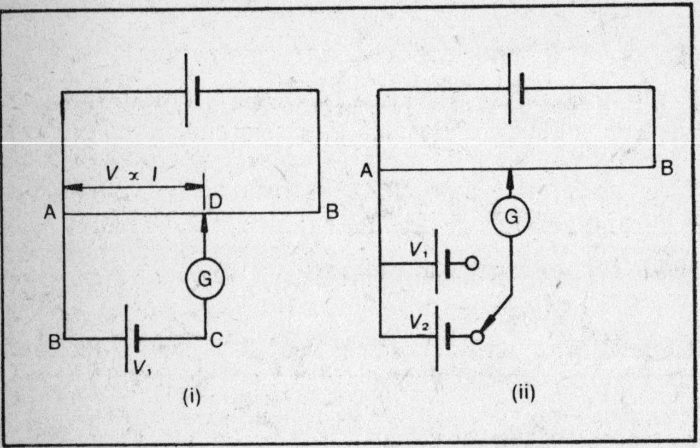

Figure 133. Potentiometer

If the resistance of the wire is $k\ \Omega\ m^{-1}$ then the p.d. across l metres will be given by

$$V = IR = Ikl \qquad \text{i.e. } V \propto l$$

The two p.d.s, V across the wire and V_1 across the unknown cell, will be balanced when the galvanometer reads zero, because then there is no resultant p.d. to cause a current to flow through it round ABCD.

Two unknown p.d.s may be compared by finding the corresponding lengths of the potentiometer wire against which they balance (fig. 133ii).

$$V_1 \propto l_1 \qquad V_2 \propto l_2$$

$$\frac{V_1}{V_2} = \frac{l_1}{l_2}$$

It must be stressed that the sole purpose of the driver cell is to provide a steady current. Its p.d. must, of course, be greater than that of the unknown p.d. under test, but its value need **not** be known. The driver cell is **never** one of the cells under test.

The potentiometer has distinct advantages over ordinary voltmeters:

(i) it draws no current.

(ii) it is far more accurate than dial instruments.

Uses of the potentiometer

(i) **Comparison of two e.m.f.'s** Since the potentiometer draws no current it is possible to compare the e.m.f.s of two cells. This may be done by balancing each in turn against the potentiometer wire. If one cell is a standard cell then the e.m.f. of the other cell may be found accurately (fig. 133ii).

(ii) **Comparison of two resistances** A separate circuit is set up with the two resistances in series supplied by another driver cell *D* (fig. 134i). The current is common to both

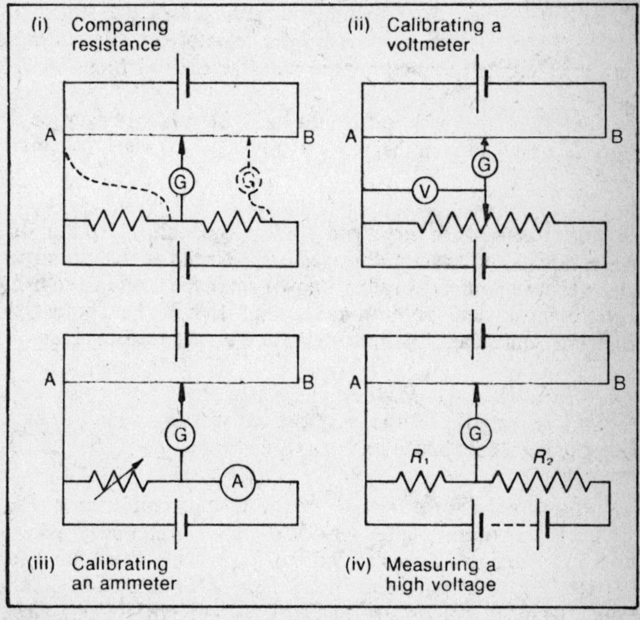

Figure 134. Potentiometer applications

resistors.

$$\frac{l_1}{l_2}=\frac{V_1}{V_2}=\frac{ir_1}{ir_2} \qquad \text{i.e.} \qquad \frac{l_1}{l_2}=\frac{r_1}{r_2}$$

In the following uses the potentiometer is calibrated against a standard cell.

(iii) **Calibration of a voltmeter** Using the circuit of fig. 134ii the p.d. across the voltmeter can be varied. The potentiometer is first calibrated by finding the balance point across a **standard cell** (a cell whose e.m.f. is known very accurately).

Then
$$\frac{V_{\text{voltmeter}}}{V_{\text{cell}}}=\frac{l_{\text{voltmeter}}}{l_{\text{cell}}}$$

(iv) **Calibration of an ammeter** (fig. 134iii). The circuit is similar except for the ammeter which measures the current through a standard resistor whose resistance is accurately known. Again the potentiometer is calibrated with a standard cell, and it is then used to find the p.d. across the standard resistor. Knowing the p.d. across the resistor the current can then be calculated and compared with the dial reading.

The same circuit could be used to measure a low resistance if a large known current is passed through the resistor, since $R = V/I$.

(v) **Measurement of large p.d.** In this application, a potential divider consisting of standard resistors is placed across the large p.d. so that only an accurately known small fraction of the p.d. appears across the potentiometer (fig. 134iv). The potential which is balanced against the potentiometer is therefore given by

$$V=\frac{R_1}{R_1+R_2}V_{\text{HIGH}}$$

The potentiometer is used as in application (i).

(vi) **Measurement of small e.m.f.** In this application the length of the potentiometer wire is effectively increased many times by inserting a series resistance R (which is equivalent to the extra length of wire coiled up) (fig. 135). The standard cell is first balanced against the resistor plus potentiometer wire. By adjusting the variable resistor S a balance point can be found on the wire. If the resistance of R and the wire are known, the p.d. per unit length of the wire can be calculated. The unknown small e.m.f. is then balanced against the wire alone, and hence the e.m.f. can be calculated.

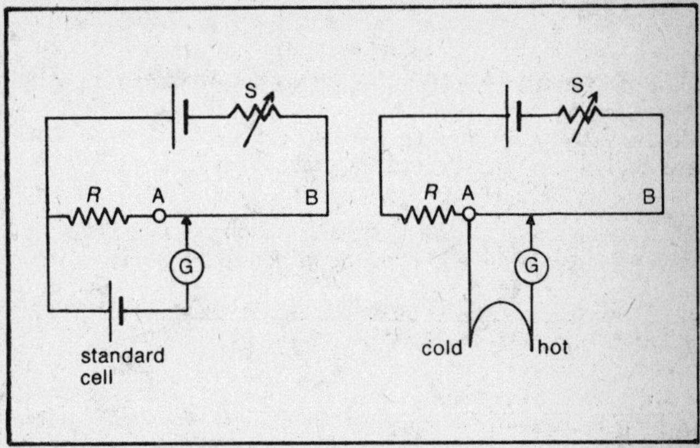

Figure 135. Measurement of small e.m.f.

Example A potentiometer is used to find the internal resistance of a cell and the following results are obtained; e.m.f. of cell E balances 50 centimetres of wire; p.d. across cell V, when a 10 Ω resistor is connected across it, balances 40 centimetres of wire.

$$\frac{E}{V} = \frac{50}{40} \qquad \therefore \quad V = 0{\cdot}8E$$

Now $\quad V = I \times R \quad$ where $R = 10\ \Omega$ load

$$= I \times 10 \quad \text{i.e. } I = V/10$$

Also $\quad V = E - Ir \quad$ within the cell

$$V = E - \frac{Vr}{10}$$

Dividing by V:

$$1 = \frac{E}{V} - \frac{r}{10} \quad \text{but} \quad \frac{E}{V} = \frac{5}{4} \qquad \text{i.e. } 1 = \frac{5}{4} - \frac{r}{10}$$

$$\therefore \quad r = 2\tfrac{1}{2}\ \Omega$$

The Wheatstone bridge

This is a development of the potentiometer idea. If two potentiometers were placed side by side sharing a common driver cell, then there would be a balance when the ratios of lengths of the two potentiometers was the same (fig. 136i). The Wheatstone bridge circuit is identical, except that resistors are used instead of potentiometer wires, and it is usually drawn theoretically as a diamond (fig. 136ii). The bridge is again balanced when the ratio of p.d.s across the two resistor chains is the same.

$$\frac{I_1R_1}{I_1R_2}=\frac{I_2R_3}{I_2R_4}\quad \text{i.e.}\ \frac{R_1}{R_2}=\frac{R_3}{R_4}$$

If R_1, R_2, R_3, are standard resistors then R_4 can be found accurately. Again the e.m.f. of the driver cell is immaterial.

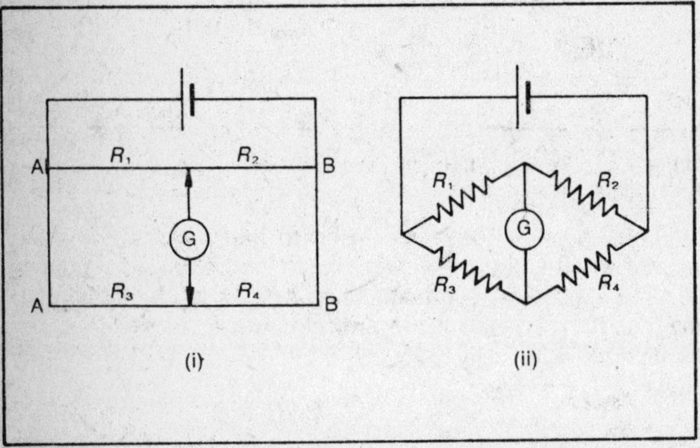

Figure 136. Wheatstone bridge

Power

The power dissipated in a load follows directly from the definition of the volt

$$\text{Volts}=\frac{\text{joules}}{\text{coulombs}}$$

Hence Joules per second = volts × coulombs per second

i.e. Watts = volts × amps

$$P=V\times I$$

But since $V = IR$ this can be rewritten as $P = I^2R$ or $P = V^2/R$.

The total energy dissipated in a circuit element in a time t is therefore given by VIt joules, where V is the p.d. across the element and I is the current through it.

High voltage transmission When power is transmitted through cables some power is dissipated in the resistance of the cables (fig. 137i). The power lost in the cables (and also the drop in useful p.d. across the load at the far end of the cables) can be greatly reduced if the transmission p.d. is raised as high as possible thus reducing the current, since power = $V \times I$.

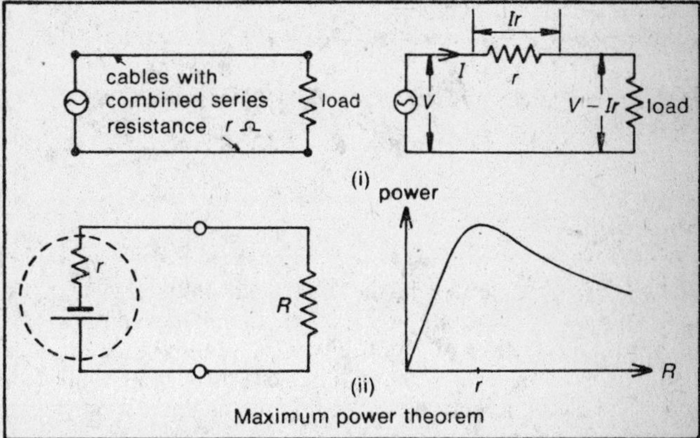

Figure 137. Power

Example If $V = 240$ V, $I = 10$ A, $r = 10\ \Omega$, calculate (i) the drop in p.d., (ii) the p.d. at the far end, and (iii) the power loss in the cables. Recalculate for $V = 2400$ V.

(i) Drop in p.d. $= Ir = 10 \times 10 = 100$ V
p.d. at far end $= 240 - 100 = 140$ V
Power loss $= I^2r = 10^2 \times 10 = 1000$ W

(ii) If p.d. is now 2400 V, current $= \frac{1}{10} \times 10 = 1$ A
(providing the same power at the supply end)
Drop in p.d. $= Ir = 1 \times 10 = 10$ V
p.d. at far end $= 2400 - 10 = 2390$ V
Power loss $= I^2r \times 1^2 \times 10 = 10$ W

Maximum power theorem The power which a generator can deliver is determined by the load, and the generator's internal resistance. The power delivered varies with load, and reaches a maximum when the resistance in the load is equal to the internal resistance of the generator (fig. 137ii). Making the two equal, known as **matching**, is very important in electronics.

Example Find the power and voltage of the brightest lamp which can be run from a 4·5 V battery of internal resistance 2 Ω.

$$\text{Maximum power is when } R = r$$

$$\therefore \text{Lamp resistance} = 2\,\Omega$$

$$\text{Total resistance in circuit} = 4\,\Omega$$

$$\therefore \text{Current} = \frac{V}{R} = \frac{4{\cdot}5}{4} = 1{\cdot}125\text{ A}$$

$$\text{Power of lamp} = I^2R = 1{\cdot}125^2 \times 2 = 2{\cdot}53\text{ W}$$

$$\text{Voltage of lamp} = IR = 1{\cdot}125 \times 2 = 2{\cdot}25\text{ V}$$

Electronics

Electronics is concerned in the main with devices in which a small signal can control a much larger one. These devices are based on conduction of electricity in a semi-conductor, in a vacuum or in a gas, although all but the semi-conductor devices are now largely obselete except for special purposes, e.g. cathode ray tubes.

Thermionic emission

When a metal is heated the kinetic energy of the free electrons is increased and they move faster. If their kinetic energy is large enough they can escape from the metal completely by overcoming the potential barrier caused by the unbalanced positive charges of the protons they leave behind. Electrons are literally 'evaporated' out of the metal. If the temperature is increased, more electrons will acquire the necessary energy and escape. The energy required per electron is the **work function** of the surface and can be reduced by chemical treatments e.g. oxide coatings, so that a surface at only red heat can emit large numbers of electrons. An electrode which produces electrons in this way is called a **cathode** and is usually heated by a low voltage heater inside.

The thermionic diode

A thermionic diode is a device which will allow current to pass in one direction only. It consists of an evacuated envelope containing a cathode which emits electrons, and an anode to collect them. The practical layout of a diode and the theoretical circuit diagram are shown in fig. 138i.

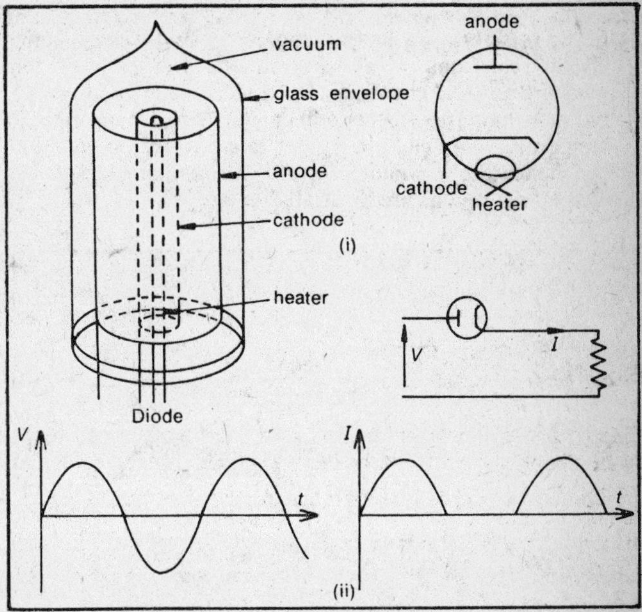

Figure 138. Diode

If an alternating supply is connected to a load via the diode then the current will flow only when the anode is positive. The graph of current against time will therefore be as in fig. 138ii.

The variation of current with p.d. (the characteristic curve) for a diode can be found with a circuit of fig. 139. The curve has two regions.

(i) In the **space charge limited region**, the number of electrons able to leave the cathode is limited by the existence of a **space charge** consisting of electrons in transit to the anode forming a cloud between cathode and anode. The space charge, being negative, will repel electrons back into the cathode if the electric field it produces near the cathode is greater than that of the anode. As the anode is made more positive so more electrons can enter the space between the electrodes (as the electric field produced by the anode increases) and hence the current increases.

(ii) In the **temperature limited region** the anode is collecting all the electrons which the cathode can emit at that temperature, and consequently an increase in anode potential will have no further effect. An increase in cathode temperature will cause a greater rate of electron emission, and hence the maximum current will be increased.

These two regions are illustrated in fig. 139.

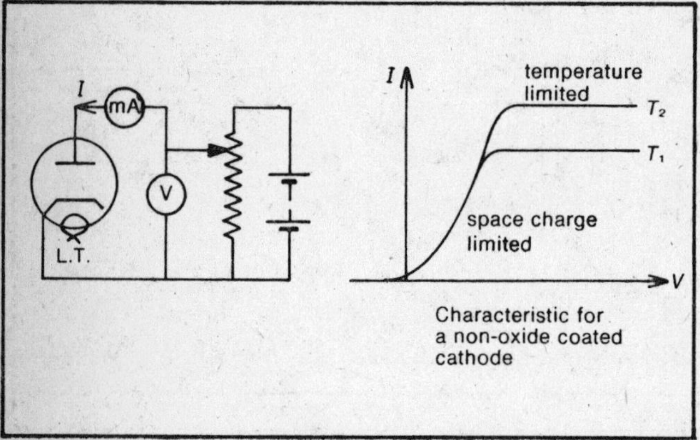

Figure 139. Diode characteristics

Semiconductor diode

If the doping of a crystal of silicon is changed from p-type to n-type during growth a p-n junction is formed. In the junction region the holes and electrons diffuse and combine leaving no charge carriers in the resultant depletion layer (fig. 140). The n-type side of the depletion layer is now positively charged (because of the absence of negative charge carriers) whilst the p-type side is negatively charged. As a result there is an electric field as shown in fig. 140ii and the resultant potential distribution is shown in fig. 140iii. Because of the depletion layer the junction will not normally conduct, but a current will flow if a p.d. greater than the potential hill is applied across the junction (i.e. p-type positive relative to n-type). A p.d. in the reverse direction (i.e. p-type negative) will only widen the depletion layer, and a current will still not flow. The junction thus acts as a diode, only conducting when it is biased in the forward direction.

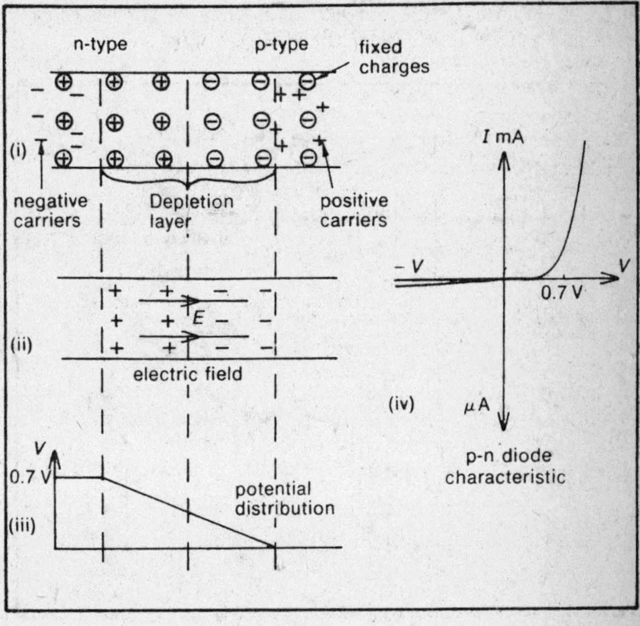

Figure 140. p–n junction diode

In a semiconducting diode, however, there is a small reverse current due to the existence of charge carriers produced, not by doping, but by the normal process of hole-electron pair production by heat, which occurs in intrinsic semiconductors. These charge carriers are known as **minority carriers**. The hole or electrons produced by doping are called the **majority carriers**.

The variation of current with p.d. for a semiconductor diode is shown in fig. 140iv. The vast majority of diodes now in use are of this type.

The transistor

In a semiconductor diode, the current flow depends on the polarity of the applied p.d. In a transistor, however, this current flow can be varied, depending on the presence of a small control current. A transistor consists of two p–n junctions formed back to back in a single crystal (fig. 141i). They can be p–n–p or n–p–n, and are usually made of silicon. The most common form of construction is to evaporate impurity layers on to the surface of a chip of silicon through holes in a silicon oxide layer (fig. 141ii).

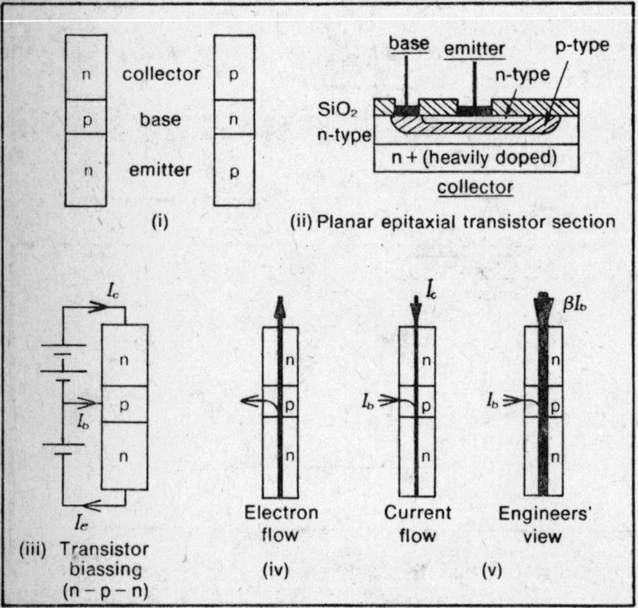

Figure 141. Transistor currents

A n–p–n transistor works in the following way. One p–n junction is forward biased, the other is heavily reverse biased (fig. 141iii). At room temperature some electrons in the first n-type section will have high enough energy to be able to cross the first p–n junction despite the naturally produced reverse field in the depletion layer. Increasing the forward bias increases the number of electrons which are able to cross the junction because the reverse field in the depletion layer has been reduced. The n-type region is known as an **emitter** because it acts as a source of electrons, rather like the cathode in a thermionic diode.

In passing through the p-type material (or **base**) which contains a large number of holes, a few electrons will recombine with holes, but the rest will cross the second p–n junction gaining energy since it is biased to prevent electrons passing in the opposite direction. The second n-type region is therefore known as the **collector**. As holes and electrons recombine in the base region electrons will flow out of the base to maintain the balance of charge (fig. 141iv). Thus the stream of electrons leaving the emitter appears to split – the majority going to the collector, the rest leaving the base.

The equivalent conventional currents are shown in fig. 141v. The ratio between I_b and I_c is nearly constant (typically 1:100) and is called the **current gain** β (fig. 142ii).

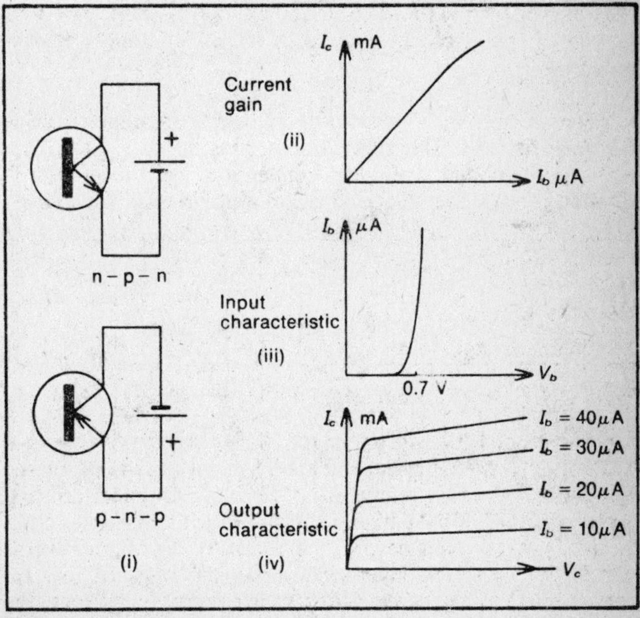

Figure 142. Transistor characteristics

A p–n–p transistor works in the same way except that the charge carriers are holes instead of electrons, i.e. the emitter emits holes. As a result, the current flow and the d.c. supply connection are opposite in the two cases. The symbols for transistors are given in fig. 142i. The arrow, which is always on the emitter, represents the direction of conventional current flow. The supply connections are as shown in fig. 142i.

A transistor's behaviour electrically can be summarized by its characteristic curves. The relationship between I_b and I_c already discussed is linear except at large currents (fig. 142ii).

The **input characteristic** is the variation of I_b with V_b (relative to emitter) and is generally similar to that of a semiconductor diode (fig. 142iii). In particular it can be seen that V_b remains at roughly 0·7 volt for the majority of currents above a certain minimum.

The **output characteristics** are the variation of I_c with V_c (relative to emitter) with I_b as a parameter (since I_c depends on I_b as well as V_c) (fig. 142iv). The effect of variation of V_c is very small and I_c can be seen to be controlled almost entirely by I_b.

A suitable circuit for measuring transistor characteristics is shown in fig. 143. The configuration illustrated is that of the transistor in common emitter connection, i.e. the emitter is common to both the input and the output circuits. The charac-

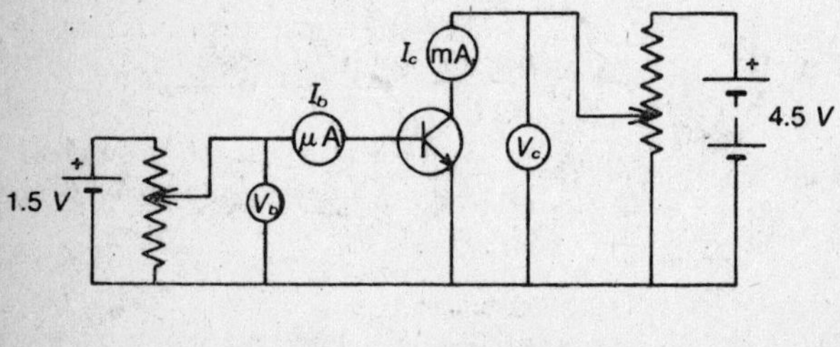

Figure 143. Circuit for transistor characteristics

teristic curves given in figs. 142ii, iii and iv are for a transistor in this connection.

The transistor amplifier An amplifier is a device for reproducing an electrical signal at an increased power. The extra power of the output signal comes from a d.c. supply. Amplifiers can be voltage amplifiers or current amplifiers, but are most commonly a combination of both.

The transistor itself is a linear current amplifier

$$\delta I_c = \beta I_b$$

It can be turned into a linear voltage amplifier for small signals by the addition of resistors (fig. 144i).

When I_c passes through the collector load resistor R_c a p.d. is developed across it.

$$V_{OUT} = V_o - I_c R_c \quad \text{where } V_o = \text{supply p.d.}$$

Hence for a small signal δI_c

$$\delta V_{OUT} = -\delta I_c R_c \quad \text{since } V_o \text{ is constant}$$

$$\delta V_{OUT} = -\beta R_c \delta I_b \quad \text{since } \delta I_c = \beta \delta I_b$$

Thus, the small change in p.d., δV_{OUT}, varies linearly with the small change in base current δI_b.

Now because of the non-linear input characteristic (fig. 142iii) (i.e. the fact that base/emitter 'resistance' $R_{IN} = \dfrac{\delta V_b}{\delta I_b}$ varies with I_b) a change of p.d., δV_b, at the base will not produce a linear change of base current, δI_b. This problem can be overcome by inserting the resistor R_B whose fixed resistance is very much greater than the varying input resistance of the transistor R_{IN} (i.e. swamping the variation in R_{IN}).

Thus $$\delta I_b = \frac{\delta V_{IN}}{R_B + R_{IN}}$$

$$\approx \frac{\delta V_{IN}}{R_B} \quad \text{since } R_{IN} \ll R_B$$

and hence $$\delta I_b = \frac{\delta V_{IN}}{R_B}$$

i.e. δI_b now varies **linearly** with δV_b

Therefore $\delta V_{OUT} = \dfrac{-\beta R_c \delta V_{IN}}{R_B}$ from above

and the voltage gain $\dfrac{\delta V_{OUT}}{\delta V_{IN}} = \dfrac{-\beta R_c}{R_B}$

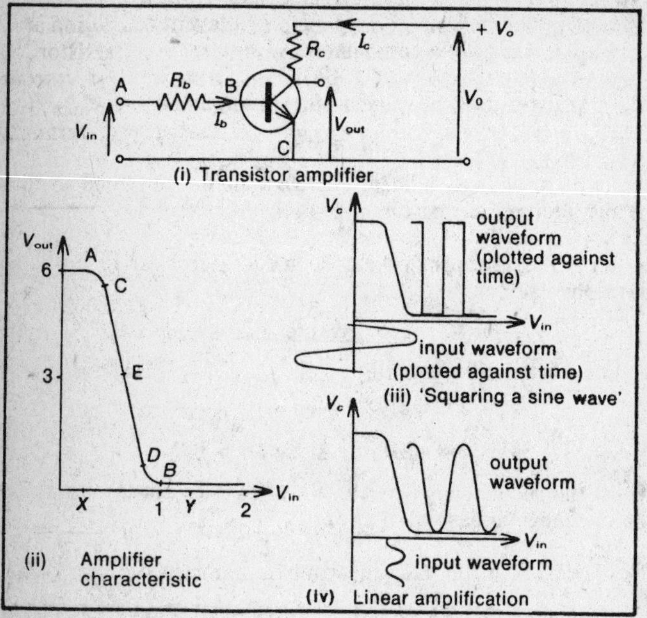

Figure 144. Transistor amplifier

Amplifier characteristics Figure 144ii is a complete plot of the variation of V_{OUT} against V_{IN}. At A, the transistor is not conducting and is said to be **cut off.**

V_{OUT} is therefore the supply p.d. since

$$V_{OUT} = V_o - I_c R_c \quad \text{and} \quad R_c I_c = 0$$

At B, the transistor is carrying the maximum current such that $R_c I_c \approx V_o$ and hence $V_{OUT} \approx 0$ (i.e. resistance from collector to emitter is now very low compared to R_c). The transistor is then said to be **bottomed**. Between A and B is a region in which V_{OUT} changes linearly with V_{IN}. For **linear** voltage amplification, the changes in V_{OUT} and V_{IN} must fall between the limits of linearity *CD.* If they do not fall within these limits, then the waveform being amplified will be **clipped.** This is in fact a good way of making an approximately square waveform from a sinusoidal input (fig. 144iii). For the majority of the time the transistor is either cut off or bottomed.

Biassing To keep a signal centralized in the linear region at *E* it is necessary to apply a bias current to the transistor. A simple way of doing this is to provide a steady bias current I_{BIAS} from the d.c. supply through a bias resistor R_{BIAS} (fig. 145i). In fact more complex methods of biassing are normally used but are beyond the scope of this book.

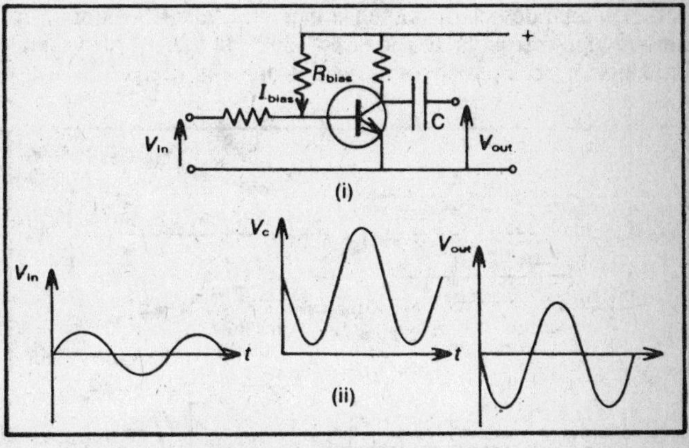

Figure 145. Transistor biassing

The output is normally taken through a capacitor to remove the d.c. component of the collector p.d. so that only alternating changes occur at the output terminals. The voltage waveforms are shown in fig. 145ii.

There is a phase reversal between the input and the output, i.e. the output is in antiphase with the input, and the output decreases as the input increases. This arises since

$$V_{OUT} = V_o - R_c I_c$$

Therefore, as I_c increases (within increasing V_{IN}) V_{OUT} **decreases**. Thus the simple voltage amplifier is also a **phase inverter.**

A transistor can also be used as a **switch** and for this application no bias is applied. If the input p.d. is low (i.e. zero, point X in fig. 144ii) then the transistor is cut off, the output current is low and the output voltage is therefore high, i.e. V_o since there is no potential drop across R_c. If V_{IN} is high (i.e. point Y on fig. 144ii) then the transistor is bottomed, the I_c large and V_{OUT} low, i.e. about zero volts. Thus the transistor switches the current on and off, and the collector p.d. switches from high to low. Transistors are used in this mode in digital circuits with one state representing figure 1 and the other representing figure 0 for handling binary numbers.

The cathode ray tube (CRT)

A thermionic device of immense importance is the cathode ray tube which projects a focussed electron beam of variable intensity on to a phosphor screen at one end (fig. 146i).

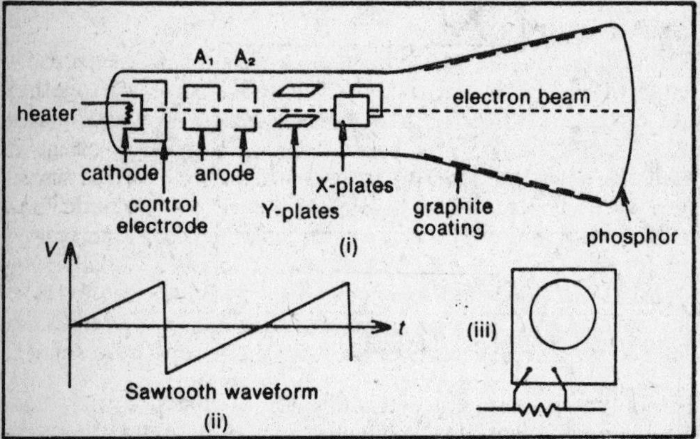

Figure 146. Cathode ray tube

Electrons are emitted by a heated cathode. The electron density in the beam (and hence the spot brightness) can be controlled by the control electrode which is held at a negative, but variable, potential. The electrons are accelerated towards the anode A_1 which has a hole in it to allow the beam through. The anode is at a large positive potential relative to the cathode. Beyond A_1 there is a further electrode A_2 at a different potential in order to focus the beam into a fine spot on the screen. The electrodes A_1 and A_2 are usually referred to as an

electron lens. The whole assembly of cathode and anodes is called an **electron gun**.

The screen is coated with a phosphor which converts the kinetic energy of the electrons into a bright spot of light. After the electrons have given up their energy, they return to the supply via the graphite coating which also serves as an electrostatic screen.

There are two ways in which the beam can be deflected. It can either be done electrostatically (as shown in fig. 146) or magnetically using external transverse fields. In the electrostatic system there are two pairs of plates, one pair to deflect the beam horizontally (X-plates), and the other pair to deflect the beam vertically (Y-plates). Thus the spot can be moved to any point on the screen by the application of suitable potential differences to the X and Y plates.

Cathode ray oscilloscope (CRO)
An oscilloscope is an instrument which enables electrical signals to be examined visually. It incorporates a CRT together with circuits for producing a sweep voltage on the X-plates and an amplified signal on the Y-plates. The sweep voltage is produced by a **time base** – an oscillator whose output waveform is a sawtooth (fig. 146ii) of variable amplitude and frequency. The spot is thus moved steadily across the screen and then flies back almost instantaneously. Usually the brightness of the beam is reduced to zero during the flyback. The waveform of the signal after amplification is applied to the Y-plate, and thus the waveform is displayed across the screen, i.e. the amplitude of the signal is plotted against time.

The CRO can be used for several other purposes.

(i) **As a voltmeter** The Y-amplifier can be calibrated, usually by rotating the gain control to a particular position. Each centimetre on the screen then corresponds to a known applied p.d.

(ii) **As a timer** The X-amplifier on the time base can also be calibrated. The frequency of the time base oscillator can be set to a known figure and X-amplifier can also be calibrated by rotating the X-gain control to the appropriate position. Each centimetre on the screen then corresponds to a known time interval. By measuring the time interval (T) between adjacent peaks of an a.c. waveform, the frequency can be calculated since $f = 1/T$.

Most CROs also have the facility of being able to replace the time base with an external signal, which is then amplified and applied to the X-plates. In this way Lissajous's figures (see p. 125) can be displayed.

Although the oscilloscope responds to potential differences, current waveforms can also be displayed by passing the current through a resistor and then examining the p.d. across it (fig. 146iii).

Key terms

Electric field strength at a point The force per coulomb of positive charge at the point. Units: $V\,m^{-1}$.
Electric potential difference between two points Work done per coulomb of positive charge taken from one point to another. Unit: Volt.
The volt P.D. between two points such that one joule of work is done if a coulomb of positive charge is moved from one to the other.
Electric potential at a point Work done per coulomb of positive charge brought up from infinity to the point.
Equipotential surface A surface over which the potential is the same at all points. It is always normal to field lines.
Coulomb's law The force between two isolated charges is proportional to their product and inversely proportional to the square of the distance between them.
Capacitance Ratio of charge of a conductor to its potential. Unit: Farad.
Dielectric An insulator which increases the capacitance of a capacitor.
Millikan's experiment The only direct method for determining the value of the electronic charge e.
Intrinsic semiconductor Pure germanium or silicon in which conduction occurs because of the production of hole-electron pairs by heat energy.
Extrinsic semiconductor Silicon or germanium to which a trace of group V or group III impurity has been added. Conduction takes place by the holes or electrons due to the impurity added.

Ionized gas A gas in which electron bombardment has produced ions.
Electrolyte A liquid containing positive and negative ions in solution.
Electromotive force The energy given to the complete circuit in electrical form per coulomb passing round it.
Resistance of a resistor Ratio between potential difference across resistor and current through it. Unit: Ohm.
Resistivity Resistance of unit length of unit cross-sectional area of a conductor. Unit: ohm-metre.
Temperature coefficient of resistance Increase in resistance per unit rise in temperature per unit resistance at 0°C.
Internal resistance The resistance of an electrical source.
Potentiometer An accurate method for comparing potential differences in which unknown p.d.s are balanced against the p.d. across a uniform resistance wire carrying a current. It draws no current and is more accurate than dial instruments.
Wheatstone bridge An accurate method for measuring an unknown resistance in which two arms possessing resistance are balanced against each other.
Thermionic emission The emission of electrons by a hot metallic surface.
Thermionic diode A vacuum tube with an anode and a hot cathode, and which allows current to pass in one direction only.
Semiconductor diode A p–n junction which allows current to pass in one direction only.
Transistor A semiconductor device in which a small base current can control a large collector current.
Common emitter connection Connection of the transistor in which the emitter is common to both input and output circuits.
Cathode ray tube A thermionic device in which a focussed electron beam is projected on to a phosphor screen at one end.
Cathode ray oscilloscope An instrument which enables electrical signals to be examined visually.

Chapter 7
Electromagnetism

Magnetic fields

A magnetic field is a region of space in which magnetic effects can be detected. The two main magnetic effects are
(i) a force on a current
(ii) an induced e.m.f. in a conductor when the field in its region changes with time.
Also, forces are exerted on the poles of permanent magnets.

Magnetic flux density (or field strength)

As with gravitational and electric fields the magnetic field strength is measured in terms of the force on a unit detector – in this case a unit current element.

Magnetic flux density (B) is the force per unit length acting on a conductor carrying a current of 1 amp placed perpendicular to the field. This is represented theoretically in fig. 15iii. Practical methods for measuring B are discussed on page 245. The direction of a magnetic field is the direction in which a magnetic north pole would move if placed in the field. The unit of B is the tesla (T).

Magnetic flux lines Physicists and engineers find it easier to visualize a magnetic field in terms of magnetic flux lines. These represent the field in both strength and direction. The flux lines are imagined such that the number of flux lines per unit area over an infinitely small area perpendicular to the flux lines is equal to B (fig. 147i). It can be shown that magnetic flux lines are always continuous loops and patterns of flux lines can be drawn for various current configurations (fig. 147ii).

Earth's magnetic field

The earth has a weak magnetic field which behaves as if the earth contained a magnet. The earth's magnetic poles do not coincide with the geographical poles, and vary their position gradually over the years. The earth's field is not parallel to the surface, but dips towards the north in Britain.

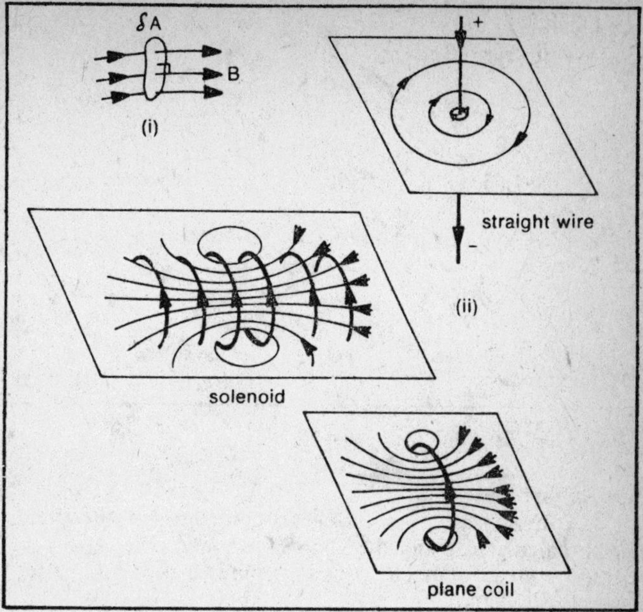

Figure 147. Magnetic fields

Maxwell's corkscrew rule

This rule of thumb gives the direction of the field relative to the current producing it. If the direction of movement of a corkscrew represents the current then the motion of the thumb represents the direction of the field (fig. 148i).

Magnetic fields due to currents

Using the corkscrew rule the fields near certain current configurations can be deduced.

(i) **Long straight wire** The flux lines are concentric circles with the greatest density near the wire (fig. 147).

(ii) **Plane coil** The flux lines are like a doughnut but the density is again greatest near the wire (fig. 147).

(iii) **Long solenoid** The flux lines are uniformly spaced at the centre of a solenoid but the density of lines decreases to half at the ends by progressively 'leaking' through the sides (fig. 147).

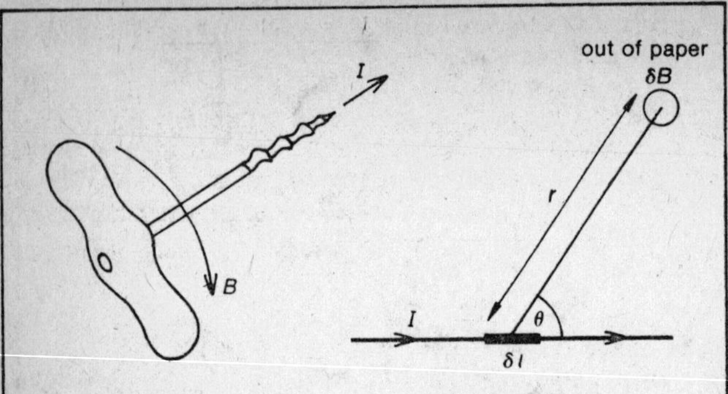

Figure 148. Field due to a current

Biot-Savart law

The flux density at any point near a configuration of currents can be calculated using the Biot-Savart law which gives the field in vacuo a distance r from an infinitesimally small current element of length δl (fig. 148ii).

$$\delta B = \frac{\mu_0}{4\pi} \cdot \frac{I\delta l \sin\theta}{r^2}$$

where μ_0 is a constant called the **permeability of free space** (or **magnetic constant**). Its value is $4\pi \times 10^{-7}\,\mathrm{H\,m^{-1}}$. Using the Biot-Savart law, and performing the necessary integrations, it can be shown that

(i) at a distance r from a long straight wire carrying a current I, in vacuo

$$B = \frac{\mu_0 I}{2\pi r}$$

If I is in amps and r in metres B is in tesla.

(ii) at the centre of a single plane coil of radius r carrying a current I, in vacuo

$$B = \frac{\mu_0 I}{2r}$$

(iii) inside a long solenoid with n **turns per metre** carrying a current I, in vacuo

$$B = \mu_0 n I$$

The length of the solenoid must be many times greater than its diameter for this to be true.

The field at the ends of a long solenoid can readily be deduced by considering the field at the centre to be made up of that due to two solenoids placed end to end at that point. The field at the end of each must therefore be half of the total and is given by

$$B_{end} = \frac{\mu_0 nI}{2}$$

Forces on currents

From the definition of B (p. 232), the force acting on a long straight wire of length L carrying a current I perpendicular to a field of B tesla will be given by

$$F = BIL \text{ newtons}$$

since the length is now L times as long and the current is I times as great.

If the current is not perpendicular to the field, then the force acts only on the component of the conductor's length perpendicular to the field, i.e. $L \sin \theta$ in fig. 149i, where θ is the angle between the conductor and the field, i.e.

$$F = BIL \sin \theta$$

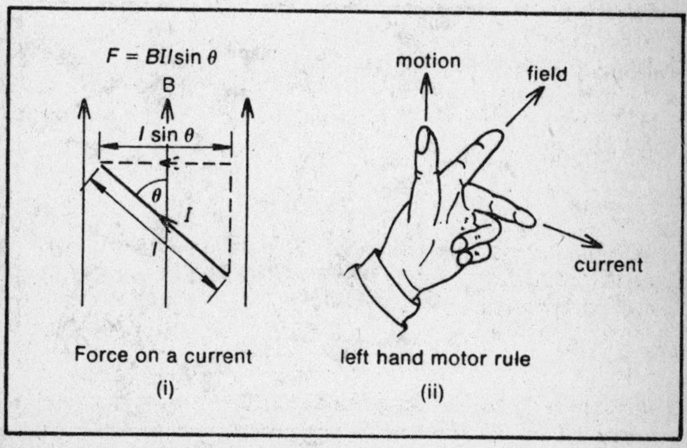

Figure 149. Forces on currents

The left-hand motor rule

This is a rule which gives the direction of the force on a current relative to the direction of the field and the direction of the current. Since the three are mutually perpendicular, they can be represented by the thumb and first two fingers of the left hand as shown in fig. 149ii.

thumb = motion (force)

forefinger = field

second finger = current

Forces between parallel currents

Consider two infinite straight conductors r metres apart in vacuo carrying currents I_1 and I_2 (fig. 150i).

Conductor 2 is in the field of conductor 1 which is given by

$$B_1 = \frac{\mu_0 I_1}{2\pi r}$$

The force on unit length of conductor 2 is therefore given by

$$F = B_1 I_2 L = \frac{\mu_0 I_1}{2\pi r} \times I_2 \times 1 = \frac{\mu_0 I_1 I_2}{2\pi r}$$

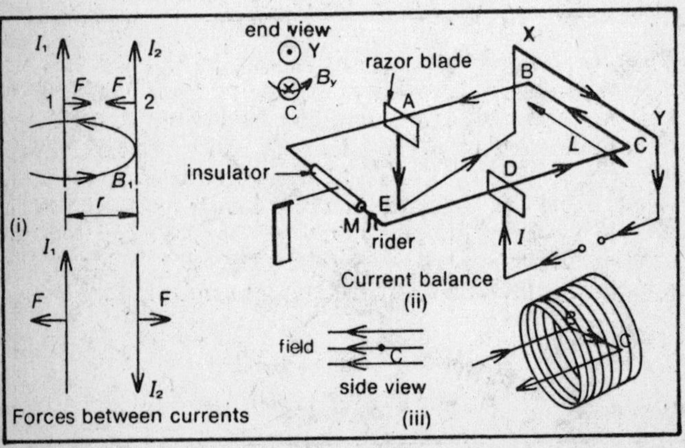

Figure 150. Force between currents

If the two currents are in the same direction then by the left-hand motor rule the force will be one of attraction.

Definition of the ampere

If both currents are equal to 1 amp and the distance between them is 1 metre then

$$F = \frac{\mu_0 I_1 I_2}{2\pi r} = \frac{4\pi \times 10^{-7} \times 1 \times 1}{2\pi \times 1} = 2 \times 10^{-7}\ \text{N}$$

The ampere is defined in terms of this force between currents.

The **ampere** is that constant current which if maintained in two straight parallel conductors, of infinite length and negligible circular cross-section and placed one metre apart in a vacuum, would produce on each of them a force of 2×10^{-7} newtons per metre length.

Current balance

An absolute measurement of current (i.e. not using previously calibrated meters) can be made with a current balance. It consists basically of a sensitive balance to measure the force on a current in a magnetic field. The magnetic field is also produced by the same current.

Since $\quad F = BIL$ and $B \propto I \quad \therefore \quad F \propto I^2$

So if F is measured, and the relationship between B and I is calculated, I can be found.

There are several forms of simple current balance. The simplest is shown in fig. 150ii in which the force between two straight conductors is measured by loading tiny masses (e.g. rider of mass m) on to the other side of the balance. When it balances, $F = mg$ if DC and DE are equal (XY is fixed). In this form of balance it is important to realize that there is no vertical force on the side limbs AB and CD and the only vertical force is that down on BC. The field of XY can be calculated at BC and hence the current can be found.

$$F = BIL = \frac{\mu_0 I \times IL}{2\pi r}$$

$$I^2 = \frac{2\pi r F}{\mu_0 L}$$

Alternatively XY could be replaced by a solenoid (fig. 150iii).

Couple on a rectangular coil

Consider a rectangular coil of sides a and b carrying a current I (fig. 151i). The forces are as shown and constitute a couple as they are equal and opposite.

Force on each vertical limb $\qquad F = BIL = BIa$

Perpendicular distance from axis $d = \frac{b}{2} \cos \theta$

where θ is the angle between the **plane** of the coil and the field.

Moment of couple is given by

$$T = 2Fd = 2BIa \times \frac{b}{2} \cos \theta$$

$$= BIA \cos \theta$$

where A = area of coil (ab).

So for N turns $\qquad T = NBIA \cos \theta$

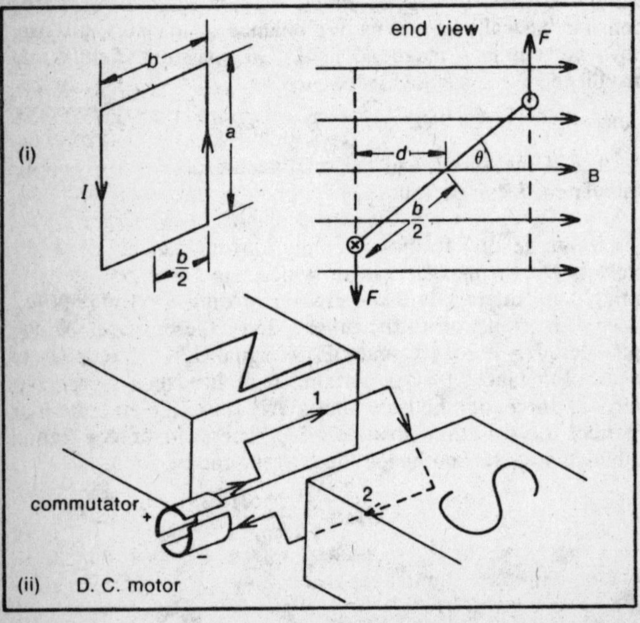

Figure 151. Force on a coil and D.C. motor

Example A narrow solenoid 1 metre long wound with 1000 turns carries a current of 5 amps. A square coil with 3 centimetre sides has 50 turns and is suspended from the middle of the solenoid. If 0·5 amp is passed through the coil, calculate the maximum couple acting on the coil.

$$B = \mu_0 n I = 4\pi \times 10^{-7} \times 10^3 \times 5 = 6{\cdot}28 \text{ m T}$$

Maximum couple is when $\theta = 0°$ (fig. 151i)

$$T = NBIA \cos\theta$$

$$= 50 \times 6{\cdot}28 \times 10^{-3} \times 5 \times 10^{-1} \times (3 \times 10^{-2})^2 \times 1 = 141\ \mu\text{N m}$$

The two following devices utilize the couple on a rectangular coil.

D.C. motor

In this application the coil is allowed to turn continuously (fig. 151ii). When conductor 1 is as shown, it is moving downwards. When it has moved round to the position of conductor 2 it is moving upwards. Applying the left-hand motor rule it can be seen that for the moment acting still to be in the right sense, the current must be reversed. This is achieved by the split-ring commutator which reverses the current each half cycle. In this way the couple on the coil always acts in the same direction. The rotating coil is carried through the vertical change-over position by its inertia. In practice, motors are far more complicated than this, but the basic principles are the same. The back e.m.f. in a motor is discussed on page 254.

Moving coil galvanometer

In this application the coil's motion is opposed by a spring. Since a linear scale is required, the couple must be independent of the angle through which the coil has rotated. This is achieved by using a radial field produced by curved pole pieces in conjunction with a fixed cylindrical soft iron core (fig. 152i). Thus $\theta = 0$ at all positions in the operating region and hence

$$T = NBIA$$

This couple is opposed by the hair springs (through which the current also enters and leaves the coil) (fig. 152ii). The restoring couple is given by

$$T = k\theta$$

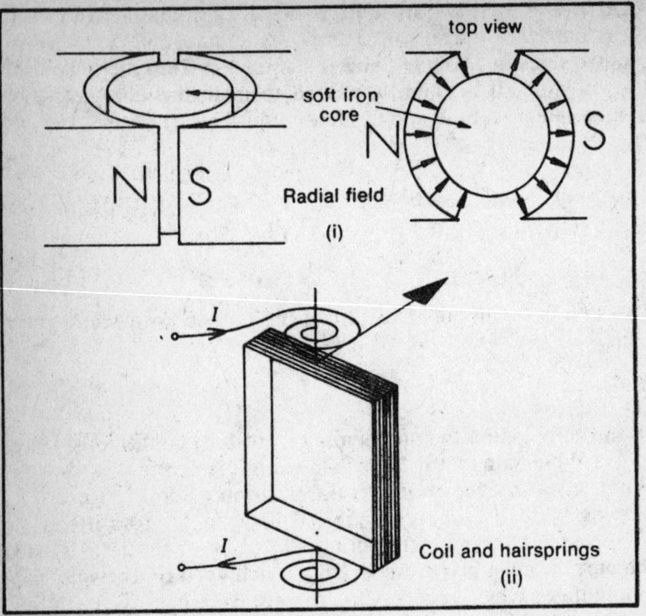

Figure 152. Moving coil galvanometer

where k is the spring constant (couple per radian to rotate the coil against the hair springs).

Therefore $$k\theta = NBAI$$

An important quantity in a galvanometer is the **current sensitivity** which is the angle through which the coil turns per amp. This is given by

$$\frac{\theta}{I} = \frac{NBA}{k}$$

Therefore to make the galvanometer more sensitive, the number of turns, the strength of the field and the area of the coil should be increased, and the spring constant decreased. Sometimes the **voltage sensitivity** is quoted, and this is the angle per volt. If the resistance of the galvanometer is R then since $I = V/R$

$$\frac{\theta}{V} = \frac{NBA}{kR}$$

Forces on moving charges

Consider a wire of cross-sectional area A in a magnetic field of flux density B containing n charges per unit volume of charge q coulombs each. Let them be travelling at v metres per second (fig. 153i). The current is the charge per second passing some point P and this will be the charge contained in the 'slug' of charge which passes P in one second. The length of this 'slug' is therefore v metres.

Volume of 'slug' $= Av$
Number of charges in 'slug' $= Avn$
Charge in 'slug' $= Avnq$
But charge in 'slug' = charge passing P in 1 second = current I
But force acting on a length of wire $= BIL = BAvnqL$
and number of charges in length L $= ALn$

$\therefore$ Force on a single charge $= \dfrac{BAvnqL}{ALn} = Bqv$

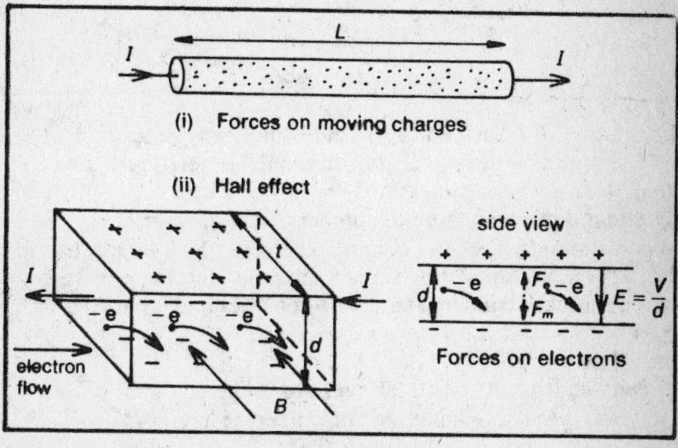

Figure 153. Forces on moving charges

This force is important in the following cases.

Hall effect

When a conductor which is carrying a current is placed in a magnetic field the force acting on the moving charges gives rise to a redistribution of charge and hence a p.d. between opposite faces of the conductor. Consider the configuration in fig. 153ii. The force on moving electrons will act in the direction shown and as a result positive charge will accumulate on the upper surface of the conductor and negative charge will accumulate on the lower surface. Consequently an electric field will come into existence between the two surfaces, and ultimately equilibrium will be established when the magnetic force F_m on the charge equals the electric force F_e acting on it i.e. $F_m = F_e$

But $$E = \frac{V}{d}$$

So $$Bqv = qE = qV/d$$

$$\therefore \quad V = Bvd$$

where V is the potential difference between the two surfaces.

Now since $$I = Avne \quad \text{(see p. 241)}$$

$$v = \frac{I}{neA}$$

but $$A = td$$

$$\therefore \quad V = Bvd = \frac{BId}{netd} = \frac{BI}{net}$$

This is called the **Hall voltage,** and is inversely proportional to the density of charge carriers (since smaller n needs greater v for the same current). The significance of using semiconductors in Hall effect devices is that the number of charge carriers is small and consequently the Hall voltages are very much larger than in metallic conductors. A tiny slab of semiconductor can therefore be used for measuring magnetic flux densities and is called a **Hall probe.**

Rearranging the equation above, for a given slab of semiconductor, *net* is constant, so for a fixed value of I

$$B \propto V_{\text{Hall}}$$

This can be used to compare values of B, or if calibrated, it can measure B. The Hall effect can also be used to determine both the sign of charge carriers, and their density.

Determination of the specific charge of the electron (e/m)

In this experiment an electron beam is deflected by a magnetic field, and the radius of curvature is measured. There are several versions of the apparatus. In the one illustrated in fig. 154 the electron beam in the fine beam tube is deflected through a complete circle by the uniform field produced by Helmholtz coils, and is detected by the glow due to the excitation of molecules in the gas which is at low pressure.

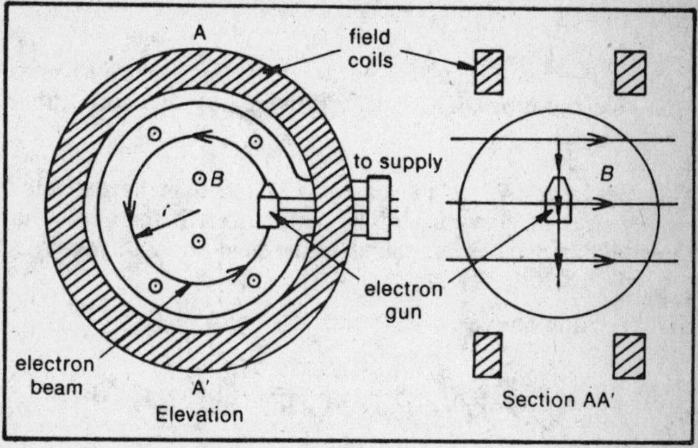

Figure 154. Determination of e/m

e/m is found as follows:
Let accelerating potential be V, velocity of electron be v, flux density be B and radius of electron path be r.

Then, by conservation of energy, as the electron was originally accelerated by p.d. V

$$\text{Electrical energy} = \text{kinetic energy}$$

$$eV = \tfrac{1}{2}mv^2$$

$$v = \sqrt{\frac{2eV}{m}}$$

Since the magnetic force keeps the electron moving in a circle:

$$\text{Magnetic force} = \text{centripetal force}$$

$$Bev = \frac{mv^2}{r}$$

$$v = \frac{Ber}{m} \quad \left(\text{or } r = v\,\frac{m}{eB}\right)$$

Equating these two expressions for velocity:

$$\sqrt{\frac{2eV}{m}} = \frac{Ber}{m} \qquad \text{Squaring:} \quad \frac{2eV}{m} = \frac{B^2e^2r^2}{m^2} \qquad \therefore \frac{e}{m} = \frac{2V}{B^2r^2}$$

and B can be calculated from the current in the coils and their geometry, V, B, and r can all be readily measured. Hence e/m can be found.

Magnetic fields are widely used for deflecting electron beams in cathode ray tubes. The field is provided by two coils either side of the CRT.

Example In a TV set the electron beam must be deflected with a radius of curvature of 10 centimetres. If the accelerating voltage is 3000 volts, calculate the field strength required. ($e/m = 1{\cdot}76 \times 10^{11}$ C kg^{-1}).

From equation above $$B^2r^2 = 2V\frac{m}{e}$$

$$\therefore \; B = \sqrt{\frac{2Vm}{r^2e}} = \sqrt{\frac{2 \times 3 \times 10^3}{0{\cdot}1^2 \times 1{\cdot}76 \times 10^{11}}} = 1{\cdot}85 \times 10^{-3}\,\text{T}$$

The mass spectrometer

The mass spectrometer is an instrument for measuring the atomic masses of elements which can be formed into a beam of ions. It consists basically of an ion source, an electric field to accelerate the ions and a powerful magnetic field to separate them according to specific charge. The whole instrument is under vacuum. One version is illustrated in fig. 155.

The electron gun directs a beam of electrons into the cavity A where the material being examined is introduced as a gas or vapour. Ions are formed by electron bombardment and are drawn toward B by making it slightly negative relative to A. They are then accelerated by the large electric field between B and C (C negative relative to B because the ions are positive). A narrow beam of ions emerges from the slit in C into the magnetic field (out of the paper) which causes the beam to move in a circular path the radius of which depends on the mass of the ions assuming that they are all singly ionized. The magnetic field also has a focusing effect on the ion beam. At the far end of their path in the magnetic field the ions meet a second slit behind which is a collector connected to a sensitive electrometer.

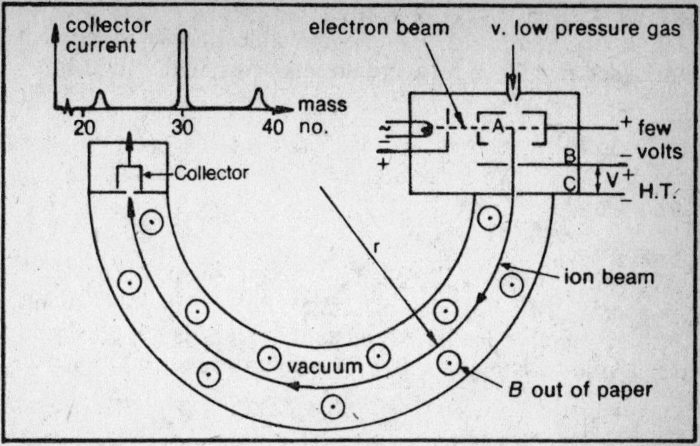

Figure 155. Mass spectrometer (schematic)

The calculation is identical to that for the measurement of e/m. In particular

$$v = \sqrt{\frac{2eV}{m_{\text{Ion}}}}$$

(assuming single ionization, i.e. assuming atoms have lost only a single electron). There is therefore a spread of velocities when the ions leave the accelerating field due to their masses, the heavier ions travelling more slowly than the lighter ions.

As before $$\frac{e}{m_{\text{Ion}}} = \frac{2V}{B^2r^2}$$

Since e is known m_{Ion} can be found. In practice, the position of the collector slit remains fixed, i.e. r is constant. The ion beam can be scanned across the slit to admit ions of different mass by varying either B or V. The mass spectrum can then be displayed using a pen recorder (fig. 155).

Measurement of *B*

There are a number of different methods available for measuring B, some already discussed and some depending on electromagnetic induction.

Current balance
A simple method is to use the movable part of a current balance (see p. 237) to measure an unknown field (fig. 150).

Then $$F = BIL = mg$$

So $$B = \frac{mg}{IL}$$

Hall probe
The Hall effect has already been discussed (see p. 242). A Hall probe consists of a tiny slab of semiconductor suitably mounted with connecting leads. A constant current is supplied and the Hall voltage is measured with a high resistance voltmeter.

Search coil
A search coil is a small coil with many turns. The field near current carrying conductors can be measured with a search coil in two ways:

D.C. method The conductor is connected to a D.C. supply. The search coil is connected to a ballistic galvanometer. The charge induced in the search coil is proportional to the change of flux (p. 252). The search coil is suddenly withdrawn from the field and the throw of the galvanometer is recorded.

Then $$Q \propto B \quad \text{and} \quad \theta \propto Q$$

$$\therefore \quad B \propto \theta \quad \text{i.e.} \frac{B_1}{B_2} = \frac{\theta_1}{\theta_2}$$

The method can be used to compare fields at various points.

A.C. method The conductor is connected to an a.c. supply. As shown on p. 252 the e.m.f. induced in the search coil is proportional to the rate of change of flux, i.e. depends on both the frequency of the supply and B.

The e.m.f. is measured by connecting the coil to a calibrated oscilloscope, and measuring the amplitude of the waveform. For fixed supply frequency $V \propto B$ so amplitude $\propto B$. Again, the method can be used for comparing fields at various points.

Permeability
If an iron rod is placed in a search coil in a magnetic field it is found that the induced e.m.f. can be up to 1000 times greater,

i.e. the value of B is greatly increased. This increase in magnetic flux when a material is present is due to the lining up of the magnetization in the magnetic domains within the material with the applied field. For an infinite solenoid, for instance, the field would no longer be given by

$$B = \mu_0 nI$$

but would be written

$$B = \mu_r \mu_0 nI$$

where μ_r is the factor by which the value of B has been increased and is called the **relative permeability**.

$\mu_r \mu_0$ can be replaced by a single constant μ called the **absolute permeability**, i.e. $\mu = \mu_r \mu_0$.

Ballistic galvanometer

A moving coil galvanometer can also be used to measure charge. In this application the coil is given an impulse by a current flowing for a short time. The impulse gives the coil angular momentum, and hence kinetic energy, and this is transferred to elastic energy in the hair springs at maximum deflection, or throw. This is described as the **ballistic use** of a galvanometer. It can be shown mathematically that

$$\text{throw } (\theta) \propto \text{charge } (Q) \quad \text{provided}$$

(i) the duration of the impulse is very short compared with the period of oscillation of the coil;
(ii) there is no damping.

In practice these conditions are met by
(i) making the period of oscillation of the coil at least two seconds by increasing its mass.
(ii) reducing the damping as far as possible by using an insulating coil former, as a metal former will cause electromagnetic damping according to Lenz's law. A galvanometer specially constructed to have these features is called a **ballistic galvanometer**. The use of the ballistic galvanometer to measure flux density is given on p. 252.

Electromagnetic induction

E.M.F. induced by flux cutting

Consider a conductor of length l being moved with a velocity v

through a uniform magnetic field (fig. 156i) and imagine a single electron within the conductor. As the conductor moves, so the electron moves with it. Because a moving charge is equivalent to a current, the electron will experience a lateral force F_m due to its motion in the magnetic field.

$$F_m = Bev$$

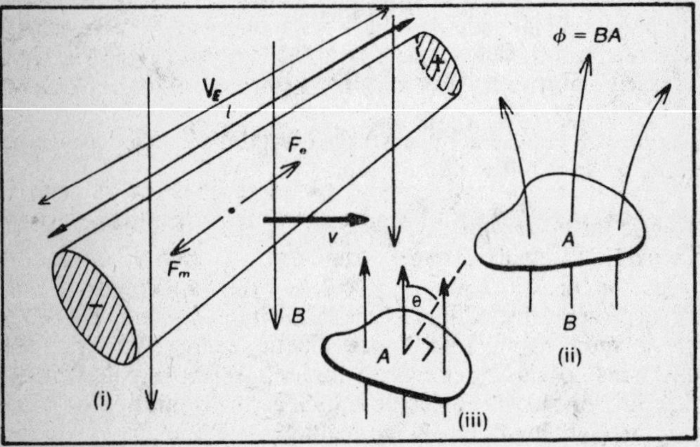

Figure 156. Electromagnetic induction

The direction of the force, given by the left-hand motor rule, will be as shown. Remember that the moving negative electron is equivalent to a conventional current moving in the **opposite** direction to that of the electron. This force will cause electrons to collect at one end of the conductor, and therefore one end will be charged negatively and the other positively as shown. There will now be an electric field between the two charges. This field E will produce an electric force F_e on the electron as shown, the negative end repelling the electrons.

$$F_e = eE$$

But $E = \frac{V_E}{l}$ where V_E = e.m.f. across the ends of the wire

$$\therefore \quad F_e = \frac{eV_E}{l}$$

The redistribution of the electrons continues until equilibrium is set up and then the two forces on an electron are equal and opposite, i.e.

$$F_m = F_e$$

$$Bev = \frac{eV_E}{l}$$

So the e.m.f. $$V_E = Blv$$

Example An aircraft of wingspan 20 metres flies at 300 m s^{-1}. Calculate the induced e.m.f. between its wing tips if the vertical component of the earth's field is 4×10^{-5} T. Could this e.m.f. be measured and used to calculate the aircraft's ground speed?

$$V = Blv = 4 \times 10^{-5} \times 20 \times 300 = 240 \text{ mV}$$

No, an equal e.m.f. in the same direction would be induced in the wires to the meter. There would therefore be no net e.m.f. round the circuit and no current flow.

Now the **magnetic flux** ϕ linking a circuit normally is defined as the product of magnetic flux density (B) and the area of the circuit (A) (fig. 156ii). It can be thought of as the total number of magnetic flux lines linking the circuit.

Thus $$\phi = BA$$

The unit is the Weber (Wb). If the normal to the plane of the circuit is at an angle θ to the flux, this becomes $\phi = BA \cos \theta$ (fig. 156iii).

Now the area swept out per second = lv

Hence Blv = the flux cut per second

i.e. induced e.m.f. = rate of cutting flux, i.e. $V = \frac{d\phi}{dt}$

This can be looked at in another way. Consider the movable conductor to be a sliding side of a circuit (fig. 157i). As the side moves an e.m.f. is generated across the ends of the circuit. The circuit now encloses a quantity of flux, and the effect of the movement of the sliding side is to change the flux linkage by changing the area of the circuit. It would therefore be true to say

induced e.m.f. = rate of change of flux linkage

Since $\phi = BA$, an obvious extension is to ask whether the rate of change of flux linkage can be due to changing B instead of changing A.

$$\frac{d\phi}{dt} = B\frac{dA}{dt} \text{ but does } \frac{d\phi}{dt} = A\frac{dB}{dt}?$$

Experiment does indeed show this to be the case and the operation of a transformer depends on it. Figure 157i, ii illustrates this difference. The first case is definitely flux cutting but can be looked upon as changing flux linkage as well. The second case can only be regarded as changing flux linkage.

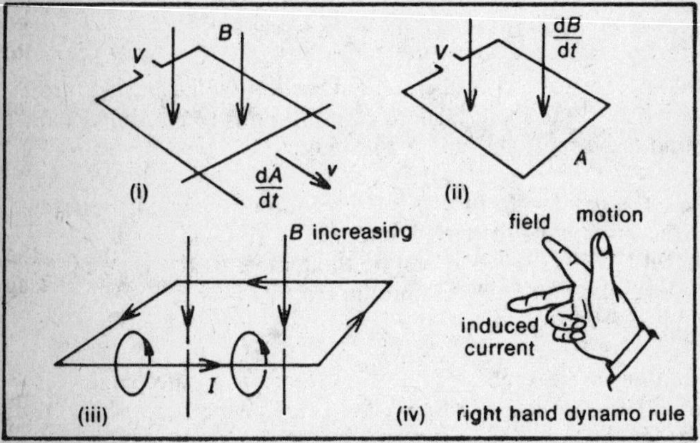

Figure 157. Faraday's and Lenz's laws

Faraday's law summarizes this, and states that induced e.m.f. is proportional to the rate of change of magnetic flux linking the circuit, or rate of cutting lines of flux, i.e.

$$V_E = \frac{d\phi}{dt}$$

Example A metal disc of radius 10 centimetres is rotated at 1000 r.p.m. in a magnetic field of 0·2 T. What e.m.f. is induced between the centre and its rim?

$$V = -\frac{d\phi}{dt} = \text{area swept out} \times B \times \text{no. of revolutions per second}$$

$$= \pi r^2 Bn = \pi(10^{-1})^2 \times 2 \times 10^{-1} \times \frac{1000}{60} = 105 \text{ mV}$$

Lenz's law

The direction of the induced e.m.f. can be deduced from the direction of the force on the electrons in the wire as discussed above. But it is easier to use a version of the law of conservation of energy known as Lenz's law. **Lenz's law** states that the direction of the induced e.m.f. is such that any current it produces will oppose the change to which it is due. As an example of the use of this, consider the case above. As the conductor is moved increasing the circuit size, and hence the flux linked, the current induced in the circuit will itself produce a field. By Lenz's law the flux produced by this current will oppose the increase in flux linkage caused by the moving conductor, i.e. it will be in the opposite direction. The direction of the induced current which produces this opposite flux can thus be deduced by the corkscrew rule (fig. 157iii).

Lenz's law and Faraday's law are normally combined in **Neumann's law** which states

$$V = -\frac{d\phi}{dt}$$

In the case where there are many turns, ϕ is, of course, the total flux linking the circuit, i.e. number of turns × flux linking a single turn.

Example A heart pacing device consists of a coil of 50 turns and radius 1 millimetre just inside the body, with a coil of 1000 turns and radius 2 centimetres placed concentrically just outside the body. Calculate the induced e.m.f. in the internal coil if a current of 1 amp in the external coil collapses in 10^{-2} second.

For internal coil $$V_2 = -\frac{d\phi}{dt} = N_2A_2\frac{dB_1}{dt}$$ where B_1 = flux density due to external coil

For external coil $$B_1 = \frac{\mu_0 N_1 I}{2r_1}$$

$$= \frac{4\pi \times 10^{-7} \times 10^3 \times I}{2 \times 2 \times 10^{-2}} = \pi \times 10^{-2} \times I\,\mathrm{T}$$

$$\therefore \quad \frac{dB_1}{dt} = \pi \times 10^{-2} \times \frac{dI}{dt} = \pi \times 10^{-2} \times \frac{1}{10^{-2}} = \pi\ \mathrm{T\,s^{-1}}$$

For internal coil $V_2 = N_2A_2\frac{dB_1}{dt} = 50 \times \pi \times (10^{-3})^2 \times \pi = 493\ \mu V$

Right-hand dynamo rule

This is an easy rule of thumb for the determination of the direction of the induced current in a situation where the moving wire is cutting flux (fig. 157iv). Here

thumb = motion of the wire.

forefinger = magnetic field.

second finger = induced current.

Coil in an alternating magnetic field

If a coil of area A with N turns is placed in an alternating field of amplitude B_0, and frequency $\omega/2\pi$, an alternating e.m.f. will be induced across its ends.

$$V = \frac{d\phi}{dt}$$

But $\phi = BAN$ and $B = B_0 \sin \omega t$

$$\therefore \quad V = \frac{d}{dt}(ANB_0 \sin \omega t)$$

$$= ANB_0\omega \cos \omega t$$

$$V = V_0 \cos \omega t$$

where the amplitude $V_0 = ANB_0\omega$.

Search coil for measurement of *B*

D.C. method The flux density of a magnetic field can be measured by placing a search coil in the field and then suddenly moving it away to where the field is negligible. The coil is connected to a ballistic galvanometer. Let R = total resistance in the circuit (coil + galvanometer), I = current and Q = total charge which passes.

Now $V = \frac{d\phi}{dt}$

But $V = IR$ and $I = -\frac{dQ}{dt}$

$$\therefore \quad \frac{dQ}{dt}R = -\frac{d\phi}{dt} \quad \text{i.e.} \quad R\,dQ = -d\phi$$

Integrating to find the total charge which has flowed from ϕ at $t = 0$ to $\phi = 0$ at $t = t$

$$\int_0^Q \mathrm{d}Q = -\frac{1}{R}\int_\phi^0 \mathrm{d}\phi$$

$$Q = \frac{\phi}{R}$$

But $$\phi = BAN$$

$$\therefore \quad Q = \frac{BAN}{R} \quad \text{i.e. } B = \frac{RQ}{AN}$$

Q can be found from the throw of the galvanometer. Hence B can be calculated.

A.C. method In this case, the conductors producing the field are connected to an a.c. supply and the field consequently alternates. The search coil does not need to be moved to produce an e.m.f. across its ends. It is connected to a calibrated oscilloscope.

Amplitude of induced e.m.f. = $ANB_0\omega$ from which B_0 can be found (p. 252).

The simple dynamo

Consider a single coil of area A rotating with angular velocity ω in a uniform field B (fig. 158i). The area linked by the flux at any angle θ between the plane of the coil and the lines of flux is $A\sin\theta$.

$\therefore$ Total flux linked, ϕ, is given by

$$\phi = NBA \sin\theta$$

But $\theta = \omega t$ $$\therefore \quad \phi = NAB \sin \omega t$$

$$V = \frac{\mathrm{d}\phi}{\mathrm{d}t} = NAB\omega \cos \omega t$$

$$= V_0 \cos \omega t$$

where $$V_0 = NAB\omega$$

Thus the e.m.f. between the ends AB of the coil varies with time as shown in fig. 158ii between the limits $\pm NBA\omega$ when $\cos \omega t = \pm 1$. Note that the e.m.f. is a maximum when $t = 0$, i.e. when the rate of cutting flux is greatest (i.e. coil is horizontal between magnetic poles).

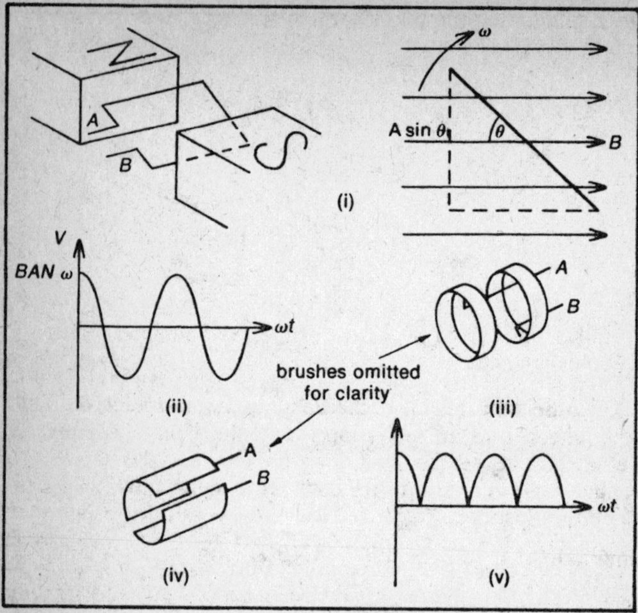

Figure 158. Simple dynamo

In an **a.c. dynamo** the ends of the coil are connected to the outside circuit via slip-rings (fig. 158iii) so that the output is as shown in fig. 158ii.

In a **d.c. dynamo** the connection is via a split-ring commutator (fig. 158iv) so that the direction of the current from the coil is reversed twice per revolution giving the output shown in fig. 158v. This waveform is more correctly described as uni-directional (but pulsating) but with a greater number of coils and a more complex commutator the output can be made very nearly smooth or steady d.c.

Back e.m.f. in motors

A simple d.c. motor and a simple d.c. dynamo are identical in construction. Hence, since the motor armature is rotating, an e.m.f. is induced in it which, by Lenz's law, must be a back e.m.f. (i.e. opposing the current causing rotation). The back e.m.f. is usually large, e.g. 80% to 90% of the applied e.m.f. and the current is driven through the armature resistance R by

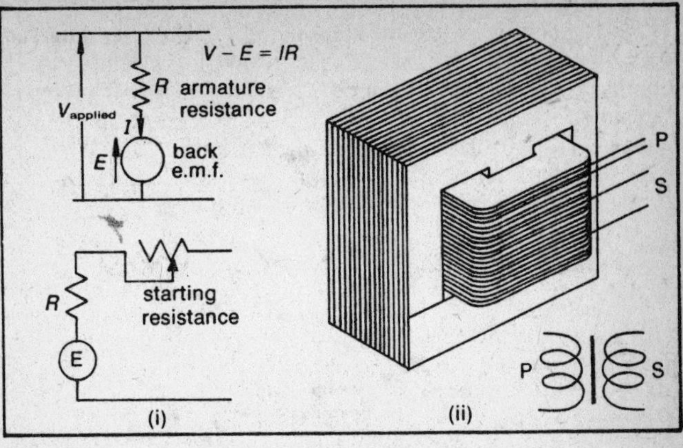

Figure 159. Motor back e.m.f. and transformer

the difference between the applied voltage and the back e.m.f. (fig. 159i). Stalling a motor, or starting it from rest, may result in an excessive current which could burn out the windings, so a series starter resistance may be used to limit the starting current to a safer value (fig. 159ii). The starting resistance is progressively removed once the armature starts rotating.

Example A d.c. motor working from 240 volt mains has an armature resistance of 2 Ω and draws a current when rotating at full speed of 10 amps. (i) What is the back e.m.f. when it is rotating (ii) what current would it draw if it were stalled (iii) what would be a suitable maximum value of a starter resistor?

(i) Volts drop across armature resistance $= IR$

$$= 10 \times 2 = 20 \text{ V}$$

$$\therefore \quad \text{Back e.m.f.} = 240 - 20 = 220 \text{ V}$$

(ii) Current in armature when stalled, $\frac{V}{R} = \frac{240}{2} = 120$ A

(iii) A suitable starter resistor would drop the 220 V, instead of the back e.m.f., when it is at rest

$$\therefore \quad R = \frac{V}{I} = \frac{220}{10} = 22\ \Omega$$

The transformer

A transformer is a device for stepping up or stepping down an alternating voltage. It consists of two coils, a primary and a secondary wound on the same core (fig. 159ii). The usual arrangement is to wind both coils on a centre limb. The primary current causes an alternating flux in the core. If all the flux passes through both coils, then the e.m.f. induced in the primary and secondary coils will be given by

$$\text{Primary} \quad V_p = n_p \frac{d\phi}{dt} \qquad \text{Secondary} \quad V_s = n_s \frac{d\phi}{dt}$$

Thus

$$\frac{V_s}{V_p} = \frac{n_s \dfrac{d\phi}{dt}}{n_p \dfrac{d\phi}{dt}} = \frac{n_s}{n_p}$$

i.e. the ratio of the e.m.f. δ is the same as the turns ratio n_s/n_p.

The primary e.m.f. will approximately equal the applied voltage as the primary current and hence the flux will increase until the two are nearly equal. (The two are not exactly equal because of the resistance of the primary coil.)

When the secondary is connected to a load, the primary current increases. If the transformer is 100% efficient then the power into the transformer will equal the power out, i.e.

$$V_p I_p = V_s I_s$$

$$\frac{I_s}{I_p} = \frac{V_p}{V_s} = \frac{n_p}{n_s}$$

The ratio of the currents is thus the reciprocal of the turns ratio.

In practice these relationships are approximate. The flux linkage is not quite perfect, and because of electromagnetic losses in the core and heat losses in the resistance of the windings, most transformers are only about 98% efficient. To reduce the eddy current losses transformer cores are laminated as shown in fig. 159ii.

Example A transformer of turns ratio 300 : 1 and 98% efficiency is used to transform the output of a generator of 5 MW at 440 volts to a higher voltage for transmission. Calculate (i) the transmission voltage (ii) the power delivered by the transformer (iii) the current into and out of the transformer.

(i) $V_2 = \frac{n_2}{n_1} V_1$

$= 300 \times 440$

$= 132\,000$ V

(ii) Power out $=$ efficiency $\times$ power in

$= 0.98 \times 5 \times 10^6$

$= 4.9$ MW

(iii) Current out $= \frac{P}{V} = \frac{4.9 \times 10^6}{1.32 \times 10^5} = 37.1$ A

Current in $= \frac{P}{V} = \frac{5 \times 10^6}{440} = 11\,364$ A

Note that the currents are not related by the turns ratio because the transformer is not 100% efficient.

Self Inductance

Consider a coil with an increasing current flowing through it (fig. 160i). The current will cause a magnetic flux to link the coil, and this changing flux will in its turn induce an e.m.f. in the coil. By Lenz's law, this e.m.f. will be such as to oppose the change to which it is due, i.e. it will oppose the increasing current, and will therefore be in the direction shown.

There is a relationship between this induced e.m.f. and the rate of change of current causing it, which will depend on the geometry of the coil.

i.e. $$E \propto -\frac{dI}{dt}$$

(because E and δI are acting in opposite directions round the circuit)

or $$E = -L\frac{dI}{dt}$$

where L is called the **self inductance** of the coil.

The unit of inductance is the henry.

Since
$$L = \frac{E}{\frac{dI}{dt}}$$

1 henry is an inductance such that an e.m.f. of 1 volt is induced by a rate of change of current of 1 amp per second.

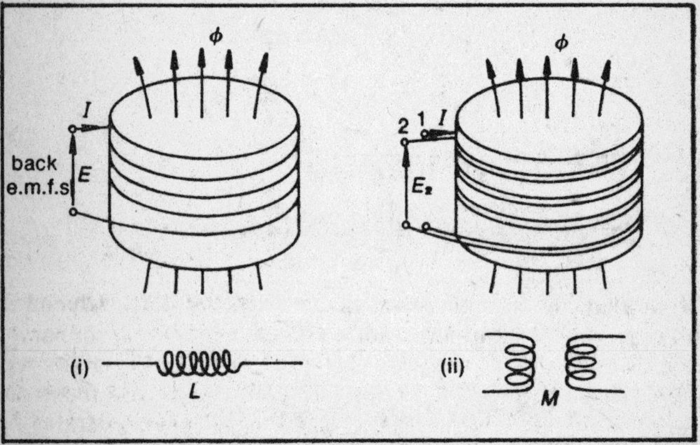

Figure 160. Self and mutual induction

Mutual Inductance

Now consider two coils wound on the same former (fig. 160ii). The current I in coil 1 produces a magnetic flux ϕ which links both coils. The flux linking the secondary will be changing and hence an induced e.m.f. will appear across its ends. If the coils are wound in the same direction and the flux links both coils the e.m.f. in coil 2 will be in the direction shown, by the argument given in the previous section. There is a relationship which depends on the geometry of the coil between this induced e.m.f. and the rate of change of current causing it.

$$E_2 \propto \frac{dI_1}{dt}$$

or
$$E_2 = M\frac{dI_1}{dt}$$

where M is the mutual inductance of the coil. The unit is again the henry.

Energy stored in an inductance

Energy is stored in the magnetic field of an inductance. This energy is calculated by summing the work done by the current against the back e.m.f. as the current rises in the coil from 0 to I. The instantaneous power is EI. Now energy is given by

$$dW = EI\,dt \qquad \text{but } E = L\frac{dI}{dt}$$

$$\therefore \quad dW = LI\frac{dI}{dt}dt = LI\,dI$$

$$\therefore \quad \int_0^W dW = \int_0^I LI\,dI$$

$$W = \tfrac{1}{2}LI^2$$

(compare with $W = \tfrac{1}{2}CV^2$ for a capacitor).

Eddy currents

If a magnetic field is changing, an e.m.f. will be induced in any conductor in the field, whether it is a separate wire, or part of a larger piece of solid metal (fig. 161i). Resultant currents will flow round all possible loops within the metal, and these are called **eddy currents**. Their existence can be demonstrated by the quite rapid electromagnetic braking of a thick copper plate swinging between the poles of a powerful magnet, or a copper cylinder spinning between the poles (fig. 161ii, iii). If the copper

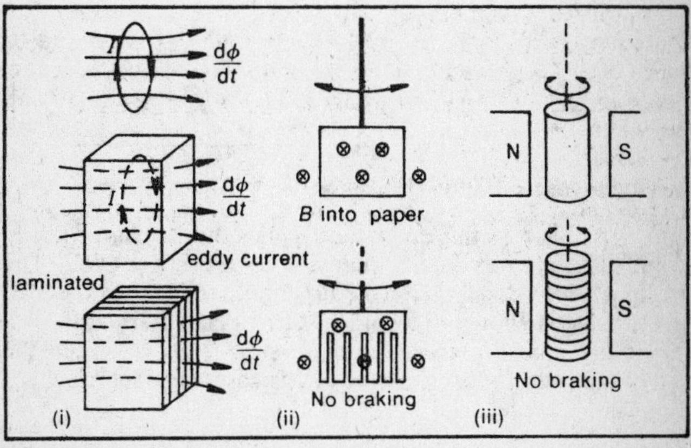

Figure 161. Eddy currents

plate has slots cut as shown, or if the copper cylinder is replaced by a pile of insulated coins, the eddy currents are very substantially reduced, and the braking becomes negligible. Eddy currents in transformer cores, and in motor and dynamo armatures can also be reduced substantially by laminating (fig. 161i).

Time varying currents

This section concerns currents which are either transient (short term variations) or continuously varying (a.c.).

Discharge of a capacitor

When a charged capacitor is connected to a resistor (fig. 162i) the current which flows will depend on the p.d. across the capacitor ($I = V/R$).

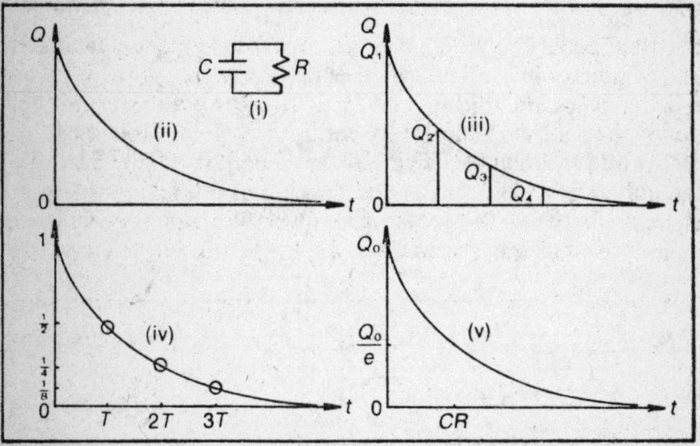

Figure 162. Exponential decay

But the p.d. across the capacitor depends on the charge left in it, and this changes as the charge decreases ($V = Q/C$). The resultant plot of charge, p.d., or current (since $Q \propto V \propto I$) against time is shown in fig. 162ii. This is called an **exponential decay** and it is common in physics. It occurs when the rate of change of a quantity (Q in this case) is proportional to the quantity present, i.e.

$$\frac{dQ}{dt} = -kQ$$

the minus sign indicating a decay, i.e. decreasing Q.

An important property of an exponential decay is that the ratio of the quantities present at the beginning and end of equal time intervals is always the same (fig. 162iii)

$$\frac{Q_1}{Q_2} = \frac{Q_2}{Q_3} = \frac{Q_3}{Q_4} \quad \text{etc.}$$

If this ratio is made equal to half, then an exponential curve is easy to construct (fig. 162iv), i.e. the value of Q halves after equal time intervals.

In capacitative decay a more convenient ratio is e (=2·718). The time interval T for the quantity to decay to $1/e$ of the original quantity is called the **time constant** and $T = CR$ where T is in seconds, C is in farads and R is in ohms (fig. 162v). The time constant is a useful measure of the response of an RC circuit. Mathematically:

$$I = -\frac{dQ}{dt}$$

(the minus sign indicating charge decreasing with time.)

$$I = \frac{V}{R} \quad \text{and} \quad V = \frac{Q}{C}$$

Combining these:

$$\frac{dQ}{dt} = -\frac{V}{R} = -\frac{Q}{CR}$$

Rearranging and integrating:

$$\int_0^t dt = -CR \int_{Q_0}^{Q} \frac{dQ}{Q}$$

since $Q = Q_0$ when $t = 0$, and $Q = Q$ when $t = t$

$$[t]_0^t = -CR[\ln Q]_{Q_0}^{Q}$$

$$t = -CR \ln \frac{Q}{Q_0}$$

$$\ln \frac{Q}{Q_0} = -\frac{t}{CR} \qquad \therefore \quad \frac{Q}{Q_0} = e^{-t/CR}$$

$$Q = Q_0 e^{-t/CR}$$

Also, since $$V = \frac{Q}{C}$$

$$V = V_0 e^{-t/CR}$$

After a time interval $t = CR$, $Q = Q_0 e^{-1} = \frac{Q_0}{e}$

i.e. the value of Q is reduced to $1/e$ of its original value after a time CR (fig. 162v).

Example In a reed switch experiment a 50 μF capacitor discharges through a 100 Ω resistor. If the frequency of the reed switch is 100 Hz, does the capacitor discharge completely each cycle?

$$CR = 50 \times 10^{-6} \times 10^2 = 5 \times 10^{-3} \text{ sec}$$

After 5×10^{-3} sec it has discharged to $\frac{V}{e}$

After 10×10^{-3} sec it has discharged to $\frac{V}{e^2} = \frac{V}{7{\cdot}4}$

i.e. 13·5% of its initial value. It is therefore not discharged sufficiently.

Charging a capacitor

If a capacitor is connected through a resistor to a source of steady e.m.f., the current which flows will depend on the p.d. across the resistor. This p.d. is the difference between the steady e.m.f. E and the changing p.d. across the capacitor V.

Initially, when the capacitor is uncharged V will equal zero (since $V = Q/C$) and the charging current will therefore be E/R. After a time when the capacitor is fully charged, V will equal E, the p.d. across the resistor will be zero and the charging current will be zero. The resultant graph of p.d. across the capacitor (or charge) plotted against time is shown in fig. 163.

Mathematically $E = V + IR$ at any time

$$I = \frac{E - V}{R}, \quad V = \frac{Q}{C} \quad \text{and} \quad I = \frac{dQ}{dt}$$

$$\therefore \quad \frac{dQ}{dt} = \frac{E}{R} - \frac{Q}{CR}$$

The solution of this differential equation is

$$Q = EC(1 - e^{-t/CR})$$

or since $V = Q/C$ $\quad V = E(1 - e^{-t/CR})$

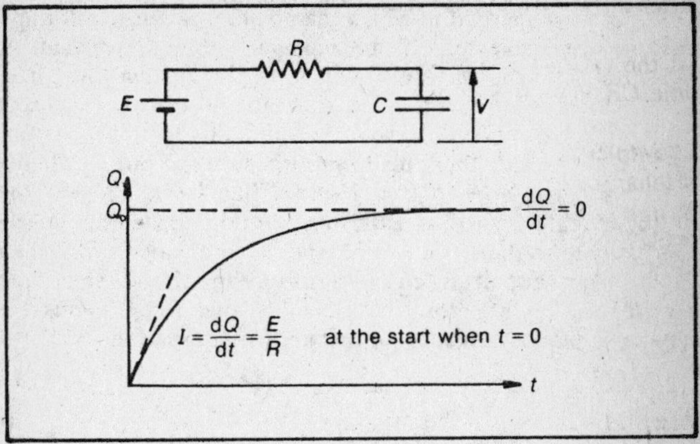

Figure 163. Charging a capacitor

Circuits involving capacitative decay

Consider the circuit of fig. 164i. Depending on the time constant relative to the period of a square wave applied to it,

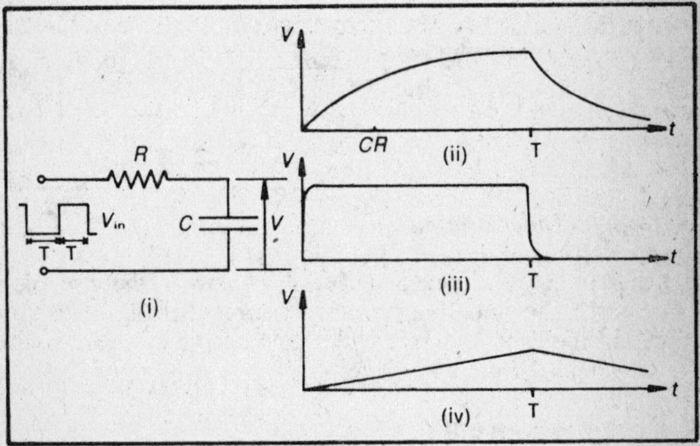

Figure 164. Integrating circuit

the response of the circuit can vary widely. Let T be the half period of the square wave. If $CR \gg T$ the circuit is an **integrating circuit** since the waveform is that of the integral of the square wave i.e. the sum of the area beneath it (fig. 164iv). If $CR \ll T$ the square waveform is hardly affected (fig. 164iii). Consider now a circuit in which the position of the resistor and capacitor are reversed. If the voltage across the resistor is measured, then the waveform will be that of the current (since $V = IR$). From the section on capacitative discharge this is initially E/R and falls to zero after a time. If the time constant CR is short enough then the output is a series of pulses when a square wave is applied (fig. 165iii). Thus when $CR \ll T$ the circuit is called a **differentiating circuit**, since the pulses approximate to the slope of the input square waveform. When $CR \gg T$ the circuit is called a **coupling circuit** since the output is a faithful copy of the input (fig. 165iv). Thus the capacitor, whilst transmitting the a.c. waveform, blocks d.c.

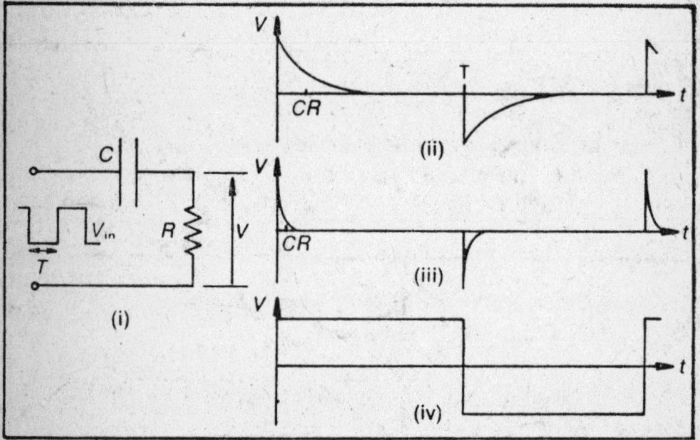

Figure 165. Differentiating circuit

Another example of capacitative discharge is the use of a capacitor in the smoothing circuit for a rectifier (fig. 167iv). In this case the time constant needs to be large compared with the frequency of the half waves.

Alternating current

The instantaneous value of an alternating p.d. is given by

$$V = V_0 \sin \omega t \quad \text{(fig. 166i)}$$

where ω is the angular frequency (see p. 114).

$$\omega = 2\pi f$$

where f = frequency of supply.

It could equally well be given by $V = V_0 \cos \omega t$ depending upon the moment at which the p.d. is zero (fig. 166ii). The waveform is the same, but the zero of p.d. is a quarter of a cycle earlier in time.

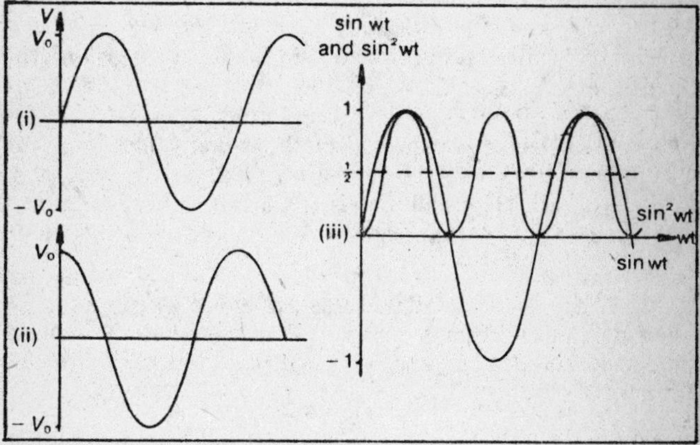

Figure 166. A.C. waveforms

The average value of the p.d. is zero, since the sinusoidal waveform is symmetrical about zero.

The peak value of the p.d. is the maximum it reaches i.e. V_0.

The r.m.s. value of the p.d. is the p.d. of a d.c. supply which would produce the same heating effect as the a.c. in a resistor. Since the power dissipated as heat in a resistor varies as V^2 (power = V^2/R or I^2R), the graph of power against time is as shown in fig. 166iii. The $\sin^2 \omega t$ graph is also sinusoidal but of twice the frequency and symmetrical about $\frac{1}{2}$ (i.e. the average value is $\frac{1}{2}$). This follows from the trigonometrical identity:

$$2 \sin^2 \omega t - 1 = \cos 2\omega t$$

i.e.

$$\sin^2 \omega t = \tfrac{1}{2} - \tfrac{1}{2} \cos 2\omega t$$

and the average value of $\sin^2 \omega t = \frac{1}{2}$ since average value of $\cos 2\omega t = 0$.

The average value of V^2 is thus $\frac{1}{2}V_0^2$

$$\sqrt{(V^2)_{\text{mean}}} = \frac{V_0}{\sqrt{2}}$$

$\sqrt{(V^2)_{\text{mean}}}$ is called the root mean square, $V_{\text{r.m.s.}}$ (square root of the mean of the squares)

$$V_{\text{r.m.s.}} = \frac{V_0}{\sqrt{2}} = 0{\cdot}707\,V_0$$

By identical reasoning we can obtain similar expressions for currents.

Thus r.m.s. values can be used exactly as d.c. values in power calculations, e.g. the power dissipated in a resistor = $v_{\text{r.m.s.}} \times i_{\text{r.m.s.}}$, etc. Normally, it is implicit that a.c. p.d.s and currents are r.m.s. values, e.g. 240 V a.c. **means** 240 $V_{\text{r.m.s.}}$.

Example A solenoid of 1000 turns per metre carries an alternating current of 10 amps at 50 Hz. What is the e.m.f. induced in a coil of area 10^{-3} m^2 and 100 turns placed at its centre?

$$I = I_0 \sin \omega t$$

$$B = \mu_0 n I$$

$$\frac{dB}{dt} = \mu_0 n \frac{dI}{dt}$$

$$= \mu_0 n \omega I_0 \cos \omega t$$

$$V = \frac{d\phi}{dt} = NA\frac{dB}{dt}$$

$$= NA\mu_0 n \omega I_0 \cos \omega t$$

$$= 100 \times 10^{-3} \times 4\pi \times 10^{-7} \times 10^3 \times 2\pi \times 50 \times 10 \cos \omega t$$

$$= 0{\cdot}395 \cos \omega t$$

$$\therefore \quad \text{r.m.s. voltage} = \frac{\text{peak voltage}}{\sqrt{2}}$$

$$= \frac{0{\cdot}395}{\sqrt{2}} = 279 \text{ mV}$$

Rectification
The process of producing d.c. from a.c. is called rectification. It needs two stages

(i) a diode in series with an a.c. supply produces a uni-directional current (pulses but all in the same direction).
(ii) a storage or reservoir capacitor in parallel with the output smooths d.c. to an almost steady direct current (fig. 167iv). The effect of the smoothing capacitor is to store up charge, as a tank would store water, releasing it when the diode ceases to conduct. This process can be improved by using a full-wave rectifier circuit which uses both positive and negative parts of the waveform (fig. 167iii). This diagram can be understood by following each current round through the appropriate diodes. The output waveform is shown in fig. 167v.

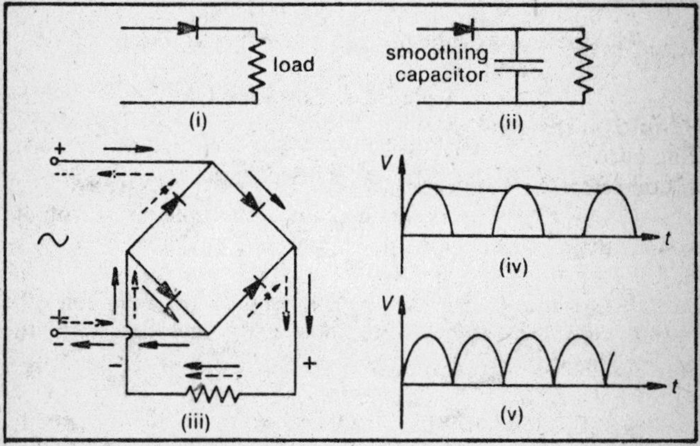

Figure 167. Rectification

A.C. measurements
A moving coil galvanometer is useless with a.c. unless modified since the torque on the coil alternates and consequently the coil just trembles.

Diode instruments feed the current to a moving coil galvanometer through a rectifier 'before' the meter. The scale is appropriately calibrated to read r.m.s. values (fig. 168i).

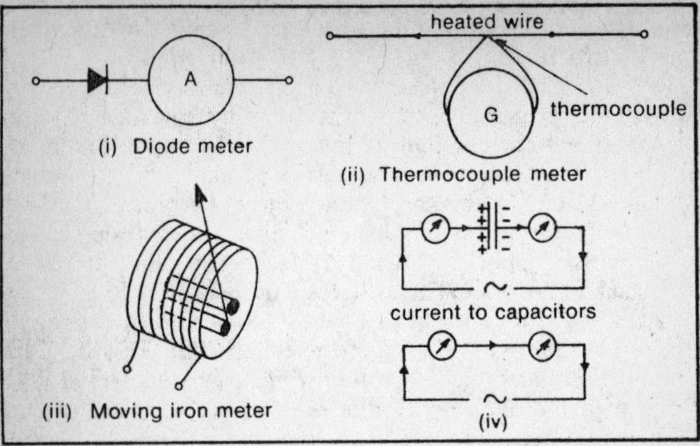

Figure 168. A.C. meters

Thermocouple instruments use a moving coil galvanometer to measure current due to the e.m.f. generated by a thermocouple attached to a piece of resistance wire heated by the a.c. current (fig. 168ii).

Moving iron instruments have two pieces of soft iron side by side in a coil carrying the a.c. current. As the pieces of iron are always magnetically identical they will always repel (fig. 168iii). The disadvantage with these instruments is that the scales are non-linear since the repulsion between the magnetized iron strips does not vary linearly with the magnetizing current.

Electrostatic instruments discussed on page 180 can also be used on a.c. as the plates will always attract each other since they always carry opposite charges to each other.

Capacitors

An alternating current appears to 'pass through' a capacitor. The current is in fact charging the plates (fig. 168iv) and it can be seen that the current flowing on to the plates is the same as if the capacitor were not there but replaced by a resistor. There is a ratio between the amplitude of the applied p.d. and the amplitude of the resulting current, and this is called the **reactance** (**not** a resistance since there is a phase difference of 90° between the p.d. and the current).

The reactance can be calculated as follows:

$$Q = CV \quad \text{and} \quad V = V_0 \sin \omega t$$

$$I = \frac{dQ}{dt} = C\frac{dV}{dt}$$

$$\therefore \quad I = C\omega V_0 \cos \omega t$$

i.e.

$$I = I_0 \cos \omega t \quad \text{where } I_0 = \omega C V_0$$

Thus reactance $$X_c = \frac{V_0}{I_0} = \frac{V_0}{\omega C V_0} = \frac{1}{\omega C}$$

The current leads the p.d. by 90° since $\cos \omega t = \sin(\omega t + 90°)$. This is because the current is zero when the capacitor is fully charged (i.e. the p.d. is a maximum).

Example What current will flow if a 100 μF capacitor is connected across 240 volt, 50 Hz a.c. mains?

$$\text{Reactance } X_c = \frac{1}{\omega C} = \frac{1}{2\pi \times 50 \times 100 \times 10^{-6}} = \frac{10^2}{\pi} = 31{\cdot}8\ \Omega$$

$$\text{Current} = \frac{V}{X_c} = \frac{240}{31{\cdot}8} = 7{\cdot}55\ \text{A}$$

Inductors

When an a.c. current passes through an inductor, a back e.m.f. is induced which equals the applied e.m.f. V.

$$V = L\frac{dI}{dt}$$ (p. 257)

Let $$I = I_0 \sin \omega t \quad \text{then} \quad \frac{dI}{dt} = I_0\omega \cos \omega t$$

$$V = LI_0\omega \cos \omega t$$

$$= V_0 \cos \omega t \quad \text{where } V_0 = \omega L I_0$$

Hence the reactance $$X_L = \frac{V_0}{I_0} = \frac{\omega L I_0}{I_0} = \omega L$$

The voltage leads the current by 90° (or the current lags the voltage by 90°).

Vector representation

The most convenient analysis of phase differences is by using rotating vectors or phasors. Referring back to the section on SHM (see p. 113) it was shown that a displacement which varies sinusoidally with time could be obtained by projecting the image of a rotating arm on to a screen. The projection of a rotating phasor on the y-axis represents the instantaneous value of a sinusoidally varying quantity (fig. 169i). A second sinusoidally varying quantity which leads the first by 90° is represented by a phasor 90° ahead anticlockwise. Both phasors rotate anticlockwise at an angular velocity ω ($=2\pi f$) radians per second. Thus the phasor diagram for a capacitor is as shown in fig. 169ii and that for an inductor is shown in fig. 169iii.

A convenient mnemonic for remembering the phase relationships in inductors and capacitors is CIVIL.

In Capacitors I leads V, V leads I in Inductors (L).

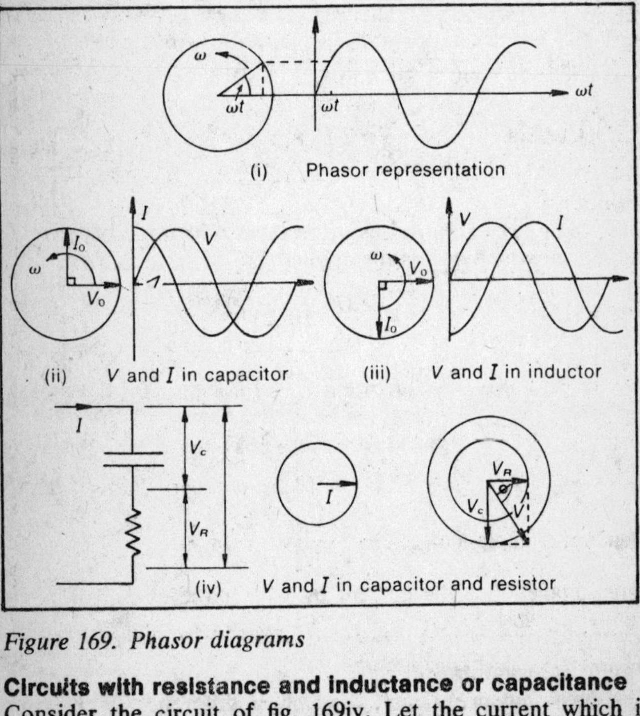

Figure 169. Phasor diagrams

Circuits with resistance and inductance or capacitance
Consider the circuit of fig. 169iv. Let the current which is

common to both resistor and capacitor be $I = I_0 \sin \omega t$. Then since the current leads the p.d. across the capacitor V_C, whilst the current through the resistor is in phase with the p.d. across it V_R, the phasor diagrams will be as shown in fig. 169iv. The magnitude of the resultant of the two phasors V is given by

$$V = \sqrt{V_C^2 + V_R^2}$$

and the phase difference ϕ is given by

$$\tan \phi = \frac{V_C}{V_R} \quad \text{i.e.} \quad \phi = \tan^{-1} \frac{V_C}{V_R}$$

The ratio of peak voltage to peak current is called the **impedance** when ϕ is neither 0° nor 90°.

Resonant circuits—Parallel resonance

An interesting situation arises when an inductor and a capacitor are connected in parallel (fig. 170i). The p.d. is common to both and the phasor diagrams are as shown in fig. 170i.

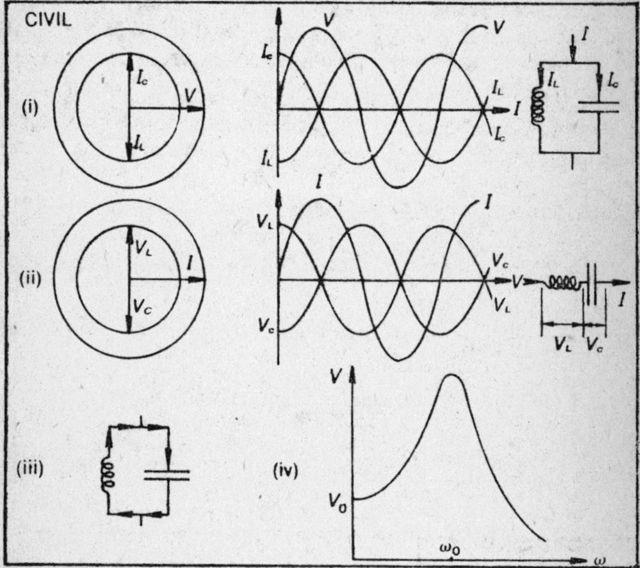

Figure 170. Resonant circuits

If $I_C = I_L$, the two cancel out i.e. $I = 0$.

Thus the reactance of the combination is given by

$$X = \frac{V_0}{I_0} = \frac{V_0}{0} = \infty$$

i.e. on resonance the reactance of the combination is infinite and no current will flow. In practice because of resistance of the inductor, a small current will flow. Parallel circuits are used for tuning in radio circuits. The response of a parallel tuned circuit to changing frequency is shown in fig. 170iv.

The condition for resonance is $I_C = I_L$ since one is 180° out of phase with the other, i.e.

$$\frac{V}{X_L} = \frac{V}{X_C} \quad \therefore \quad \frac{1}{\omega L} = \frac{1}{\frac{1}{\omega C}}$$

$$\therefore \quad \omega^2 LC = 1 \quad \text{i.e.} \quad \omega = \frac{1}{\sqrt{LC}} \quad \text{or} \quad f = \frac{1}{2\pi\sqrt{LC}}$$

What is happening in practice is that there is a large current **round** the circuit (fig. 170iii) and only a small current **through** it which tops up the energy lost per cycle. It could be said that charge 'sloshes' to and fro round the circuit from one plate of the capacitor to the other.

Example A parallel tuned circuit for a radio receiver is to be constructed with a 500 pF variable capacitor and a coil. If the longest wavelength which is to be received is 600 metres what should the inductance of the coil be?

$$f = \frac{c}{\lambda} = \frac{3 \times 10^8}{600} = 500 \text{ kHz}$$

Resonance occurs when $\quad \dfrac{1}{\omega C} = \omega L$

i.e. $\quad L = \dfrac{1}{\omega^2 C} = \dfrac{1}{(2\pi \times 5 \times 10^5)^2 \times 5 \times 10^{-10}}$

$$= \frac{1}{(2\pi \times 5)^2 \times 5} = 203 \ \mu\text{H}$$

Series resonance

In this case a similar situation arises when the current is common to both, and the p.d.s across the capacitor and the inductor are in antiphase. The phasor diagrams become those of fig. 170ii. Thus the reactance of the combination is given by

$$X = \frac{V_0}{I_0} = \frac{0}{I_0} = 0$$

i.e. on resonance the reactance of the combination is zero. The circuit can be used to pass the resonant frequency, and to stop others.

Energy is stored in a resonant circuit entirely in the capacitor at one moment, and entirely in the inductor a quarter of a cycle later, and at other times partly in both – the total energy in the circuit remaining constant in theory; in practice energy is dissipated in resistance in the circuit.

Power in reactive elements

The instantaneous power absorbed in an inductor is the product of the instantaneous current and the instantaneous p.d. (fig. 171). The power curve is now symmetrical about zero and hence the average power absorbed is zero, and the current is known as a **'wattless' current**. In fact the inductor gives back to the circuit all the energy it has absorbed in the previous quarter cycle. This can be shown mathematically:

$$P = V_0 \sin \omega t \times I_0 \cos \omega t = \tfrac{1}{2} V_0 I_0 \sin 2\omega t$$

The mean value of $\sin 2\omega t = 0 \quad \therefore \quad P_{mean} = 0$

Exactly the same is true of the power absorbed in a capacitor.

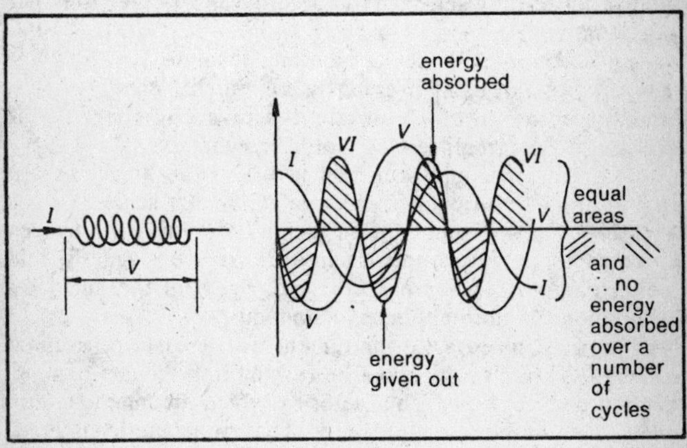

Figure 171. Power in a reactive element

If resistance is present, then the phase difference will no longer be 90° but ϕ so that

$$V = V_0 \sin \omega t \qquad I = I_0 \sin(\omega t + \phi)$$

$$\therefore \quad P_{mean} = V_0 I_0 \sin \omega t \sin(\omega t + \phi)$$

$$= \tfrac{1}{2} V_0 I_0 [\cos \phi - \cos (2\omega t + \phi)]$$

The mean value of $\cos(2\omega t + \phi) = 0$

$$\therefore \quad P_{mean} = \tfrac{1}{2} V_0 I_0 \cos \phi = V_{r.m.s.} I_{r.m.s.} \cos \phi.$$

Cos ϕ is called the **power factor.**

Key terms

Magnetic flux density Force per unit length acting on a conductor carrying a current of one amp placed perpendicular to the field.

Corkscrew rule Rule of thumb giving direction of magnetic field relative to current.

Biot-Savart law The mathematical relationship which gives the magnetic field due to an infinitesimally small current element.

Left-hand motor rule A rule of thumb for determining the direction of the force acting on a current in a magnetic field.

Ampere The constant current which, if maintained in two straight parallel conductors of infinite length and negligible circular cross-section and placed one metre apart in vacuo, would produce between them a force of 2×10^{-7} newtons per metre length.

Current balance A device for making absolute measurement of current, i.e. not using previously calibrated meters.

Split-ring commutator A device for reversing the flow of current into the armature of a motor or dynamo.

Radial field A non-uniform field in which the flux lines are radial in order to produce a linear galvanometer scale.

Hall effect The phenomenon in which two opposite surfaces of a current-carrying conductor in a transverse magnetic field develop charges. To increase the p.d. between the surfaces, the conductor is normally a semiconductor.

Mass spectrometer An instrument for measuring atomic masses of elements which can be formed into a beam of ions.

Relative permeability The factor by which the magnetic flux density is increased by the presence of a ferromagnetic material.

Ballistic galvanometer A specially adapted galvanometer for measuring charge. Charge passed is proportional to throw.

Magnetic flux linking a circuit The product of magnetic flux density normal to the circuit and area of a circuit. Unit: weber.

Faraday's law The induced e.m.f. is proportional to the rate of change of magnetic flux linking a circuit.

Lenz's law The direction of any current caused by an induced e.m.f. is such as to oppose the change to which it is due.

Right-hand dynamo rule A rule of thumb for determining the direction of an induced current.

Back e.m.f. A rotating motor armature also acts as a dynamo and the e.m.f. produced, which opposes the applied e.m.f., is called the back e.m.f.

Transformer A device for stepping up or stepping down alternating voltages.

Self-inductance Ratio of self-induced e.m.f. to rate of change of current.

Mutual inductance Ratio of induced e.m.f. in one circuit to rate of change of current in another.

Eddy current Small induced current in a conductor when subjected to a varying magnetic field. Can be reduced by lamination.

Lamination Construction of a magnetic core from sheets of material insulated from each other to reduce eddy current loss.

Exponential decay A form of decay in which the rate of decay of a quantity is proportional to the quantity still present.

Angular frequency The product of 2π and the frequency of an alternating supply.

Peak current Maximum value the current reaches.

R.M.S. current That alternating current which will produce the same heating effect as a d.c. current of the same value.

Rectification Process of producing direct current from alternating current.

Reactance The ratio of peak voltage to peak current where the voltage and the current are 90° out of phase.

Impedance The ratio of peak voltage to peak current when the voltage and current are neither 90° out of phase, nor in phase.

Resonant circuits Circuits consisting of an inductor and a capacitor in either series or parallel. When on resonance the inductor reactance equals the capacitor reactance.

Wattless current Current in an inductor or a capacitor which dissipates on average no energy.

Power factor The factor by which the product of r.m.s. voltage and r.m.s. current must be multiplied to give power. For a resistor in which voltage and current are in phase the power factor is 1. The power factor is the cosine of the phase angle between voltage and current.

Chapter 8
Nuclear and Quantum Physics

Nuclear physics

This section is concerned with radiation emanating from the nucleus and with the nuclear model of the atom.

Radioactivity

Early work showed that the radiation from radioactive sources consists of three types: α, β and γ, distinguished by their range in solids and gases and their behaviour in a magnetic field. Furthermore, the radiation was found to cause ionization, a property on which radiation detectors depend.

Radiation detectors are of two types – those which detect the arrival of a single particle or photon, and those which display the paths of particles.

Ionization chambers were the original detectors used. An ionization chamber, which consists of a can fitted with a

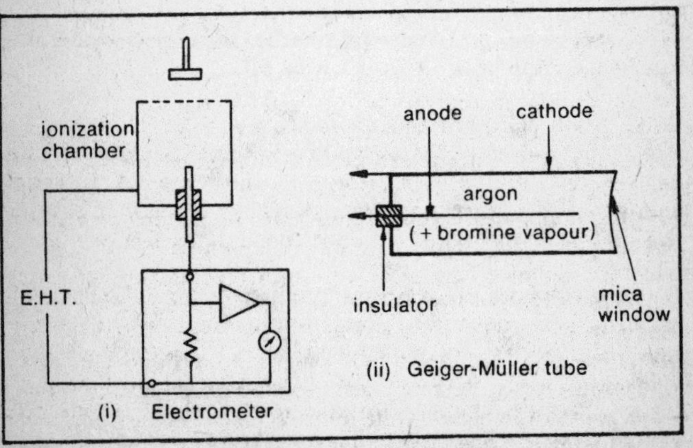

Figure 172. Radiation detectors

central insulated electrode, can be fitted onto an electrometer and is connected to a high voltage supply (fig. 172i). If ionizing radiation is introduced into the chamber, for instance, from a source of a radioactive gas, then a small current will flow because of the ionization of the air in the chamber. This current, which flows through a very high resistor (typically 10^3 MΩ), will develop a voltage across the ends of the resistor and this is measured by the electrometer, which draws virtually no current.

The Geiger–Müller tube makes use of gas amplification to enhance the ionization caused by a single particle. It consists of a case with a mica window at one end (fig. 172ii) and a central conductor which is raised to a positive potential of about 400 volts. The tube is filled with argon at low pressure with a trace of bromine. The arrival of a particle causes an argon atom to be ionized. The electric field accelerates the electron produced, which acquires sufficient energy to ionize a further atom. These two electrons will also accelerate causing further ionization and so on, with the result that an avalanche occurs and a large number of electrons reaches the anode. The resultant pulse is amplified and fed into a scaler (which counts pulses) or a ratemeter (which produces an output proportional to the average pulse rate). α- and β-particles cause direct ionization in a G–M tube, but γ-rays are detected by the secondary electrons emitted from the walls of the tube when struck by γ-rays. α-particles appear to have shorter ranges in air with G–M tube experiments than they do in a cloud chamber (3 cm instead of 7 cm). This is due to the energy needed for them to penetrate the mica window of the tube.

Solid state detectors are a more recent development and consist of a reverse biassed p–n junction. Ionizing radiation will remove electrons from atoms, forming hole-electron pairs, and hence charge carriers will be able to flow across the junction which otherwise will not conduct. (p. 220).

Cloud chambers show up the tracks of ionizing particles by using the phenomenon of condensation from critically supersaturated vapours onto charged particles – ionized air molecules left in the wake of an α-particle, for instance. The supersaturated vapour is produced by cooling a saturated vapour (usually alcohol) either by sudden expansion or by setting up a temperature gradient with no convection.

The Wilson or expansion cloud chamber (fig. 173i). Rapid withdrawal of the pump handle produces the expansion required to cool the vapour to the critical degree of supersaturation. An instantaneous pattern of vapour trails will mark the paths of the particles. The trails rapidly dissipate.

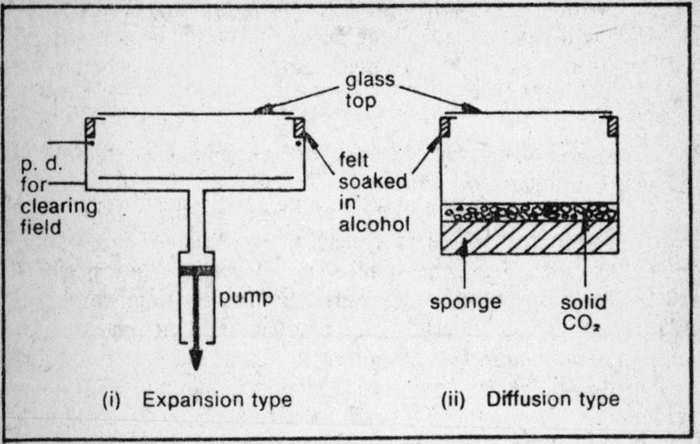

Figure 173. Cloud chambers

The diffusion or continuous cloud chamber is shown schematically in fig. 173ii. Since the solid CO_2 keeps the bottom very cold and cold air does not rise, a temperature gradient is set up, and at one particular level, the vapour will be in the necessary state of supersaturation. Vapour trails then form (and dissipate) continuously.

Identification of α-, β- and γ-rays

These types of radiation can be identified in several ways.

Photography is widely used. All types of radiation can cause the formation of an image. Special photographic film is placed, for instance, behind a cracked pipe irradiated by γ-rays. Film with a thick emulsion can also be used to study particle tracks.

Absorption of radiation by solids or gases shows three different types of behaviour. Using a Geiger counter, a radium source and various thicknesses of aluminium foil (fig. 174i) the results shown in fig. 174ii can be produced. Foil thicknesses for these purposes are usually measured in mg cm^{-2}.

The combination of a Geiger–Müller tube and a scaler is usually termed a Geiger counter.

Type 1 is due to α-particles with a short range (stopped by very thin aluminium foil). The cut off is quite sharp leaving types 2 and 3. α-particles have a range of several cm in air.

Type 2 is due to β-particles with a longer range (a few mm in aluminium) but again with a fairly sharp cut off leaving type 3. The range of β-particles in air is several tenths of a metre.

Type 3 is due to γ-rays with a very long range, capable of penetrating a considerable thickness of lead. The intensity of γ-rays decreases exponentially with distance. One centimetre of lead will absorb about half the γ-radiation incident on it.

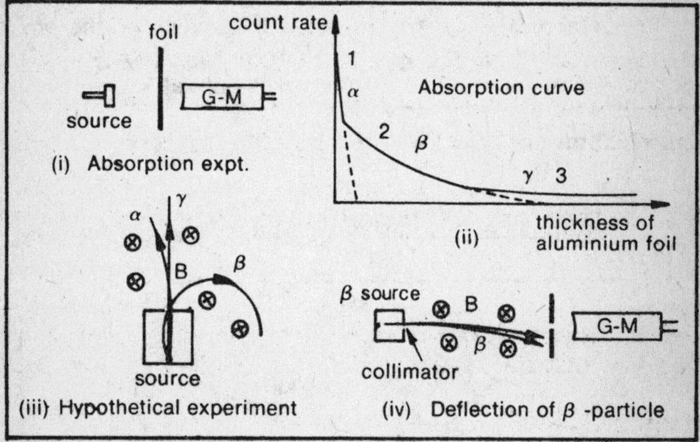

Figure 174. Radioactivity experiments

Behaviour in magnetic fields gives another sharp distinction between the three types of radiation. A hypothetical experiment to illustrate this is shown in fig. 174iii. Although β-particles have about twenty times the velocity of α-particles, they have only about $\frac{1}{4\times2000}$ their mass and half their charge. From page 243, the radius of curvature of the path of a charged particle is given by

$$r = v\frac{m}{q}\frac{1}{B}$$

Now $v_\beta = 20v_\alpha$, $\frac{q_\alpha}{m_\alpha} = \frac{2}{4 \times 2000} \cdot \frac{q_\beta}{m_\beta}$ $\therefore$ $\frac{m_\alpha}{q_\alpha} = 4000 \cdot \frac{m_\beta}{q_\beta}$

$$\therefore \quad r_\beta = 20v_\alpha \times \frac{1}{4000} \cdot \frac{m_\alpha}{q_\alpha} \times \frac{1}{B} = \frac{1}{200} r_\alpha$$

i.e. the radius of β-particle tracks is about two hundred times less than that of α-particles.

β-particles carry a negative charge whilst α-particles carry a positive charge and consequently α- and β-particles are deflected in opposite directions by a magnetic field. γ-rays are unaffected by magnetic fields.

The deflection of β-particles is readily illustrated using a collimated source (fig. 174iv) and a slit in a brass plate in front of the G–M tube. A magnet can easily deflect the particles away from the slit and the count rate will drop considerably. A similar experiment can be performed with α-particles, but path lengths of about 0·5 metre are needed because of the large radius of curvature, and it must therefore be under vacuum because the range of α-particles in air is only about 7 cm.

Cloud chamber tracks illustrate differences in ionizing power (fig. 175).

α-particles produce very heavy ionization, and because they

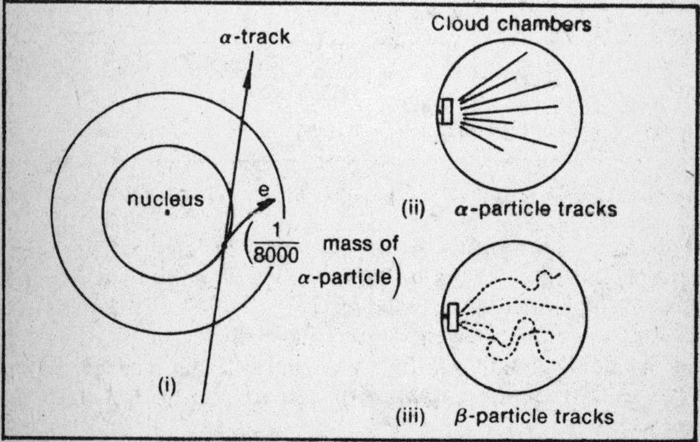

Figure 175. Cloud chamber tracks

are massive relative to electrons, their paths are little affected by ionizing collisions with electrons as they pass through atoms (fig. 175i). (Most α-particles are hardly deflected as they pass through gold films.) With energies of several MeV, they can make many ion-electron pairs in their short paths (7 cm for radium α-particles). As different substances produce α-particles of different energies, track lengths will vary.

β-particles although having similar energies have about ten times the range and hence produce about a tenth of the ionization per cm. The tracks are very much more difficult to see and because β-particles are electrons, ionizing collisions with other electrons in the atoms cause changes of course, occasionally with deflections of 90° or more (fig. 175iii).

$\beta+$ (positron) tracks are similar, but they will curve in the same direction as α-particles in a magnetic field.

γ-rays produce little ionization and cannot really be observed in school cloud chambers.

The nature of the radiation

α-particles are helium nuclei (doubly ionized helium atoms). They contain two protons and two neutrons and therefore have a double positive electronic charge. The final iden-

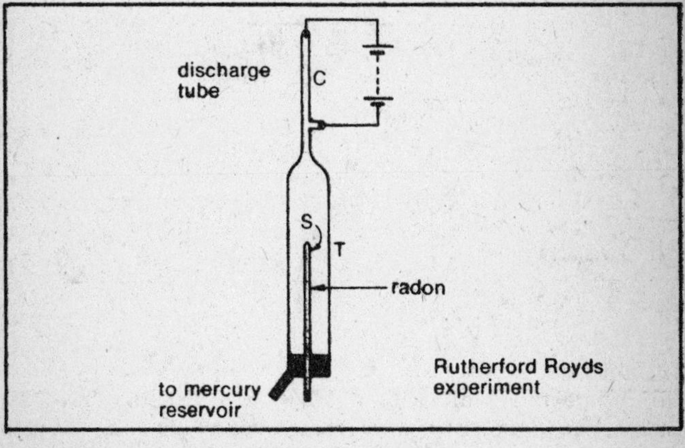

Figure 176. Rutherford Royds experiment

tification was made in the Rutherford Royds experiment (fig. 176). Radon (a radioactive gas) was placed in the thin wall glass tube S. α-particles passing through S reached the tube T, where they recombined with electrons to become helium atoms. After six days the resultant gas was compressed into the discharge tube C at the top by filling tube T with mercury. The resultant gas discharge between the electrodes showed the spectral lines of helium. A subsequent test in which the tube S was filled with helium failed to reveal any trace of helium in the outer tube T. α-particles have energies in the range of several MeV and velocities of about $\frac{1}{200}$ that of light. Their mass is 4 unified atomic mass units (u.).

β-particles are electrons with energies in the range of several MeV and velocities of up to two-thirds that of light. Their rest mass is $\frac{1}{1836}$ u. but their mass increases as their velocity approaches the velocity of light according to the theory of relativity. The value of e/m consequently varies with velocity.

γ-rays are electromagnetic radiation of very high frequency. Photon energies are in the MeV range, and wavelengths vary from about 4×10^{-10} m to 5×10^{-13} m. They are not affected by either electric or magnetic fields.

Type	**Nature**	**Typical Energies** MeV	**Atomic Mass** u.	**Charge** e	**Range**	**Ioniz-ation**	**Velocity**
α	He nuclei	1–9	4	+2	10^{-1} mm in Al	heavy	up to $\frac{1}{200}c$
β	electrons	0·01–13	$\frac{1}{1836}$	−1	1 mm in Al	10^{-1} that of α	up to $\frac{2}{3}c$
γ	electro-magnetic radiation	0·01–7	0	0	1 cm lead reduces by half	10^{-4} that of α	c

Table 3. Types of radiation

Radioactive decay

The disintegration of unstable nuclei is a statistical process. Each disintegration produces characteristic radiation. The rate of radioactive decay is unaffected by physical conditions.

The probability λ of a nucleus disintegrating in 1 second is given by

$$\lambda = \frac{\text{no. of particles disintegrating}}{\text{total no. of particles present}} = \frac{-\delta N_1}{N}$$

So no. of particles disintegrating in 1 second $\delta N_1 = -N\lambda$

$\therefore$ no. of particles disintegrating in δt sec $\delta N = -N\lambda\delta t$

The minus sign indicates a **decrease** in N.

This can be rewritten $\frac{dN}{dt} = -\lambda N$ as $\delta t \to 0$

which is the condition for exponential decay, i.e. the rate of decay is proportional to the number of unstable nuclei present. λ is called the **decay constant** (see also p. 261).

The expression can be rearranged and integrated from $t = 0$ when $N = N_0$ to $t = t$ when $N = N$

$$\int_{N_0}^{N} \frac{dN}{N} = -\lambda \int_0^t dt$$

$$[\ln N]_{N_0}^{N} = -\lambda [t]_0^t$$

$$\ln \frac{N}{N_0} = -\lambda t \quad \therefore \quad \frac{N}{N_0} = e^{-\lambda t}$$

i.e. $$N = N_0 e^{-\lambda t}$$

This function is plotted in fig. 177.

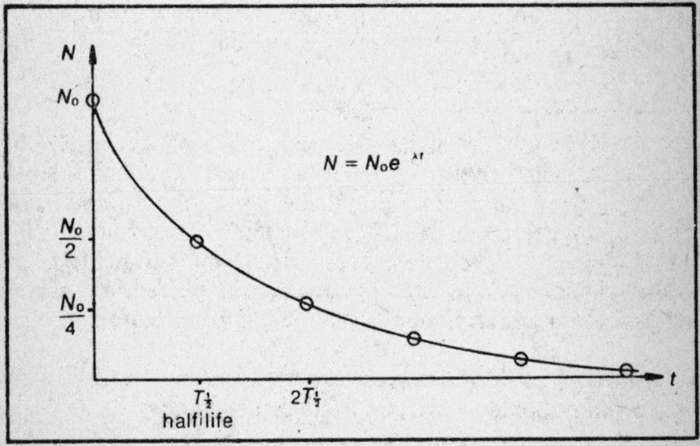

Figure 177. Radioactive decay

In dealing with radioactivity a convenient measure of the decay curve is the half life, $T_{1/2}$, which is the time taken for the radioactive material to decay to half its original quantity. The quantity present therefore halves after equal intervals of one half life (i.e. half the parent nuclei have become daughter nuclei) (fig. 177).

There is a relationship between half life and decay constant. Substituting the conditions after one half life in the above expression

$$\ln \frac{\frac{1}{2}N_0}{N_0} = -\lambda T_{1/2} \qquad \therefore \quad \ln 2 = \lambda T_{1/2}$$

$$\lambda = \frac{0{\cdot}693}{T_{1/2}}$$

Thus if the half life is known λ can be found and hence the quantities present after any period can be calculated.

This relationship also enables the half life to be calculated from the rate of decay since

$$\frac{dN}{dt} = -\lambda N$$

dN/dt can be found by counting the number of disintegrations per second on a scaler and allowing for the fact that the scaler only counts the disintegrations which send particles in its direction. N can be calculated from the number of moles of material present, n, and Avogadro's number N_A

$$N = N_A n$$

The half life of thoron (a radioactive gas produced by the decay of thorium hydroxide) can be found by puffing a small quantity of the gas from a polythene bottle into an ionization chamber connected to an H.T. supply and an electrometer (fig. 172). By plotting the decay curve, the half life is found to be 52 seconds. Alternatively, a G–M tube can be placed in a closed container into which a thoron sample has been puffed.

Activities of radioactive sources used to be measured relative to the notional activity of 1 gram of radium.

The Curie (Ci) is the activity of a radioactive material which undergoes $3{\cdot}7\times10^{10}$ disintegrations per second. School sources are usually less than 10 μCi.

The Becquerel (Bq) is the new S.I. unit of activity however, and is the activity of a radioactive material which undergoes 1 disintegration per second.

Example 1 Radioactive phosphorus-32 has a half life of 14 days. A source containing this isotope has an initial activity of 10 μCi.

(i) what is the activity of the source after 42 days?

(ii) what time elapses before the activity of the source falls to 2·5 μCi?

(i) 42 days = 3 half lives

$$\frac{dN}{dt}=\left(\frac{1}{2}\right)^3\left(\frac{dN}{dt}\right)_0$$

where $\left(\frac{dN}{dt}\right)_0$ = initial rate of decay

$$\therefore\quad \frac{dN}{dt}=\frac{10\times10^{-6}}{8}=1{\cdot}25\ \mu\text{Ci}$$

(ii)

$$\frac{\text{final activity}}{\text{initial activity}}=\frac{2{\cdot}5\times10^{-6}}{10\times10^{-6}}=\frac{1}{4}$$

Time to decay to $\frac{1}{4}$ initial activity = 2 half lives = 28 days

Example 2 Radioactive protoactinium-234 has a half life of 72 seconds. How much protoactinium is left of a source of initial mass 1 milligram after 2 minutes.

$$\lambda=\frac{0{\cdot}693}{T_{1/2}}=\frac{0{\cdot}693}{72}=9{\cdot}6\times10^{-3}$$

$$\lambda t=9{\cdot}6\times10^{-3}\times120=1{\cdot}152$$

$$N=N_0e^{-\lambda t}$$

$$\therefore\quad N=10^{-3}\times e^{-1{\cdot}152}=0{\cdot}316\ \text{mg}$$

Carbon-14 dating is a good example of the use of a radioactive decay curve. A radioactive isotope of carbon (carbon-14) is continuously formed by cosmic rays acting on the earth's atmosphere. This forms radioactive carbon dioxide which is absorbed by living organic matter in the ordinary way but the absorption stops as soon as the matter dies. If the proportion of radioactive carbon-14 to normal carbon-12 in the atmosphere is assumed to have been constant throughout history, then the initial proportion of carbon-14 in a sample of organic matter which has just died is known (although it is minute – about 1 in 10^{12}). By very careful measurement of the radiation emitted by the specimen, it is possible to estimate what proportion of carbon-14 is left. Since the half life of carbon-14 is known to be 5600 years, the age of the specimen can be calculated from the decay law.

Biological effects and safety precautions

α-, β- and γ-rays, together with X-rays are called **ionizing radiation** because they all cause ionization which can be detected in detectors like those described. However, their ability to ionize extends to living cells as well. They can cause burns and destruction of living cells. They can initiate serious diseases and can even cause genetic changes. Furthermore, the effects are to some extent cumulative with the result that the total exposure over a long period of time can cause irreparable damage, and also exposure to radiation does not normally cause any pain at the time.

α-particles do not normally penetrate the surface layers of skin but α-active materials are dangerous if swallowed or breathed in. β-particles, although producing less ionization, can penetrate further. Again the main danger is ingestion. γ-rays, however, are more dangerous because of their greater penetration and sources should be as weak as possible.

The following precautions should be observed:

1. Always keep sources as far from the body as possible using long forceps, and point them away from people.
2. Return sources immediately after use to the lead caskets.
3. No eating or drinking in the laboratory.
4. Sources should be carefully labelled and kept in a locked labelled cupboard in a little frequented area.

Provided these precautions are observed the dangers from school sources are reduced to negligible proportions.

The nuclear model of the atom

The early theories of atomic structure due to J. J. Thomson

regarded the atom as a 'plum pudding' consisting of a sphere of positive charge with electrons embedded in it like raisins, the whole structure being electrically neutral (fig. 178i).

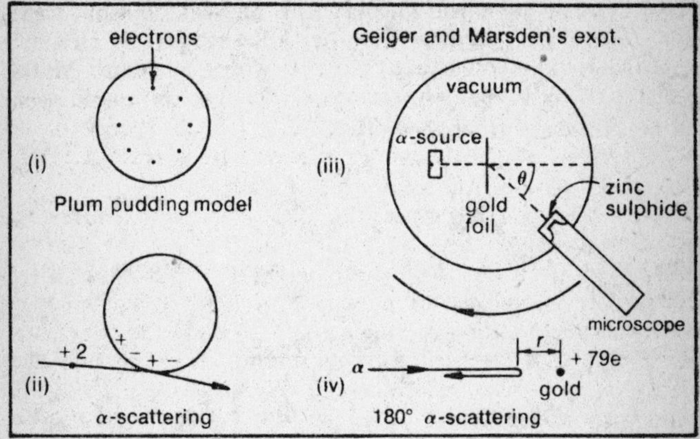

Figure 178. α-particle scattering

It was known that α-particles when passed through thin foils of heavy metals were scattered through small angles (less than a degree). This was consistent with the plum pudding model in which the charged particle could only be affected by individual negatively charged electrons within the atom when very close to it, or by its diffuse positive charge (fig. 178ii). Rutherford, however, suggested an experiment to see if α-particles could be scattered through wide angles.

The α-particle scattering experiments of Geiger and Marsden, which no one expected to work, showed that for a metal foil 4×10^{-7} m thick about one α-particle in 20 000 was scattered through more than 90°. Rutherford was astonished and stated that it was as incredible as if a 15″ shell fired at a piece of tissue paper had bounced back. The apparatus consisted of a very strong source of α-particles enclosed in a container with a slit, a gold foil and a zinc sulphide screen viewed through a microscope (fig. 178iii). Source, foil and screen were enclosed in an evacuated box (to increase the path length of the α-particles). As particles struck the zinc sulphide screen, tiny spots of light or scintillations were seen. Rutherford, assuming that the inverse square law of electrical repulsion was still valid down to such minute dimensions, concluded that the forces necessary to produce the observation could only occur if the whole of the positive charge of an atom were to be found in a very small volume in the middle of the atom.

A rough calculation will illustrate this and estimate the maximum size of the nucleus. Consider a 8.4 MeV ($1{\cdot}34 \times 10^{-12}$ J) α-particle, travelling exactly in line with the centre of the nucleus, being brought to rest by the charge on a gold atom before being repelled back (fig. 178iv). Then energy of α-particle equals electrical energy of α-particle at rest.

$$W = q_1 V = \frac{q_1 q_2}{4\pi\epsilon_0 r}$$

Now $W = 1{\cdot}34 \times 10^{-12}$ J, $q_1 = 2e$, $q_2 = 79e$ for gold and $e = 1{\cdot}6 \times 10^{-19}$C

$$\therefore \quad r = \frac{q_1 q_2}{4\pi\epsilon_0 W} = \frac{9 \times 10^9 \times 158 \times (1{\cdot}6 \times 10^{-19})^2}{1{\cdot}34 \times 10^{-12}} = 2{\cdot}7 \times 10^{-14}\ \text{m}$$

This is of the order of 10^{-4} of the radius of the atom ($\approx 10^{-10}$ m) and is still larger than the likely radius of the nucleus ($\approx 10^{-14}$ m). At this point the force acting on the α-particle will be 50 N – equivalent in terms of acceleration produced to a force of about 10^{24} tonnes weight acting on a mass of 1 kg!

α-particle paths not in line with the centre of the nucleus are

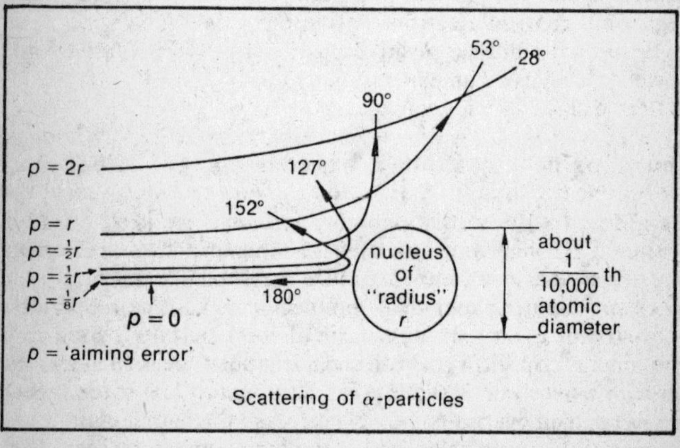

Figure 179. Angles of scatter

calculated to have the form shown in fig. 179. Clearly, in view of the extremely small ratio of the volume occupied by the nucleus to that of the atom (like a fly in a cathedral), it is not surprising that so few α-particles suffer 90° deflection in spite of passing through a couple of thousand layers of atoms in the very thin foils used. The results of the scattering experiment are found to agree closely with the scattering theory. The full theoretical expression also enables the charge of the nucleus (+79*e* for gold) to be estimated and thus the number of protons in the nucleus can also be estimated. It is found to equal the atomic number in the periodic table of elements.

Protons are hydrogen nuclei (ionized hydrogen atoms) and can be produced by bombarding hydrogen gas with α-particles. Another method of production is to bombard a hydrogen rich material like polythene with α-particles. This will produce 'knock on' protons which can be detected by having a longer range and producing less ionization than α-particles. Protons are a constituent of the nucleus of all atoms. The mass of a proton is approximately one unified atomic mass unit and it has a single positive electric charge (+ *e*).

The unified atomic mass unit (u.) is defined as $\frac{1}{12}$ the mass of a carbon-12 atom. Since one mole contains $6{\cdot}022 \times 10^{23}$ atoms and has a mass of 0·012 kg, the mass of 1 carbon atom is $\dfrac{0{\cdot}012}{6{\cdot}022 \times 10^{23}}$ kg.

$$\therefore \quad 1\text{ u.} = \frac{1}{12} \times \frac{0{\cdot}012}{6{\cdot}022 \times 10^{23}} = 1{\cdot}6605\text{ kg}$$

Atomic number (*Z*) is now defined as the number of protons in the nucleus.

Neutrons are uncharged particles and were first produced by bombarding beryllium with high energy α-particles. They do not cause ionization and can only be detected indirectly by producing ionizing particles – for instance 'knock on' protons in polythene or in a hydrogen filled cloud chamber. Neutrons are also a constituent of the nucleus and have a mass of approximately 1 u. Protons and neutrons within the nucleus are called **nucleons.**

Within the nucleus the neutron is stable, but a free neutron has a half life of $15\frac{1}{2}$ minutes, decaying into a proton and a β-particle (plus an anti-neutrino). Thus in radioactive decay which produces β-particles, neutrons become protons and the atomic number increases.

Mass number (*A*) is the number of nucleons in the nucleus. The number of protons is roughly equal to the number of neutrons for light nuclei ($Z < 30$) and for stable nuclei of higher atomic number the proportion of neutrons increases.

For describing nuclear reactions a nucleus is represented by ${}^{A}_{Z}\mathrm{X}$ where A is the mass number, Z is the atomic number and X is the chemical symbol. Thus in addition to the elements the following symbols are also used

α-particle is written ${}^{4}_{2}\mathrm{He}$

β-particle is written ${}^{0}_{-1}\mathrm{e}$

a proton is written ${}^{1}_{1}\mathrm{H}$

a neutron is written ${}^{1}_{0}\mathrm{n}$

Radioactive decay involves the emission of α- and β-particles. In α-particle emission A is reduced by 4 and Z by 2, e.g.

$${}^{226}_{88}\mathrm{Ra} \longrightarrow {}^{222}_{86}\mathrm{Rn} + {}^{4}_{2}\mathrm{He}$$

In β-particle emission A remains the same (same number of nucleons) and Z increases by 1 (as a neutron becomes a proton), e.g.

$${}^{210}_{82}\mathrm{Pb} \longrightarrow {}^{210}_{83}\mathrm{Bi} + {}^{0}_{-1}\mathrm{e} + \nu$$

Another example is the transmutation of nitrogen to oxygen when nitrogen is bombarded with α-particles, leaving a proton as a product of the collision.

$${}^{14}_{7}\mathrm{N} + {}^{4}_{2}\mathrm{He} \longrightarrow {}^{17}_{8}\mathrm{O} + {}^{1}_{1}\mathrm{H}$$

Nuclear reactions can also be represented by a form of short-hand. For example, the reaction quoted for the transmutation of nitrogen is represented by

$${}^{14}_{7}\mathrm{N}(\alpha, \mathrm{p}){}^{17}_{8}\mathrm{O}$$

Within the bracket, α means that the transmutation is caused by an α-particle, and p means that the transmutation produces a proton as well as oxygen-17, i.e.
Initial nucleus (incoming particle, outgoing particle) final nucleus

Isotopes of an element have the same number of protons (giving the atom its chemical identity) but a different number of neutrons.

Chlorine, for instance, has two isotopes·

$^{35}_{17}Cl$ with 17 protons and 18 neutrons
$^{37}_{17}Cl$ with 17 protons and 20 neutrons

They occur naturally in the ratio of about 3:1, and since they are indistinguishable chemically, the measured atomic weight of chlorine is the mean atomic mass of the sample.

$$\therefore \quad \text{Atomic weight} = \frac{3 \times 35 + 1 \times 37}{3 + 1} = 35{\cdot}5$$

Isotopes can be produced artificially by bombardment of nuclei with various particles. In practice artificial radioactive isotopes are produced by placing the raw materials in a nuclear pile, in which there is a high neutron flux, for a period of about 6 half lives of the desired radioactive material.

Isotopes cannot be separated chemically but they can be distinguished in a mass spectrometer (see p. 244). Isotopes (e.g. uranium-235 and uranium-238) can be separated because of the slight difference in their rates of diffusion. However, the process is very slow and very costly.

Uses of radioactive isotopes

The uses of radioactivity are now very widespread. Generally radioactive isotopes which have been produced artificially are better for most purposes. Typical uses are as follows:

1. **β-radiation** is used to follow biological processes. Phosphorus-32 which is a good source of β-particles is introduced into the organism by injection or as a nutrient. The spread of the tracer can then be checked by examining various parts for β-radiation – either by using a Geiger counter or by placing the specimen (e.g. a leaf) on a suitable photographic plate.

2. **β-radiation** is used for thickness gauges. Strontium-90 which is a good source of β-particles is placed on one side of a continuous sheet of paper during manufacture. β-particles are detected on the far side using a Geiger counter and the decrease in intensity caused by the thickness of the paper is noted.

3. γ**-radiation** is used instead of X-rays for convenience in checking metal structures for cracks, e.g. the welding of an oil pipeline. Cobalt-60 which is a good source of γ-rays is used and the radiation is detected by placing a suitable photographic film in contact with the section of metal under examination.

Positrons

Positrons (β+) are positive electrons. These 'anti-particles' of the electron were first observed in 1932 in cloud chambers bombarded by cosmic rays – very high energy particles reaching Earth from space. They were later found to be products of many artificial radioactive disintegrations. A proton (with the addition of a neutrino) decays into a neutron plus a positron. A γ-ray photon passing near an atomic nucleus may vanish and produce in its place an electron–positron pair, i.e. energy is transformed into mass. Conversely a positron travelling through matter will soon annihilate itself in combination with an electron and the energy is carried away as two γ-ray photons. The positron is represented by ${}_{-1}^{0}e$.

Stability of nuclei

There is an optimum ratio of neutrons to protons for each mass number. If the number of neutrons ($A-Z$), or **neutron number** (N), is plotted against the number of protons (Z) for stable isotopes, it is found that the points fall within fairly narrow limits (fig. 180). Initially, the ratio is 1 but it gradually

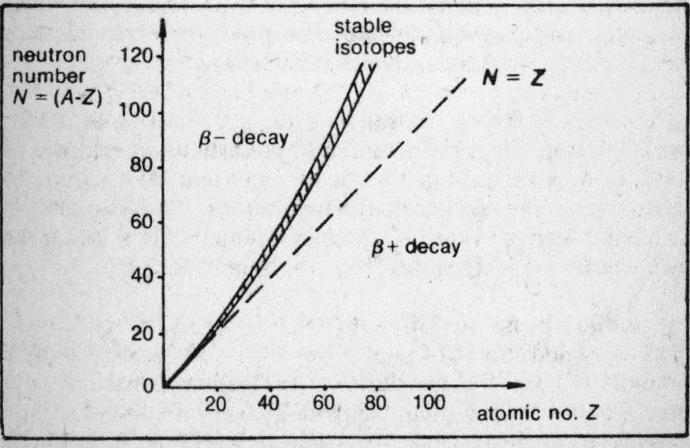

Figure 180. Stability of nuclei

increases to about 1·5. Any nucleus plotted either side of the stable region will be radioactive and the nucleus will attempt to restore the ratio to that needed for stability by either a neutron becoming a proton (β- decay) or a proton becoming a neutron (β+ decay),

$$^{29}_{13}Al \longrightarrow ^{29}_{14}Si \quad \text{or} \quad ^{25}_{13}Al \longrightarrow ^{25}_{12}Mg$$

or by α-decay which can increase the ratio of neutrons to protons (assuming more neutrons than protons in the nucleus initially).

Mass and energy

One of the major conclusions of Einstein's Special Theory of Relativity is that mass and energy are equivalent. The theory predicts that $E = mc^2$ where E is the amount of energy gained by a body, m is the resultant increase in mass and c is the velocity of light.

1 u. ($1{\cdot}66 \times 10^{-27}$ kg) is thus equivalent to $14{\cdot}9 \times 10^{-11}$ J = 931 MeV. The energy equivalent of an electron is 0·5 MeV. Thus for energies on a macroscopic scale, the increase in mass is quite undetectable but on an atomic scale it is considerable.

Binding energy

Nucleons in a nucleus are bound together by the nuclear force due to the **strong interaction** – a force 137 times stronger than the electrostatic repulsion between the protons and of very short range (10^{-15} m). This attractive force means that nucleons coming together gain energy in much the same way as a spaceship moving towards the Earth will gain kinetic energy from the Earth's gravitational field. The spaceship will dissipate its energy as heat when it enters the atmosphere; and the nucleons will emit radiation in the form of γ-rays as they come together. This energy loss corresponds to a mass loss or **mass defect** i.e. the nucleus is less massive than its constituents, and it is found that when nuclei fuse together or disintegrate the mass of the isolated constituents is not equal to the mass of the nucleus.

To re-separate the nucleons would require this energy to be supplied and in this sense, it is a measure of the energy holding the nucleus together and is called the **binding energy**. It could be compared with the energy which would be needed for a spaceship to escape from the Earth, which is in a sense the energy binding the spaceship to the Earth's surface.

For example, consider the mass of an α-particle and its constituents.

$$\begin{aligned} \text{Mass of 2 neutrons} &= 2{\cdot}01732 \text{ u.} \\ \text{Mass of 2 protons} &= \underline{2{\cdot}01566} \\ & \quad 4{\cdot}03298 \\ \text{Mass of } \alpha\text{-particle} &= \underline{4{\cdot}00260} \\ \therefore \quad \text{Mass defect} &= 0{\cdot}03038 \text{ u.} \end{aligned}$$

$$\therefore \quad \text{Binding energy} = 0{\cdot}03038 \times 931 = 28{\cdot}28 \text{ MeV}$$

Binding energy per nucleon

If the binding energy of a nucleus is re-expressed as the binding energy per nucleon (e.g. $\frac{28{\cdot}28}{4}$ for α-particle) it is found that it is not constant but rises to a maximum at around mass number 56 (iron) which indicates that it is a measure of the stability of the nucleus after which it decreases slightly to an average value of about 8 MeV per nucleon (fig. 181). This behaviour has a profound effect on the processes of fission and fusion.

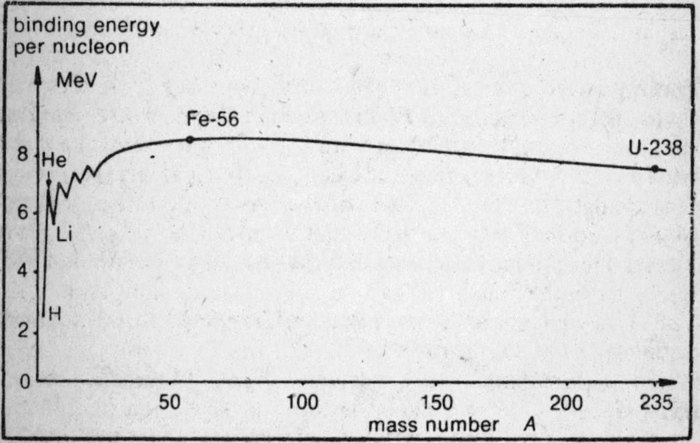

Figure 181. Binding energy curve

Fusion and fission

Fusion is the process of joining nuclei together. If two nuclei of low mass number could be joined together to form a larger nucleus, then since the binding energy of the nucleons of the heavier nucleus is greater than the total binding energy of the light nuclei, energy would be released. The figures quoted for an α-particle do, of course, apply to the formation of helium. This process will work in general until the maximum of the binding energy curve is reached at Fe-56. Beyond this point energy would be needed to cause fusion.

The difficulty in the fusion process, however, lies in forcing two positive charged nuclei together against immense electrostatic forces (see p. 186) i.e. until the strong but very short range nuclear attraction takes over. This can only be done by giving the nuclei immense kinetic energy by heating. To cause fusion, temperatures of many millions of kelvin are required. This has been possible in the hydrogen bomb, where a plutonium fission bomb is used as a detonator. It is also the process whereby the stars produce their energy. In the sun, for instance, the reaction is thought to take place in its core at 14 million K with the outer surface radiating energy at 5500 K. There are several possible reactions which might be used if a controlled reaction could be maintained for producing power – fusion of deuterium, for instance:

$$^{2}_{1}H + ^{2}_{1}H \rightarrow ^{3}_{1}H + ^{1}_{0}n + 3{\cdot}2\ MeV$$

Fission is the process of heavy atoms breaking up into two or more lighter nuclei of smaller mass and thus higher binding energies per nucleon. The process can continue up to the point where the binding energy starts to decrease again, i.e. it continues from U-238 up to Fe-56 on the binding energy curve (fig. 181). The fission fragments can have a wide range of mass numbers but the most common are in the region of 96 and 140.

The fission is initiated by 'injecting' a neutron into a heavy nucleus. A typical reaction is

$$^{235}_{92}U + ^{1}_{0}n \longrightarrow ^{236}_{92}U \longrightarrow X + Y + N^{1}_{0}n + 198\ MeV$$

where X and Y are the fission fragments and N is the number of neutrons produced. The reaction can be sustained if it produces sufficient neutrons to cause further fission.

Quantum physics

This section is concerned with the 'graininess' of the physical world. The particulate nature of both mass (atoms, protons, neutrons) and charge (electrons) has already been discussed. Several phenomena discovered at the turn of the century however could only be explained by extending the 'graininess' to electromagnetic radiation as well. So the Quantum Theory was born which considers amongst other things that radiation too can only be emitted or absorbed in discrete packets or 'quanta'.

The Photoelectric effect A light shining on to a clean metal surface can cause electrons to be emitted. It is found, however, that whether an electron is emitted or not depends on the **frequency** of the light and **not** on its intensity. Electrons are emitted if the **frequency** of the light is higher than a critical **threshold frequency** f_0. The intensity of the light determines the rate of emission of electrons, provided however that the frequency is high enough to cause emission.

This is not what would be expected by classical theory and can only be explained by the assumption that the light occurs in quanta (called photons) whose energy is proportional to the frequency of the light, i.e.

$$E = hf$$

where h is a constant of proportionality called **Planck's constant.** Its value is $6{\cdot}6 \times 10^{-34}$ J s. This is called Planck's law.

Example How many photons a second does a one watt torch bulb emit if it is 10% efficient and λ emitted is 500 nm?

$$\text{Frequency of light} = \frac{c}{\lambda} = \frac{3 \times 10^8}{5 \times 10^{-7}} = 6 \times 10^{14}\ \text{Hz}$$

$$\text{Photon energy} = hf$$
$$= 6{\cdot}6 \times 10^{-34} \times 6 \times 10^{14} = 3{\cdot}96 \times 10^{-19}\ \text{J}$$

Lamp emits 10^{-1} watt of light

$$\therefore \text{ no. of photons per second} = \frac{10^{-1}}{3{\cdot}96 \times 10^{-19}} = 2{\cdot}5 \times 10^{17}$$

In photoelectric emission the **whole** energy of a photon is transferred to a **single** electron and if this energy is greater than the **work function** of the surface the electron will escape. The work function Φ is the energy (often measured in electron volts) needed to remove the electron from the metal.

Thus $$\Phi = hf_0$$

If the photon energy is greater than the work function, then the excess energy appears as kinetic energy of the electron once it has escaped. This is stated in **Einstein's photoelectric equation** which states

$$\text{kinetic energy} = \text{photon energy} - \text{work function}$$
$$\tfrac{1}{2}mv^2_{max} = hf - \Phi$$

v_{max} is used because some of the energy may well be lost before the electron reaches the surface if the photon penetrates the metal some distance before giving up its energy.

A Photoelectric experiment This equation can be verified experimentally by using a commercial photoelectric cell and reverse biassing the anode so that the electrons will no longer reach it despite their kinetic energy (fig. 182i). Thus the anode current ceases to flow when electrons cannot quite reach it.

$$\text{electric energy} = \text{kinetic energy}$$
$$eV = \tfrac{1}{2}mv^2$$

If the work function is expressed in terms of threshold frequency

$$\Phi = hf_0$$

then the photoelectric equation becomes

$$eV = hf - hf_0 \quad \text{i.e.} \quad V = \frac{h}{e}f - \frac{h}{e}f_0$$

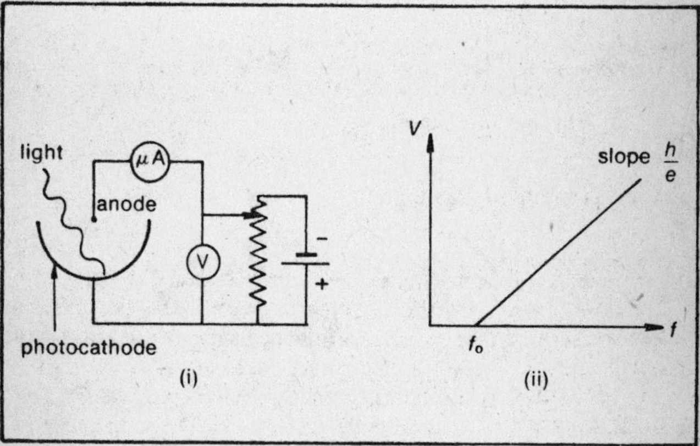

Figure 182. Photoelectric experiment

Thus, if V is plotted against f (illuminating the photocathode using different colour filters for which f is known) a linear graph is produced of gradient h/e and intercept f_0 on the frequency axis (fig. 182ii). Since e is known, a value for h can be found.

The variation of rate of emission of electrons with intensity of illumination can be checked by moving the light further away. The numbers of photons per second will decrease as the intensity of the light decreases and hence the current will be found to decrease.

Sizes of photons Table 4 gives typical values of sizes of photons and what they can do because of their particular size.

Type of Radiation	λ metres	f Hz	**Photon Energy** Joules	**Photon Energy** eV	**Atomic Effects**
Long wave radio	1000	3×10^{5}	2×10^{-28}	$1{\cdot}2\times10^{-9}$	
Very short wave radio	10^{-1}	3×10^{9}	2×10^{-24}	$1{\cdot}2\times10^{-5}$	Spins molecules
Infrared	10^{-4}	3×10^{12}	2×10^{-21}	$1{\cdot}2\times10^{-2}$	Makes molecules vibrate
Light	5×10^{-7}	6×10^{14}	4×10^{-19}	2·4	Excites atoms
Ultraviolet	10^{-8}	3×10^{16}	2×10^{-17}	$1{\cdot}2\times10^{2}$	Ionizes atoms
X-rays	10^{-10}	3×10^{18}	2×10^{-15}	$1{\cdot}2\times10^{4}$	Ionizes atoms
γ-rays	10^{-12}	3×10^{20}	2×10^{-13}	$1{\cdot}2\times10^{6}$	Disturbs nuclei

Table 4. Sizes of photons

Electronvolts (eV) are a convenient but non-S.I. unit used extensively in atomic work. An electron volt is the energy of an electron which has been accelerated through a p.d. of 1 volt.

$$\therefore \quad \text{energy} = eV = 1{\cdot}6\times10^{-19}\times1\ \text{J}$$

i.e.

$$1\ \text{eV} = 1{\cdot}6\times10^{-19}\ \text{J}$$

Atomic orbital energy levels Electrons within atoms can

only exist in certain orbitals each of which has a particular energy associated with it. The present day view of an orbital is that it is a cloud of smeared-out electric charge, the density of which at any point is proportional to the probability of finding an electron there.

The existence of discrete energy levels within the atom was demonstrated in the electron bombardment experiments of Franck and Hertz (1914).

The Franck Hertz experiment passed a beam of electrons through mercury vapour (fig. 183i). The pressure was low so that electrons would suffer relatively few collisions with mercury atoms and also that the energy of the electron could be varied by altering the accelerating potential between the filament F and the grid G. Beyond G was a collecting plate P which was slightly negative relative to G. Electrons accelerated through less than say 4 volts reached the plate P after making elastic collisions with the mercury atoms. If, however, the energy of an electron became equal to the difference between two energy levels in the atom, then the mercury atom could absorb the kinetic energy of the electron. Some of these collisions would occur next to G, so that these electrons would not be accelerated further and would therefore not be able to reach P against the negative potential. Therefore the current from P dropped. As V was increased this process could

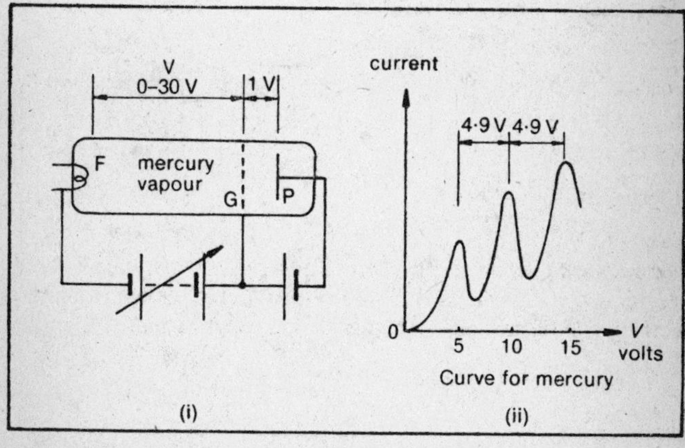

Figure 183. Franck-Hertz experiment

occur in the middle of the tube and the electron, having given up its energy, would be accelerated again and make a second inelastic collision next to G. The current therefore showed a second drop, and so on. The resulting graph is shown in fig. 183ii. The significant fact is that the distance between each point at which the current starts decreasing is the same and is equal to the difference between two energy levels in the mercury atom (4·9 eV or $7{\cdot}85 \times 10^{-19}$ J).

Subsequently, more sensitive experiments showed the existence of many energy level differences within the atom. Thus not only is electromagnetic radiation quantized but the energy levels of the orbitals within the atom are also quantized.

Excitation and ionization There are several ways in which an electron can be raised to a higher orbital – electron bombardment, molecular bombardment in a flame, etc.

There are three possibilities when an atom is struck by particles with kinetic energy:

i. an elastic collision may occur if the energy is too small.
ii. **excitation** occurs if the energy is equal to or greater than the energy needed to raise an electron in the atom to another orbital.
iii. **ionization** occurs if the energy is equal to or greater than the energy needed to remove an electron from the atom.

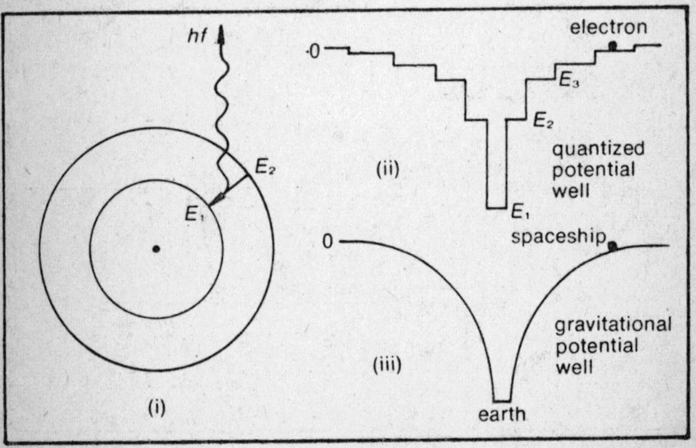

Figure 184. Energy levels

Optical line spectra One of the consequences of the quantization of both orbital energies and radiation is that if an atomic electron is raised to a higher energy level by any means then it will re-emit a photon of radiation when it returns to its original orbital (which is usually within 10^{-8} sec). The energy of the photon will be equal to the energy differences between the two orbitals, i.e.

$$hf = E_2 - E_1 \quad \text{(fig. 184i)}$$

where E_2 and E_1 are the higher and lower orbital energies respectively. Hence a sharp spectral line appears of frequency f if, say, a gas is heated. Differences between other orbital energies will also give rise to spectral lines and the resultant patterns of lines, which can be seen in a spectrum, are called **emission spectra**.

A helpful analogy is to consider a potential well with steps down the side (fig. 184ii). The electron in an orbital is represented by a ball which can sit on any step. If the ball

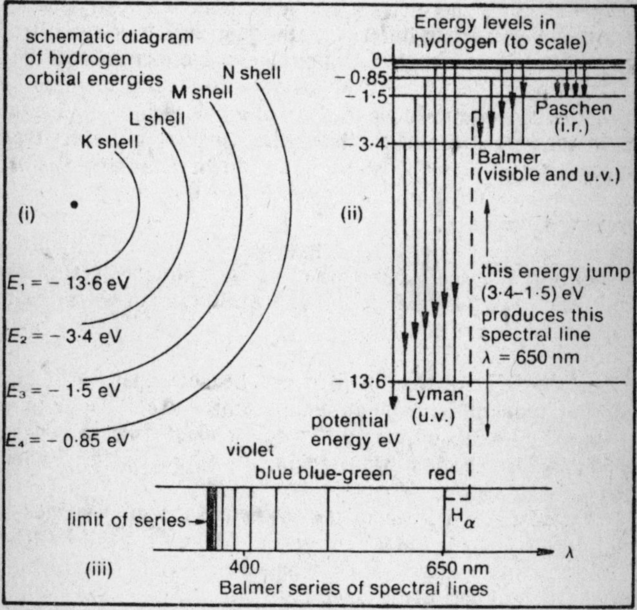

Figure 185. Energy levels and spectral lines

moves down the well it will gain kinetic energy and will dissipate this energy as heat when it strikes the next step. An electron in an atom, however, will radiate the energy it gains as a photon whose frequency is given by $hf = E_2 - E_1$. The total depth of the well can be found by adding the step heights, since it is only these which are known (from the photon energies emitted i.e. spectral line frequencies). For comparison a gravitational potential well (with all energy levels possible) is shown in figure 184iii.

The hydrogen spectrum The energy levels for the hydrogen atom have been worked out in detail (fig. 185ii), and the resultant spectral lines are due to the energy changes shown.

There are four series of spectral lines, only one of which – the Balmer series – is in the visible region. It can be shown that the energy difference between the orbitals becomes less and less, tending to zero. Thus only a finite energy is needed to raise the electron to an infinite orbital, i.e. to remove it from the atom altogether. This energy is called the **ionization energy** and the equivalent potential difference through which the electron would have to be moved is called the **ionization potential.**

Since it makes more sense to think of a free electron as having zero energy, the electron orbitals are assumed to have **negative** energies – like the steps going down from the surface (zero energy) into a potential well (corresponding to negative potential energies).

Under normal circumstances the hydrogen atom's electron will be in the lowest orbital or **ground state**. It can be raised to any orbital or **excited state**.

From the diagram (fig. 185ii) it can be seen that the largest energy jump will be from an infinite orbital (0 eV) to the inner orbital (−13·6 eV) assuming there is a place free in it. This produces the shortest wavelength, $\lambda = 91$ nm in the Lyman series, in the ultraviolet.
The longest wavelength in the visible region corresponds to the shortest jump in the Balmer series, −1·5 eV to −3·4 eV. This produces a wavelength, $\lambda = 650$ nm, the so-called Hydrogen-α line in the red part of the spectrum.

Spectra from flames The thermal energies of molecules and atoms in flames can be sufficient to cause excitation and ionization by collision. For instance, the mean kinetic energy of sodium atoms in a flame (2000 K) is $\frac{3}{2}kT$ (see p. 91).

$$\tfrac{3}{2}kT = \tfrac{3}{2}\times 1{\cdot}4\times 10^{-23}\times 2000 = 4{\cdot}2\times 10^{-20}\,\mathrm{J} = 0{\cdot}26\,\mathrm{eV}$$

The energy jump of the outer valence electron, which gives the familiar yellow sodium light, is 2·1 eV. Because of the spread of atomic velocities about the mean, some atoms will thus have the energy necessary to excite the sodium atom to emit its light.

Optical continuous spectra

When atoms are sufficiently close together, as in solids and liquids, they affect each other's orbital energy levels. As a result the discrete energy levels in the atom broaden out into energy bands which overlap (fig. 186i). This means that electrons in atoms in solid materials can have any energy and are not confined to discrete energy levels. Thus, provided there is sufficient thermal energy available, a solid will emit photons of effectively any energy and a continuous spectrum is produced. The distribution of energy within the continuous spectrum of a 'black body' has been discussed on p. 105.

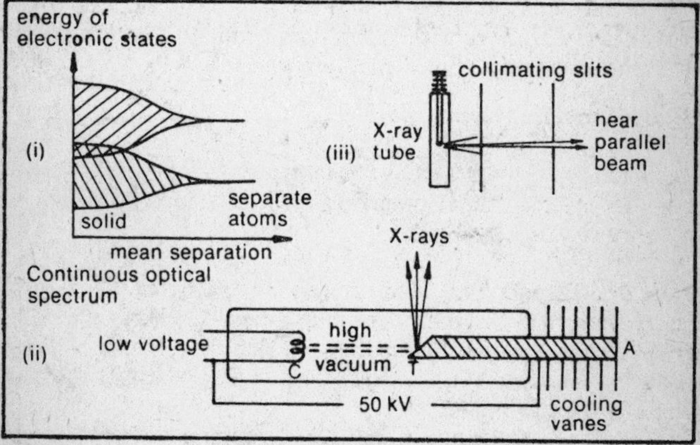

Figure 186. X-ray production

X-rays X-rays are extremely short wavelength (10^{-9} m – 10^{-11} m) electromagnetic radiation and are produced when a metal anode is bombarded by very high energy electrons.

A typical X-ray tube (fig. 186ii) consists of a heated cathode C and a target T of heavy metal (often tungsten) as part of an anode A in a vacuum tube. A high p.d. (50 kV typically) is applied between anode and cathode. The supply can be a.c. as the tube acts as its own rectifier.

Behaviour of X-rays X-rays can penetrate solid matter, although the intensity decreases with distance. They cannot be focussed and a near parallel beam is produced by collimation with two slits (fig. 186iii). Their wavelength was first measured using diffraction gratings at glancing angles but would now be found using diffraction by a crystal of known interatomic spacing (see p. 153). X-rays are usually detected using special photographic film, but ionization chambers can also be used.

X-ray line spectra Optical line spectra are a result of the excitation of the outer valence electrons of an atom. X-ray line spectra result from the excitation of the innermost K shell electrons of heavy atoms (fig. 187). This requires much energy since the inner levels are much further apart than the outer ones (about 1000 times) (fig. 185). This is possible because of the very high energies of the bombarding electrons (50 keV) compared with 2·1 eV to produce visible yellow sodium light, for example. Thus, the energies of the photons produced when the atomic electrons refill their original orbitals are very high and hence the wavelengths produced are very short.

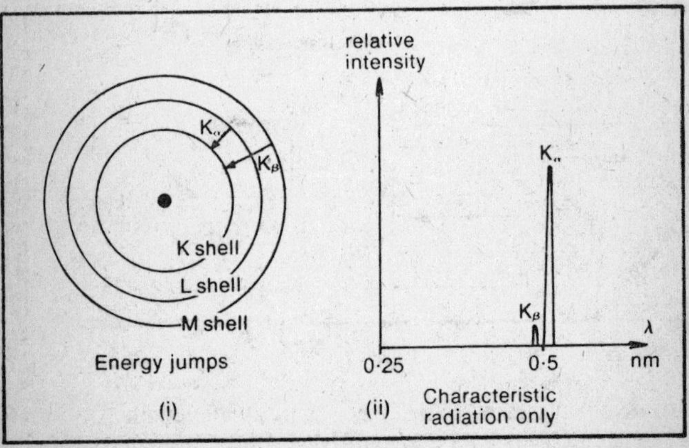

Figure 187. X-ray spectra

$$E = hf = \frac{hc}{\lambda} \quad \therefore \quad \lambda = \frac{hc}{E} \qquad \text{where } E = \text{energy jump.}$$

Typical transitions are shown in fig. 187i. The shortest wavelengths are due to the K_α and K_β transitions and a typical line spectrum is shown in fig. 187ii. The radiation is called the **characteristic radiation** of the element.

The K_α line is of greater intensity than K_β because it results from the more probable transition (K–L), and consequently more electrons are raised to the L rather than the M orbital.

For example the accelerating p.d. necessary to produce the K_α line for palladium (0·06 nm) can be calculated as follows:

$$f = \frac{c}{\lambda} = \frac{3 \times 10^8}{6 \times 10^{-11}} = 5 \times 10^{18}\ \text{Hz}$$

∴ Energy level difference K to L $= hf = 6{\cdot}6 \times 10^{-34} \times 5 \times 10^{18} = 3{\cdot}3 \times 10^{-15}$ J so minimum energy of bombarding electron needed $= eV = 3{\cdot}3 \times 10^{-15}$ J.

$$\therefore \quad V = \frac{3{\cdot}3 \times 10^{-15}}{1{\cdot}6 \times 10^{-19}} = 20{\cdot}6\ \text{kV}$$

Moseley's law It is evident from the example just quoted that the energies of the innermost orbitals depend on the atom involved. If the wavelengths of the K_α lines are measured, they are found to depend on atomic number (fig. 188i).

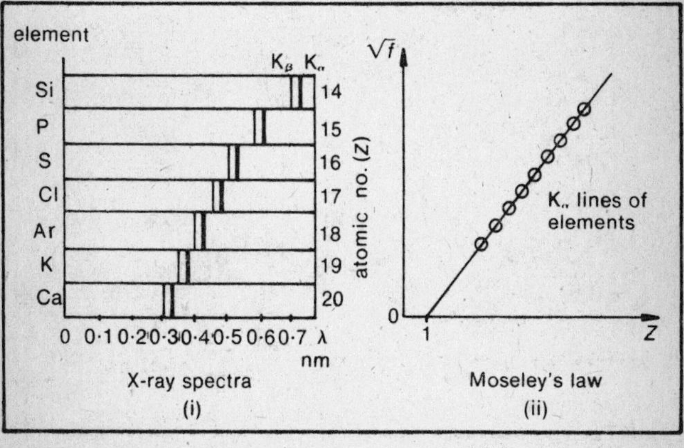

Figure 188. Moseley's law

If the square root of the K_α frequency is plotted against atomic number, a straight line results (fig. 188ii) which can be expressed as Moseley's law for the K_α line:

$$f = \tfrac{3}{4}R_0(Z-1)^2$$

where R_0 is called the Rydberg constant.

Moseley's law gives another method for finding the number of protons in the nucleus (see p. 289) and lead originally to discovering the correct order of chlorine, argon and potassium. By atomic number from Moseley's Law, the sequence is chlorine (17) – argon (18) – potassium (19) but by atomic weight it is chlorine (35·5) – potassium (39·1) – argon (39·9).

X-ray continuous spectra Another manifestation of the quantization of radiation is in the emission of X-rays (or Bremsstrahlung) caused directly by the rapid deceleration of electrons e.g. during approach to atomic nuclei. The energy of the photons is determined by the energy lost during the deceleration.

This 'braking effect' increases rapidly with the energy of the electron and the intensity of the radiation increases correspondingly (fig. 189i). A significant feature of the continuous spectrum is that there is a well defined minimum wavelength, i.e. a maximum frequency of radiation.

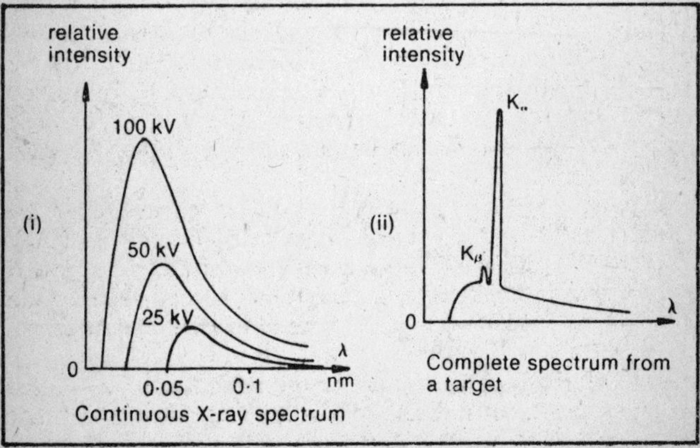

Figure 189. X-ray continuous spectra

This occurs when the entire kinetic energy of an electron is converted into a single X-ray photon. It is a relatively rare event as either the electron emits several smaller X-ray photons in successive decelerations, or it is slowed down without the production of X-rays – merely generating heat or even producing X-rays by the process which gives characteristic radiation. In fact, typically only 0·2% of the energy of the electron beam is converted into X-rays. The condition of minimum wavelength is

$$hf_{max} = \frac{hc}{\lambda_{min}} = eV \text{ (if electrons were accelerated through } V \text{ volts)}$$

$$\lambda_{min} = \frac{hc}{eV}$$

Since λ_{min} is well defined, this gives another good way of measuring Planck's constant.

Example Calculate the shortest X-ray wavelength which a 100 kV beam could generate when it strikes a target.

$$\lambda_{min} = \frac{hc}{eV} = \frac{6{\cdot}6 \times 10^{-34} \times 3 \times 10^{8}}{1{\cdot}6 \times 10^{-19} \times 10^{5}} = 12{\cdot}4 \text{ pm}$$

A full X-ray spectrum of continuous plus characteristic radiation is shown in fig. 189ii.

Ionization by electron bombardment A similar experiment to that of Franck and Hertz can be used to measure the ionization potential of atoms (fig. 183). In this experiment, the collecting plate P is connected through the milliammeter to a large negative potential so that positive ions only will be collected. In the Franck Hertz experiment only excitation occurred and no ions were produced. The grid G is made positive relative to the cathode and its potential is variable.

As the potential of G is increased, a point is reached when the current from P suddenly starts to flow and increases rapidly with potential. At this point the energy of the accelerated electron is just sufficient to remove outer electrons from the gas atoms. The value of V is then the ionization potential.

Typical ionization potentials are in the region of 6 or 7 volts. The largest is that of helium (24·5 volts) and the smallest that of caesium (3·87 volts). These are called **first ionization** potentials to distinguish them from subsequent ionization potentials corresponding to the removal of further electrons from the atom.

Gas discharge tubes work on this basis. If a large p.d. is provided between the ends of a tube containing gas at low pressure, ionization occurs near the electrodes and is followed by the acceleration of both ions and electrons, which causes further ionization and excitation. The ions and electrons constitute a highly conducting plasma and the light from the excited atoms can be used for luminous signs, etc.

Ionization in flames

The energies required to ionize atoms are also available in the thermal energies of molecules in a flame. If a flame is placed between charged plates and a shadow cast of it using a powerful lamp and a screen, two hot regions (ions and electrons) can be seen to be attracted to the negative and positive plates respectively.

Excitation by photons

Excitation can be produced not only by bombardment by particles but also by receiving photons. The main difference is that to cause excitation, the energy of the photon must equal the difference between energy levels **precisely**.

Absorption spectra are the result of white light passing

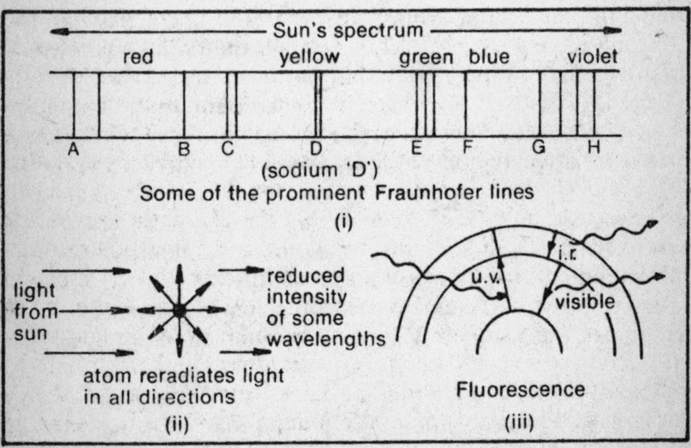

Figure 190. Absorption spectra and fluorescence

through a gas and appear as a normal white light spectrum with dark lines or 'shadows' across it. The reason for the dark lines is that photons of the suitable wavelength cause excitation of the gas atoms, which then re-radiate the energy in all directions as the electron returns to its original orbital almost immediately. Since the light is re-radiated in all directions, only a small proportion continues in the original direction, and hence the intensity of light at these wavelengths is greatly reduced. The best example of an absorption spectrum is the existence of the Fraunhofer lines in the sun's spectrum – an incredible complexity of lines due to elements in the sun's atmosphere (fig. 190i). Very prominent among the Fraunhofer lines is the hydrogen-α line (see p. 302). Because of the rapid motion of hydrogen atoms, a broadening of this line due to the Doppler effect is observed.

Fluorescent tubes also rely on excitation by photons but in a solid instead of a gas. In a fluorescent tube, a mercury vapour gas discharge provides an ultraviolet rich spectrum of lines and the phosphor coating on the inside of the tube absorbs ultraviolet. The phosphor re-radiates the energy in more than one stage, and one of the jumps produce light in the visible region (fig. 190iii).

Wave-particle duality

In considering Fraunhofer diffraction at a slit, the distribution of energy in the diffraction pattern was calculated (fig. 91iii). But what is the situation if only one photon goes through the slit? Where does it go? Clearly, it is impossible to say. Nevertheless it is found that if the experiment is conducted with such a low light intensity that only one photon at a time passes through the slit but the period over which the experiment is conducted is sufficient to give measurable blackening of a film, then the diffraction pattern still appears. Under these circumstances it can only be concluded that the diffraction pattern is due to the probability of photons going to any particular point and that this probability is determined in some way by the light waves. Thus, a maximum, according to the wave theory of diffraction, corresponds to a high probability of finding photons and a zero corresponds to zero probability of finding photons. If a large number of photons form the pattern, then a point where the probability of finding a photon is a maximum will receive a large number of photons, i.e. a maximum intensity of light at that point.

If the relationship from the Special Theory of Relativity (see p. 293) between the energy and equivalent mass of a photon is combined with the expression for the energy of a photon in terms of its frequency, a relationship between the wavelength and momentum of a photon can be deduced.

$$E = mc^2 \qquad E = hf \qquad \lambda f = c$$

$$\therefore \quad E = mc^2 = \frac{hc}{\lambda} \qquad \therefore \quad \lambda = \frac{h}{mc} = \frac{\text{Planck's constant}}{\text{momentum of photon}} \qquad \text{(i)}$$

In this expression m is the mass equivalent of the photon's energy and c is the velocity of the photon, i.e. that of light.

The momentum of light (a somewhat strange concept) has been demonstrated experimentally by detecting the difference in momentum change (i.e. force) when light is reflected ($2mc$) and when it is absorbed (mc) by polished and black surfaces of a 'windmill' in a high vacuum. The resultant pressure on a surface due to incident light (or indeed any electromagnetic radiation) is called **radiation pressure**.

Quantum mechanics

It is on the basic idea of waves of probability that quantum mechanics is built. The wave-particle duality can be extended from photons, which are basically waves but behave as if they had a particulate nature, to electrons, which are basically particles but behave as if they also had a wave nature. This theory is supported by the phenomenon of **electron diffraction.** In a school version of this experiment electrons in a vacuum tube pass through a very thin graphite film and are found to form a diffraction pattern on the phosphor screen at the end of the tube (fig. 191). The wavelength of the wave associated with the electrons can be calculated from the spacing of the atomic planes in the graphite (known by X-ray diffraction), the dimensions of the diffraction rings and the distance from graphite to the screen. The wavelength is found to be proportional to $1/\sqrt{V}$ where V is the potential difference accelerating the electrons. In this case the particle clearly has velocity as well as mass. The resultant momentum and hence the wavelength can be calculated as follows:
The velocity is found by equating the electrical energy and the kinetic energy

$$eV = \tfrac{1}{2}mv^2$$

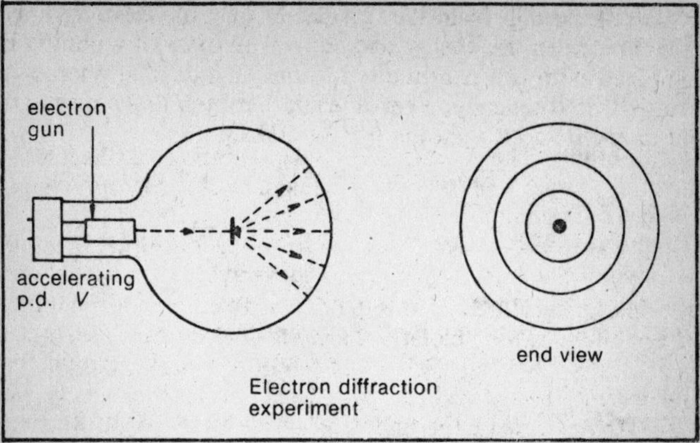

Figure 191. Electron diffraction

$$\therefore \quad v = \sqrt{\frac{2eV}{m}}$$

$$\therefore \quad \text{momentum} = mv = \sqrt{2emV}$$

If the same type of formula as (i) for photons is used

$$\therefore \quad \lambda = \frac{h}{\text{momentum}} = \frac{h}{\sqrt{2emV}}$$

i.e.

$$\lambda \propto \frac{1}{\sqrt{V}}$$

The hypothesis that wavelength is inversely proportional to momentum is thus supported, even though the electron is not travelling at the same speed as a photon.

What do these electron waves represent? They are not electromagnetic waves and can only be interpreted as 'matter waves' such that they represent the **probability** of finding an electron at a particular position. The present theory of the electron orbitals in an atom is based on standing waves of probability forming round the nucleus, like standing waves on a string.

Protons, neutrons, hydrogen and helium atoms have also been shown to have wave properties but for larger bodies the wavelength of the associated wave would be too small to show any observable effects.

Key terms

Radioactivity The spontaneous disintegration of the nuclei of some isotopes of certain elements, with the emission of ionizing radiation.
Ionizing radiation Radiation which causes ionization in gases and solids i.e. α- and β-particles and γ-rays.
Ionization chamber A container with two electrodes. Ionizing radiation is detected by the current that flows between the electrodes as a result of the ionization of the gas within the chamber.
Geiger–Müller tube An ionization detector which makes use of gas amplification to enhance the ionization caused by a single particle.
Cloud chamber A chamber in which the tracks of ionizing particles are shown up by the ions acting as centres for condensation from a critically supersaturated vapour.
Expansion (Wilson) cloud chamber A cloud chamber in which the supersaturation is caused by sudden decompression.
Diffusion (continuous) cloud chamber A cloud chamber in which the supersaturation occurs because of a temperature gradient.
Geiger counter A combination of a Geiger–Müller tube and a scaler.
α-particles Helium nuclei containing two protons and two neutrons. They have a double positive electronic charge.
β-particles Electrons with very high velocities emitted from nuclei in radioactive decay.
γ-rays Electromagnetic radiation of very high frequency.
Exponential decay A type of decay in which the rate of decay is proportional to the quantity present.
Half life The time taken for the material to decay to half its original quantity of parent nuclei (or half its initial activity).
Curie (Ci) Activity of radioactive material which undergoes $3{\cdot}7 \times 10^{10}$ disintegrations per second. (Not an S.I. unit).
Becquerel (Bq) Activity of radioactive material which undergoes 1 disintegration per second.
Carbon-14 dating A method of archaeological dating depending upon the decay of radioactive carbon-14.
Thomson's plum pudding model An early model of the

atom which regarded the atom as a sphere of positive charge with electrons embedded in it like raisins.

α-particle scattering experiment One in which the deflection of α-particles by gold foil is measured. It is the key experiment giving evidence for the nuclear model of the atom.

Nuclear model A model of the atom which consists of protons and neutrons within a very small nucleus at the centre of concentric orbitals containing electrons.

Protons Hydrogen nuclei, with single positive charge.

Unified atomic mass unit (u.) One twelfth of the mass of a carbon-12 atom. Approximately the mass of a proton or a neutron.

Atomic number (Z) Number of protons in the nucleus.

Neutrons Uncharged particles of approximately the same mass as protons.

Mass number (A) Number of nucleons in the nucleus.

Nucleons The collective term for protons and neutrons.

Isotopes Atoms having the same number of protons but a different number of neutrons, i.e. same atomic number but different mass number.

Atomic weight The average mass of atoms in an element expressed in unified atomic mass units.

Photoelectric effect The process of emission of electrons from a metal surface caused by incident light.

Threshold frequency The frequency of light above which photoelectric emission will occur from a particular surface.

Work function The energy which an electron must be given in order just to escape from a particular surface.

Electronvolt (eV) A non-S.I. unit of energy equal to the energy acquired by an electron in moving through a potential difference of one volt. It is equal to $1{\cdot}602 \times 10^{-19}$ joule.

Planck's constant The constant of proportionality in Planck's law. Its value is $6{\cdot}6 \times 10^{-34}$ J s.

Einstein's photoelectric equation Maximum kinetic energy of a photoelectron = photon energy less the work function of the material.

Photon Quantum (packet) of electromagnetic radiation.

Atomic orbital A cloud of smeared out electric charge, the density of which at any point is proportional to the probability of finding an electron there.

Franck-Hertz experiment An electron bombardment experiment for determination of ionization energies.

Excitation The process of raising an electron within an atom to a higher orbital, i.e. higher energy state.

Ionization The process of removal of an electron or electrons from an atom.
Ionization energy The energy required to remove an electron or electrons from an atom. First, second and third, etc. ionization energies correspond to the removal of the first, second and third, etc. electrons respectively.
Ionization potential Potential difference through which an electron is moved to gain ionization energy.
Ground state The lowest energy state of an atom when the atom is most stable. For example when the one electron of a hydrogen atom is in the innermost orbital.
Excited state The state of an atom when an electron has been raised to a higher orbital than it occupies in the ground state.
Line spectrum A spectrum of electromagnetic radiation from an atom consisting of lines of different wavelengths.
Continuous spectrum The spectrum from an incandescent material with all wavelengths over a particular range.
X-rays Electromagnetic radiation of extremely short wavelength (10^{-9} m to 10^{-11} m).
K_α and K_β emission X-ray emission due to transitions from the L to K and M to K orbitals respectively.
Moseley's law For certain elements, the square root of the frequency of K_α X-rays is related linearly to the atomic number.
Bremsstrahlung X-rays emitted by the braking effect when electrons are suddenly decelerated on hitting a target.
Gas discharge tube A tube containing gas at low pressure in which electron bombardment excites atoms to emit radiation.
Absorption spectrum A continuous spectrum in which lines are missing due to absorption of radiation at these wavelengths on passing through a medium.
Fraunhofer lines The lines missing from the sun's spectrum due to absorption in the sun's atmosphere.
Wave-particle duality Waves can be regarded as particles (photons), and particles (electrons etc.) can be regarded as having a wave nature.
Radiation pressure The pressure on a surface due to incident electromagnetic radiation.
Matter waves Waves of probability, which determine where a particle may be found with a certain probability.

INDEX